ORGANIZATIONAL COMMUNICATION FOR SURVIVAL

THIRD EDITION

ORGANIZATIONAL COMMUNICATION FOR SURVIVAL

Making Work, Work

VIRGINIA P. RICHMOND

West Virginia University

JAMES C. McCROSKEY

West Virginia University

LINDA L. McCROSKEY

California State University, Long Beach

PEARSON

*Boston • New York • San Francisco • Mexico City
Montreal • Toronto • London • Madrid • Munich
Paris • Hong Kong • Singapore • Tokyo • Cape Town • Sydney*

Executive Editor: Karon Bowers
Series Editor: Brian Wheel
Series Editorial Assistant: Jennifer Trebby
Senior Marketing Manager: Mandee Eckersley
Composition and Prepress Buyer: Linda Cox
Manufacturing Buyer: JoAnne Sweeney
Cover Coordinator: Kristina Mose-Libon
Editorial-Production Coordinator: Mary Beth Finch
Editorial-Production Service: Shepherd, Inc.
Electronic Composition: Shepherd, Inc.

For related titles and support materials, visit our online catalog at
http://www.ablongman.com

Between the time Web site information is gathered and then published, it is not
unusual for some sites to have closed. Also, the transcription of URLs can result in
unintended typographical errors. The publisher would appreciate notification
where these errors occur so that they may be corrected in subsequent editions.

Library of Congress Cataloging-in-Publication Data

Richmond, Virginia P., 1949–
    Organizational communication for survival: making work, work/
Virgina P. Richmond, James C. McCroskey, Linda L. McCroskey.—3rd ed.
        p. cm.
    Includes bibliographical references and index.
    ISBN 0-205-40800-1 (alk. paper)
    1. Communication in organizations. I. McCroskey, James C. II. McCroskey,
Linda L. III. Title

HD30.3R53 2005
658.4'5—dc22   2004044591

Printed in the United States of America.

10 9 8 7 6 5 4 3 2 1   09 08 07 06 05 04

CONTENTS

CHAPTER THREE

Nonverbal Behavior and Communication   33

CHAPTER FOUR

Administration, Supervision, and Communication   49

CHAPTER FIVE

Barriers to Effective Communication   60

CHAPTER SIX

Personality, Temperament, and Communication Traits   71

CHAPTER SEVEN

Organizational Orientations and Communication Traits   84

CHAPTER EIGHT

CHAPTER NINE

CHAPTER TEN

CHAPTER ELEVEN

CHAPTER TWELVE

CHAPTER THIRTEEN

CHAPTER FOURTEEN

Disagreement, Conflict, and Groupthink   175

CHAPTER FIFTEEN

Effective Supervisory and Subordinate Relationships   190

Index   205

Whether we like it or not, most of us must go to work every day. Organizations are a fact of life for most people in modern societies. People spend most of their adult lives working within and for some type of organization. Even before one joins the workforce on a permanent basis, life in organizations has become commonplace—the elementary school, the secondary school, the college or university. Organizations are such an omnipresent facet of our lives that we usually take them for granted and never recognize the impact they have on our behavior.

A relatively small proportion of the population ever studies what it means to be a member of an organization; and those who do are generally people who hope to assume some managerial role in an organization. Hence, universities have entire schools, colleges, and departments devoted to such topics as business administration, public administration, educational administration, hospital administration, sports management, and hotel management. Unfortunately, most such programs focus on how to *manage* other people, not how to *be* managed.

We have titled our book *Organizational Communication for Survival.* We have chosen to focus on communication not only because it is our area of professional expertise, but also because communication is the vehicle by which management occurs—for good or ill. In short, it takes effective communication to make our work experiences work for us.

Effective communication requires strategic choices. Strategic communicators know how to choose the communication behaviors that are most likely to improve their own chances to survive and prosper in an organization, and they make those choices. This view sometimes is derogatorily referred to as "Machiavellian," an orientation we discuss in Chapter 6. However, communicating strategically is only a negative behavior when it involves unethical practices. We never recommend that you lie, cheat, or steal—or engage in any other immoral behavior. We also do not highly recommend that you seek every possible opportunity to become a "whistle blower," constantly complain about how you are treated, or otherwise to make life difficult for others in an organization. Neither of these types of behavior are likely to be in your best interests over the long-term. However, you do need to look out for your own best interests in an organization. You should never expect that someone else will do that for you.

Our working subtitle for the first edition of this book was "A Peon Perspective." That early subtitle emphasizes our orientation: We shall direct primary attention to the roles we play in organizations as subordinates, since we are all subordinates of someone else and will be even though some day we may rise to a high supervisory position. There are always more "peons" than there are "bosses," and we are all "peons" before we become "bosses" unless our parents have the questionable sense to will us a wholly owned business before we take our first job!

As you read through this book, you may conclude that we have a pessimistic view of both organizations and people in organizations. Some of our colleagues, who have read portions of the manuscript, have labeled us "cynical" or "sarcastic." Although the distinction may be only a play on words, we prefer to describe our orientation as "realistic."

Many organizations indeed are dismal places to exist. Many managers would starve to death if they had to depend on their managerial skills to provide sustenance. And many subordinates couldn't care less about either the quality of their own work or the survival of the organization. If such observations justify labeling us as cynics, so be it. But our experiences with a variety of educational, business, and governmental organizations suggest such views are realistic. Certainly, not all organizations are dismal, all managers incompetent, or all subordinates uncaring. But these circumstances prevail a sufficiently large proportion of the time so that we cannot approach organizations with rose-colored glasses firmly in place. Were we to do so, our survival in the organization might be very brief.

This book, therefore, may be typified as a "survival guide for subordinates." Understanding and applying everything we discuss in this book will not guarantee that you will rise to a position of "boss," or even guarantee your survival in a given organization. But we think it will improve your chances of both. That is why we wrote it.

Many individuals have contributed to our thinking about communication in organizations and, hence, to the present book. We would particularly like to express our appreciation to those who reviewed this edition of this book and made excellent suggestions for improvement: Phil Grise, Florida State University; William Jong-Ebot, Florida Memorial College; Patricia J. Sotirin, Michigan Technological University; Steven Koski, College of St. Elizabeth; Steven Venette, North Dakota State University. We also wish to thank Karon Bowers, who served as editor for several of our books. As a result of her excellent work and effective communication, she has been promoted to a well-deserved position with Allyn & Bacon. Finally, we wish to thank several managers under whom we have worked for making us understand the need for this book. It is never too late to learn.

■ ■ ■ ■ ■

CHAPTER 1

THE NATURE OF ORGANIZATIONS

This is a book that proposes to talk to you about communicating competently in organizations. Although some people believe "competent communication" is "competent communication" no matter where it is practiced (whether you are trying to get a date, sell a car, teach a class, or get a job makes no real difference), we are of a mind that what makes a person a competent communicator in one environment may not make that same person a competent communicator in another environment. This is seen as a "contextual" view of communication competence.

Since we have adopted a contextual view, we are committed to the assumption that, to a major extent, what can be described as competent communication behavior is influenced by the context in which that communication behavior is performed. To understand competent communication behavior in organizations, then, you must first understand the basic nature of the context created by the presence of an organization. Although you have existed in organizations all of your life, you may never really have stopped to think about the characteristics of those organizations around you or how they function. To begin your examination of organizational communication, then, we think it important to take time for that consideration.

What is an organization? A simple definition of an organization is "a group of people working together to achieve common goal(s)." Although this seems very simplistic, it is a workable definition for many purposes. It clearly fits most work groups. However, most social groups, service groups, and religious groups also function very much like formal work-oriented organizations. They usually work together with some common goal in mind.

For definitional purposes here, let us also consider a more formalized definition of an organization. We may define an organization as "an organized collection of individuals working interdependently within a relatively structured, organized, open system to achieve common goals." The key to this definition is that people are *working together* in some organized fashion with a goal in mind. Success of each worker's efforts is dependant on the efforts of other workers in the organization. For example, in a major business corporation, although each unit may have various assignments, many of which do not overlap with other units, all units are still working to meet a common goal (produce a product or service). All units are assessed as to whether or not they can meet their individual goals as well as help the organization achieve its overall goals. In manufacturing systems, for example, there are many departments (design, production, marketing, shipping, etc.), but all work to achieve a common goal (to produce and sell a product). To work together within any organization requires communication. Communication provides the connections which keep the organization together.

TYPES OF ORGANIZATIONS

Although most organizations have many things in common, they definitely are not all alike. There are basically two types of organizations: profit and nonprofit. Profit-based organizations have a "bottom line" that is concerned with how much money the company nets in a given period of time. You probably are familiar with some of the larger profit-based organizations in the United States, such as General Motors, IBM, Ford, United Airlines, General Mills, and General Electric. You have seen their advertisements since you were a child. Profit-based organizations must make a profit from selling the goods or services they provide or they will cease to exist. They must have a profit margin that keeps them "out of the red" or they will be bankrupt or be swallowed by some larger corporation. Although they may have many goals, the overall goal of these organizations has to be to "make money" or they will be in big trouble. Corporations such as Robert Hall Clothiers, Eastern Airlines, Studebaker, and Underwood Typewriters— very large corporations that prospered in the past that you may never even have heard of—ceased to make the profits necessary to maintain themselves; hence they ceased to exist.

Nonprofit organizations have goals that are concerned with providing products or services also, but they do not have to make a profit while doing so. In fact, many nonprofit organizations are specifically designed to provide products or services for free or at a price below the actual cost of providing those products or services. Some common nonprofit groups are organizations such as churches, most educational institutions, the postal service, the social security administration, public hospitals, government-owned utilities, the military, and many charitable groups. The economic foundation of these organizations is drawn from taxes, fees, and/or contributions. These organizations survive based on the number of persons they serve and the quality of the service provided. If a college has a continuing decline in enrollment, it will have to cut back on the number of personnel it employs. Eventually, if the decline continues, the college might cease to exist, as many did across the United States in the 1970s and 1980s. If the product or service is no longer needed, the organization providing that product or service is no longer needed.

Nonprofit organizations perpetuate themselves much like profit-based organizations do. They try to create or define a need among people and provide the means to satisfy that need in order to survive. Why are some branches of the government so large? Because they have managed to convince government officials and/or the general public that they are necessary to satisfy some need(s) of the people. Further, they continue to convince those same people that they are satisfying those needs.

In recent years, a new type of organization has developed in the United States—primarily as a function of tax laws and regulations. This type is known as "not-for-profit" organizations. This type of organization often is a spin-off from a non-profit organization. When a non-profit organization is able to provide services or products for which people are willing to pay amounts well beyond the needs of the non-profit organization for survival, it can run afoul of the tax regulations which do not permit making such profits without paying taxes.

When these organizations reorganize as not-for-profit organizations, they can avoid the taxes. They can "donate" their profits to non-profit organizations of their choice. They can also pay members of their Board of Directors and other employees very high salaries and bonuses, if they choose. Many of these organizations function essentially like for-profit organizations. They can buy property, including other similar organizations, and expand into extremely large organizations. Many medical systems have followed this pattern. Although these organizations are considered not-for-profit organizations by the Internal Revenue Service (IRS), if the income (what people other than the IRS would call "profits") stops coming in, the organization will cease to exist. Hence, for our purposes here, we will consider "not-for-profit" organizations as just a special case of "for-profit" organizations. They are very much like one another, and very different than truly "non-profit" organizations.

COMMON CHARACTERISTICS OF ALL ORGANIZATIONS

All organizations have some common characteristics. Let us consider a few of those.

System. All organizations are systems. By "systems" we mean that all units or parts within the organization are interrelated and interdependent and depend on one another to make the whole organization functional. For example, to make the total organization a success, a clothing manufacturing organization depends on subsystems of designers, cutters, machine operators, packagers, sales persons, distributors, and so on. If one subsystem within the total system fails, it can impact the overall system. For example, if the cutters go on strike, the work of the machine operators might be forced to stop. If the sales persons are unable to sell the clothing, the production subsystems must be shut down. In other words, each of the parts of the overall system must work well or the larger system may fail. Your car is a system. If the fan belt in your car fails, the entire car stops, not just the fan. Any change in a system has the potential for impacting the total organization. The magnitude of the change will determine the magnitude of the impact on the system.

Systems vary in the degree to which they are open to outside influences. Closed systems tend to have limited interaction with the environment; open systems have more. The more open an organizational system is, the more communication it has with those outside the system. Closed organizational systems center their communication on the people within that system. Each organization is a system with relative degrees of openness. Some organizations are clearly more open than others. Most of the major corporations in the United States have to maintain very open systems. If they do not, they won't survive. They depend substantially on interactions with people and organizations outside their formal organizational boundaries for success, or even survival. Some organizations, however, can be more closed and still maintain themselves. For example, the Amish in Pennsylvania have been able to establish and maintain a nearly closed system while at the same time not suffering what they see to be any significant losses. They attempt to sustain a self-sufficient community that does not depend on interactions with people and organizations outside their own boundaries for success or survival. Whereas General Motors must maintain an open system in order not to suffer, the Amish do not need to do so. Thus, although there are exceptions like Amish communities, organizations generally must communicate effectively with individuals and organizations beyond their own boundaries to prosper.

Rules.   Organizations have routine patterns established through formal or informal rules which they expect members to follow. Organizations usually have a high value for the written word, particularly when it comes to formal rules. Hence, formalized routines often are distributed to new employees in an "employee handbook." These routine rules are usually well-defined policies and procedures, such as the time the workday begins or ends. Every organization has routine patterns or procedures members are expected to follow. Some organizations require that personnel file certain forms if they are sick, take a vacation, or need a day off. Other organizations require that people wear certain types of clothing while at work and not appear in other environments in their work apparel. Routine patterns may change as a person's status changes in the organization. For example, policies and patterns for a new person might not be the same as for one who has been in the organization for several years. There might be different policies for supervisors than for their subordinates. However, some routine patterns will be the same for all. The rules vary depending on the organization. The formal rules usually are explained to you when you first enter an organization. It usually is easy to learn the less-formal rules by watching others at your same level or by asking your supervisor if you are in doubt.

Roles. Every employee in every organization has assigned duties or roles he or she is expected to perform. In fact, this is usually one of the reasons a person is hired by an organization. Engineers are hired because they can perform engineering roles, salespersons are hired because they can sell, teachers are hired because they can teach, and so on. As an employee, you are likely to be evaluated in large part on your ability to perform your assigned role. Managers examine your performance periodically to determine if you are accomplishing your assigned duties (roles) in an acceptable manner. If you are not, you may be given a warning or be terminated by the organization.

Hierarchy. All organizations have a chain of command—an established hierarchy of authority levels. This structure determines who reports to whom and who is in charge of what. Usually the chain of command is very clear in an organization. In fact, many organizations provide all incoming employees with a flowchart that outlines the various levels in the organization and how they are related. Such "organizational charts" specify the formal chain of command in the organization. A representation of the formal organizational structure often is included in the employee handbook.

It is very important that you know who is your immediate supervisor, and most organizations take care to make certain that information is available to everyone. When that is not the case, major problems can result. We recall consulting with the leadership of a technical organization that believed it had a major communication problem. After interviewing employees at several levels of the organization, we found the employees thought the major problem was that no one ever knew who was in charge of what. There was a manager on paper, but in an effort to increase employee participation in decision making (certainly a desirable objective), he had delegated so many duties, without informing those below him who was delegated what, that most people did not know whom to go to when they had problems. When we asked individual employees who their immediate supervisor was, many couldn't say. The head secretary was the only one who seemed to understand most of what was going on, and she was irritated because she had "too many bosses." The organization needed a clear cut, precise breakdown of hierarchical levels. Effective organizational communication is virtually impossible in a "disorganized organization."

Norms. It is not unusual to find norms (both formal and informal) in all organizations. Norms are established patterns or standards accepted by most members of the organization. They are what people in the organization do and what they believe is the "right" thing to do. Some norms exist for such a long time they become formalized into rules—such as men wearing ties while working. However, many norms are not formally expressed. You, as a new employee, have to learn about these norms as well as you can. You may not be told about some of the norms because everyone else simply takes them for granted. It is not that they are "secret," but just that adherence to norms becomes habitual behavior that is performed regularly without much thought or reflection. For example, employees in one organization in which we consulted liked to have "bag lunch sessions" each Friday (rather than going to a restaurant, as they did the rest of the week) so they could talk frankly with their supervisor. This was done so often, it became a formalized norm. A new supervisor started off on a very bad footing when he went out for lunch the first Friday he was there. No one told him about the bag lunch norm. In the same organization, the norm was that older, more-established employees occasionally could wear bluejeans to work, but the newer, less-established employees could not. No one told this to one of the new employees. He noticed that some of his co-workers wore jeans to work, so one day he did so too. He was very surprised when he received several rather derogatory comments about his dress from co-workers, and his supervisor suggested he dress more appropriately in the future. Because he violated a norm he did not even know existed, he communicated a "superiority" attitude to his co-workers.

There are many informal norms in all organizations—all employees need to know the norms so they don't inadvertently violate them. For example, in one organization we worked with, the manager would put a "do not disturb sign" on her door when she was working on the budget. Although she generally maintained an "open door" policy, all the older employees knew the sign meant "budget time" and to leave her alone. Some of the new employees didn't, but were quickly informed about the sign so they wouldn't get in trouble. Many norms can be learned only by being in the system and listening and watching what other, more-established personnel do. Although it is not fair to you as a new employee, you are expected in most organizations to adhere to the unwritten and unspoken norms from the day you join the organization. The norms exist because the people think they are "right" and that "good" employees follow them. If you do not, you are seen as doing things "wrong" and as not being a "good" employee. The best rule to follow when you are uncertain what is considered appropriate is to ask someone who has been in the organization for some time. "When in doubt, check it out."

Many progressive organizations recognize that new employees engage in inappropriate behaviors simply because they do not know any better. Sometimes the effect of such inappropriate behaviors is so negative that the new employee has little chance for long-term success in the organization. Hence, the organization tries to prevent such problems from occurring by appointing a "mentor" for each new employee. A mentor usually is a person with experience in the organization to whom the new employee can go for advice with regard to what behaviors are appropriate and what ones are inappropriate. Unfortunately, most organizations do not have mentoring programs. Hence, it is important that you try to make friends with one or more experienced people in the organization so that you can turn to them for such mentoring assistance. In the absence of such mentoring, you are highly likely to make serious mistakes that will jeopardize your position in the organization.

Similarity.   Organizations create pressure to achieve similarity among their employees. They have a need for their employees to be similar in attitudes, beliefs, values, and goals. This is not just a form of bias that permeates organizations; increased similarity among people makes for better working relationships and better communication. Although neither the leaders of the organization nor the rank-and-file employees may have read the results of the research that has demonstrated these facts, they both are likely to be intuitively aware that people who are alike get along better with one another. Hence, if you do not fit the norms of the organization or seem deviant in some significant way, you are likely to be encouraged to leave the organization and seek work elsewhere.

Managers want people who "see eye to eye" with them on most issues. As employees, we want co-workers who think like us and have similar goals because it makes communication easier and more open. It is more difficult to communicate with someone who has goals and values that are different from your own. The principle of similarity can be succinctly stated: The more similar two communicators are, the more likely they are to interact with one another, and the more likely it is that their communication will be successful. If you wish to survive in any organization, it would be wise to emphasize your similarities with others around you and deemphasize your differences.

Status.   Organizations usually create clear-cut status distinctions between levels of employees. As we noted previously, there is a chain of command in most organizations that defines formal status in the organization. But there also is informal status. There may be managers and employees, but some managers have higher status than other managers, and some employees have higher status than other employees. The system usually is designed to permit people to earn much more status than they are initially assigned, even without assuming a position at a higher level in the organization. Sometimes, because of the length of time (tenure) one has been in the system, one employee has higher status than others. Some people have nicer offices than others; some may have windows, some do not. Some may have newer equipment than others. Some may have better parking places, a better work schedule, or more choice in assigned duties. Each organization has a variety of symbols to indicate that some employees are viewed as more valuable to the organization (have higher status) than others.

Such symbols normally are considered to have far more psychological value than their intrinsic value. What all of these status symbols have in common is that it is expected that you earn them by service to the organization. If they are acquired in any other way, they have much less value as status symbols. It is sometimes possible to acquire some of the symbols by persistent requests (after all, it is the squeaky wheel that gets the grease!) or irritating one's supervisor (commonly called "bitching," particularly if someone else is doing it). However, it is important to realize that status often does not accompany symbols acquired via such methods. Resentment from one's peers and/or supervisor is more likely to accompany symbols acquired in such manner.

In some cases, the absence of a symbol is in itself a symbol. In one organization with which we are familiar, new desks were being purchased for all senior employees. One employee requested *not* to have a new desk placed in her office. Instead, she asked to have her desk replaced by a table. In her view, a table was more useful to her. This request was viewed as strange by some others in the organization, for one of the indicators of status in that organization was the size of a person's desk. Nevertheless, since she had been there longer than some others and had been a dedicated employee, her request was honored. She had the status to make such an unusual request and have it honored. Since her office became different from everyone else's, the absence of a desk actually increased her status among the employees.

Had this employee been a pain in the neck, she probably would not have had the status to have such a request honored. Although status would probably never have been mentioned, other reasons would have been found not to honor it. Some status is granted with every job, but most of it is earned by putting in time and effort in helping the system, not hurting it. If you want higher status in your organization, normally you must earn it by demonstrating your value and commitment to that organization.

Networks. Organizations have communication networks. Understanding the communication flow and network in any organization is critical to the survival of any employee. The formal communication network follows the organizational chart we discussed previously. The informal network, which often is much more important to your success and survival in the organization, is an unseen set of connections that usually has little or nothing to do with the formal network. You need to know "who knows whom," how long they've known each other, and what they have in common. The informal network follows such friendship connections. For the first few months in an organization or in a new position, you need to do a lot of listening and asking questions but very little opinion giving. You must develop an understanding of the informal network as well as the formal one. If you fail to learn the appropriate communication channels, you might put a foot in your mouth without even knowing it. You can only imagine how much damage you could do to your career in the organization by telling a co-worker how much you dislike your supervisor, only to find out later he/she is married to the supervisor's daughter/son! If you have a well-developed relationship with a mentor, you are much more likely to obtain a good understanding of the informal network in the organization and, of course, much less likely to make such a mistake.

Organizational Culture.   *Culture* is the way a group thinks and behaves. The most common use of this term is with reference to national or ethnic groups that occupy specific geographical territories, such as the "Japanese culture" or the "American culture." Although its use with reference to organizations is primarily metaphorical, the metaphor is particularly appropriate.

Just as people in no two countries or no two ethnic groups are exactly alike, so also people in no two organizations are exactly alike. People in organizations, over time, develop distinct organizational cultures. So too do even different units within large organizations (such as IBM–New York vs. IBM–California). Knowledge about the organization and its interface with the external environment accumulates. Shared beliefs, values, and attitudes develop. Myths are created and perpetuated. Unique ways of interpreting symbols and behaviors are formed. Original words and phrases are created and new meanings are assigned to words in the language. In short, a culture, unique to the people in that organization (or unit within an organization), comes into existence.

Much of the difficulty people have when going from one country to another is a function of not understanding the cultural differences between the countries. Moving from one organization to another can be just as traumatic as moving from one country to another. Social scientists have studied organizations intensely for several decades, but they have reached few conclusions that can be generalized to all organizations. Each conclusion must be tempered with a few or many reservations based on the cultural distinctions between organizations.

In the sense in which we opened this chapter, the organizational culture is the context in which organizational communication takes place. In this section we have attempted to illustrate a few of the important characteristics of organizations that vary as a function of the particular culture of the given organization. Old, established organizations normally will have very powerful cultures, ones that are relatively easy to identify but very difficult to change. Newer, growing organizations frequently will have less well-defined cultures, ones that are more fluid and harder to pin down. Regardless of the type of organization in which you find yourself, it is critical that you learn the culture of that organization. Effective communication depends on conforming to a major extent to the cultural demands that are present.

ORGANIZATIONAL ENVIRONMENTS

All organizations exist physically somewhere; they are a part of a larger community. When you join an organization, it is easy to think of the organization as an entity unto itself since, as we have already noted, it has its own culture and way of seeing things. Employees in organizations often tend to ignore factors outside their office walls, or to recognize that they exist but to consider them irrelevant to their own job. This can be a serious mistake. Since people have lives outside as well as inside organizations, what happens on the outside can have profound impact on what happens on the inside.

The culture of the locality in which an organization exists can significantly impact the culture of the organization. Organizations will literally "pick up" aspects of the culture of the city or region because usually many of the organization's personnel come from the immediate community in which it exists. Lumber companies reflect the culture of the area in which they are located, as do telephone companies, steel mills, car manufacturers, software companies, schools and colleges, and airlines. The organizations will have examples and artifacts of the local culture throughout their premises and will often reflect the thinking of the local people. Hence, new employees, particularly those from outside the immediate area, must be very cautious about conflicting with the local culture. For example, when in Texas, never say *anything* negative about Texas. In the 1970s and 1980s a large number of Easterners relocated in Texas because of better job opportunities. The first thing they had to learn if they wanted to survive in organizations in that state was that in Texas the Texas culture dominates *everything*. "Texas, like a whole other country!"

PRELIMINARY PRINCIPLES FOR PEONS

A "peon" is a worker at or near the bottom of the organizational ladder who does the work that requires minimum skills. Virtually everyone starts at the bottom, even those with college degrees. Almost all of us are, have been, or will be peons at one time or another in our lives. To move out of peon status and into a more rewarding role in the organization, you must demonstrate that you are of value to the organization and do not present a threat to its well-being. In order to do that, you need to avoid the minefields, which are unmarked but block your way to success.

To get you started off on the right track before you have time to read the rest of this book, we have formulated seven principles that may help you on your trek toward success. These principles are not so universally true that they deserve the standing of laws, such as those our friend Murphy has advanced ("whatever can go wrong, will go wrong"), but they are valid often enough to be kept in mind as you venture into your personal organizational minefield.

The Principle of Survival: CYA.   Although the formulator of this principle was guilty of poor spelling, the principle is true nevertheless. To survive in an organization, you must learn immediately how to CYA (cover your behind). By this we do not mean lying, stealing, or blaming a colleague for your errors. We do mean that when making any decisions or carrying out tasks, always be sure to leave yourself a way out. If you make a mistake, admit it and don't make it again. If you make a poor decision, suggest there might be an alternative and go on. Always leave a way to protect yourself. Don't get backed into a corner. Never say things like "Obviously this is the best decision" or "This is the only way of doing it." This will catch up with you, and then you have no way of protecting yourself. We know a teacher who was cautioned against a particular teaching method he was planning to use. He would not admit there might be a better way of teaching the material, so we let him do it his way. He bombed and the students were very upset with him. He had left himself with no way out.

We also know a middle-level manager who would make decisions about how to improve his unit and implement them without even consulting with his supervisor. He lasted less than six months with the company. If he had obtained support for his ideas from his supervisor, his behind would have been covered even if things went wrong. He didn't, and it wasn't.

Doctors are very sensitive to CYA behavior in this age of lawsuits. In fact, some attribute the rising costs of health care in large part to doctors' CYA behaviors. If a patient or close relative of a patient thinks there is a problem, most doctors do not deny or put off the problem; they immediately get a second opinion. Then if two doctors are wrong, at least the original physician can say, "I had a second opinion that supported mine."

Risk taking is very risky for peons. If well-established people make mistakes, they have a history of good efforts to fall back on. Peons don't. Talk to your supervisor. Share your ideas. If you have a good idea, it will still be a good idea if it is approved by your supervisor. If it is a bad idea, your supervisor will either prevent you from making a mistake or at least share the error with you. Remember, if you don't give yourself a way out, someone may *show* you the way out!

The Principle of Power: To become a supervisor, you must prove to be a good subordinate.   As one of our colleagues once put it, a bit more crudely, "If you don't show you can kiss it, they won't let you kick it!" Whenever you enter a new organization, regardless of your skill, education, or experience, you are expected to demonstrate you can do the job "their" way. You may have wonderful ideas for improvement, but the organization was there before you and most likely will be there long after you are gone. Their (the organization's and the people committed to it, like your supervisor) culture says their way is best. Only after you have learned to perform their way *may* they be interested in your new ideas.

Almost everyone is hired on a trial basis in any organization—and many new employees do not survive that trial stage. You must learn the formal and informal norms, obey the rules, and do your job as well as "they" want it done. If you can accomplish all of these objectives, you will start earning some credits as a valuable employee. Remember, those who hired you expect a certain amount of deference and respect for them and their ideas. When you meet these expectations, you are on the road to a more responsible position.

The Principle of Tenure: Old boys (girls) are bigger than big boys (girls). People who have been with the organization a long time (tenure) may have influence beyond what it would seem they have by looking at the formal organizational chart. These "old boys" and "old girls" often have much more power because of their informal contacts than people who appear to be far above them on the formal charts. These are the folks who can tell you, if they chose to do so, where the bodies are buried—since they probably helped bury some of them. They can provide invaluable aid for your survival, or they can virtually seal your fate.

There is a not-too-funny joke that illustrates this point. The question is asked, "Where does an 800-pound gorilla sleep?" The answer is "Anywhere it wants to." Most of the 800-pound gorillas in an organization are old boys and old girls. They usually expect the peons to "heel," and if you do, you may be accepted. Probably the worst mistake you can make as a new member of an organization is to have a "falling out" with an old boy or an old girl. You should try to find out who they are and make friends with them. If you can't make friends, at least stay out of their way. You don't win fights with 800-pound gorillas.

The Principle of Decision Making: Never make a decision today that can be postponed until tomorrow. This is an injunction that many people in organizations think is being followed by all supervisors, but usually is not. It is not, however, as bad an idea as it might seem on the surface. In its favor is the basic fact that you are likely to have more information to base your decision on tomorrow than you do today, and at least you will have no less information. In general, then, it is a wise principle for peons to practice. If you postpone some decisions, the issues will resolve themselves and you will never need to take the risk of making any decision. Of course, this is not always so: Some decisions have to be made immediately; delays can be costly.

The primary way people get into trouble in organizations is by making hasty decisions. Many times people get rushed or pushed into making decisions without the right information or knowing all the facts. Many decisions don't need to be made immediately. Many times one can say, "Let me think about it. Can you get back to me later? I need time to get the facts. I want others' opinions on the issue," and so on. If you are not well acquainted with the system, the people, and the policies, the best advice is to wait on decisions.

The Principle of Modesty: Never appear better than your boss.   Although you might be better than your supervisor—don't go out of your way to show it. He or she might feel threatened and decide you would be "better off" in another organization. It is very naive for any employee, particularly a relatively new one, to get into competition with the person above. The chances of a subordinate succeeding in getting his or her supervisor removed and being selected to replace that person are extremely remote. A far better strategy for success is to work with one's supervisor to help that person achieve a promotion. Such efforts are much more likely to lead to one's own elevation. It is very common for a person who is promoted to a higher position in an organization to be allowed to bring some of his or her people along. Loyal supporters are likely to receive such treatment; competitors are most unlikely to receive it.

The Principle of Self-Importance: The organization got along quite well before you were hired; it can get along quite well if you are fired.   There are extremely few exceptions to the general rule that "no one in an organization is irreplaceable." And when it comes to peons, there virtually are none. No matter how well trained, highly motivated, and brilliant you are, the organization can get along without you. After all, it is getting along without the person you replaced, isn't it? It is quite likely that you need the organization much more than the organization needs you. This is not to say that even the most lowly employee in an organization does not make a contribution. Rather, it is to stress that in most circumstances there are a number of people who could be hired who could make that contribution. The organization does not have to have *you* to obtain it. During your first six months of employment, it is virtually certain that if someone wants to find a reason to fire you, one can be found. Your task is to make certain no one *wants* to. As you move up the organizational hierarchy, you will become more valuable to the organization, and hence more difficult to replace. Do not become self-important before you are important.

The Principle of Acceptance: If you want to be accepted, you must be acceptable.   Several 12-step programs designed to help people overcome various types of problems begin their meetings with a brief prayer: "God grant me the serenity to accept the things I cannot change, courage to change the things I can, and the wisdom to know the difference." New employees would be wise to consider this prayer—particularly the first portion. In the early period of one's employment in an organization, almost everything one is expected to accept is included among "the things I cannot change." If you don't accept things the way they are in the organization, there will be little opportunity for you to change them in the future.

This does not mean you have to love everything about the organization—only that you accept the organization the way it is. Whining is not acceptable. Whiners are not acceptable. Simply put, if you don't like something, you may inquire why it is as it is. But beyond that, shut up about it! As you become more acculturated, you probably will find out why the organization is what it is and does things the way it does. You are even likely to decide things are not as bad as you first thought. Most people in most organizations think their organization is good and its practices, rules, norms, etc. are reasonable. If you express your unwillingness to accept the organization, these people are not going to accept you.

As we indicated previously, these principles are advice you should consider as you enter any new position. They are not guarantees, and their effect is not usually enough to achieve your success. But if followed appropriately, they are likely to permit you to stay around long enough to employ some of the suggestions you will find in the following chapters.

VIEWING ORGANIZATIONS

We hope that the realities discussed in this chapter do not frighten you excessively. Some organizations are wonderful places to spend your working life, others are miserable places to be. Many have both positive and negative characteristics. While it is desirable to be hopefully optimistic as you take a position in an organization, it also is wise to be wary of the problems you can encounter. We have chosen to look at organizations as they often are in this book. We do not suggest how organizations *should be*. Other books on organizational behavior and communication are available that take the latter view. These academic efforts often are driven by post-modern or feminist-Marxist approaches. For more advanced studies in organizational communication these efforts are of considerable value. However, we believe "peons" need to understand the realities of modern organizations and the roles of communication before they begin to theorize about how to improve them. Hence, this book attempts to provide a realistic view of organizations that both peons and former peons can understand and deal with—warts and all.

REFERENCES AND RECOMMENDED READINGS

Adams, S. (1996). *The Dilbert principle*. New York, NY: Harper Business, A Division of Harper Collins Publishers.

Frank, A. D., & Brownell, J. L. (1989). *Organizational communication and behavior: Communicating to improve performance* (2 + 2 = 5). New York: Holt, Rinehart, and Winston.

Hickson, M., III. (1973). The open systems model: Auditing the effectiveness of organizational communication. *Journal of Business Communication, 10,* 7–14.

Katz, D., & Kahn, R. (1966). *The social psychology of organizations.* New York: John Wiley & Sons.

Koehler, J. W., Anatol, K. W. E., & Applbaum, R. L. (1981). *Organizational communication: Behavioral perspectives.* (2nd Ed.). New York: Holt, Rinehart, & Winston.

McCroskey, J. C. (1990). Fitting into the department. In J. A. Daly, G. W. Friedrich, & A. L. Vangelisti (Eds.), *Teaching communication: Theory, research, and methods.* Hillsdale, NJ: Lawrence Erlbaum, 471–480.

McCroskey, J. C., & Richmond, V. P. (1996). *Fundamentals of human communication: An interpersonal perspective.* Prospect Heights, IL: Waveland Press.

McCroskey, J. C., & Richmond, V. P. (1996). Human communication theory and research: Traditions and models. In M. B. Salwen & D. W. Stacks (Eds.). *An integrated approach to communication theory and research.* Mahwah, NJ: Lawrence Erlbaum Publishers, 233–242.

Richmond, V. P., & McCroskey, J. C. (2004). *Nonverbal behavior in interpersonal relations.* (5th Ed.). Needham Heights, MA: Allyn and Bacon.

Rogers, E. M., & Agarwala-Rogers, R. (1976). *Communication in organizations.* New York: Free Press.

Stone, G., & Singletary, M., & Richmond, V. P. (1999). *Clarifying communication theories: A hands-on approach.* Ames, IA: Iowa State University Press.

STUDY GUIDE

1. Identify and distinguish among the three types of organizations.
2. Explain what is meant when we say "an organization is a system."
3. Define and distinguish between "roles" and "rules" as they apply to organizations. Why is each important?
4. What is meant by a "disorganized organization"? Why is this concept important?
5. What is meant by "organizational norms"? Why are they important?
6. Distinguish between "similarity" and "status." Which is more important? Why?
7. Identify and distinguish between the two types of communication networks in an organization. Which is more important to a peon's survival? Why?
8. Explain the concept of "organizational culture."
9. Why is the environment in which an organization exists important?
10. What are the seven Preliminary Principles for Peons? Which of the principles is most important? Why?

CHAPTER 2

THE NATURE OF COMMUNICATION IN ORGANIZATIONS

Regardless of the type of organization, communication is the element that maintains and sustains relationships in it. What person A says to person B not only can have an impact on those two people but, since organizations are systems, it also can have a meaningful impact on the total system. Your communication with your co-workers and supervisors in the organization will be a major determinant of how satisfied you are with your work, and how satisfied *others* are with your work.

For example, in one organization where we worked, there was a very gossipy, control-oriented person who would subtly let others know what he/she thought of his/her co-workers. Eventually, this type of communication made it impossible for others to work with this individual. When asked to work with this person, others would find excuses not to or would become "ill" when the time to do the work rolled around. This, of course, had a negative impact on the work of the total unit. The communication behavior of individual employees plays a more significant role in organizational life than some think. Organizational communication is central to organization success.

MYTHS AND MISCONCEPTIONS ABOUT COMMUNICATION IN ORGANIZATIONS

Only a small proportion of the people in most organizations have ever engaged in serious study of how the process of communication works. Communication is one of those things we deal with every day, so most of us assume we know quite a bit about it. Although that assumption often is correct, most of us also know some things about communication because they are just "common sense." Unfortunately, some things that are "common sense" are just plain wrong. Before we turn our attention to some of the basic facts about communication in organizations, and some advice on how to deal with those realities, we need to look at some of the most common misconceptions about communication in organizations so we do not fall prey to these myths as we strive to survive.

Myth 1: Meanings are in words.   The idea that meanings are in words is perhaps the most common misconception about communication. This misconception can lead to much misunderstanding between two people and thwart the effectiveness of communication between supervisor and subordinate. What a particular word means to us may not be what it means to someone else. The word stimulates a meaning in our minds that is different from the meaning it stimulates in the mind of our colleague. For example, the word *evaluation* carries different meanings for people at different levels in the organization. The lower-level employees might feel this means the end of them. The upper-level management might feel this means support for their work. The point we wish to make about words and their meanings is that no word has meaning apart from the person using it. No two people share precisely the same meanings for all words. *Meanings are in people, not words.* Therefore, we must realize that what we say to others in the organization might not stimulate in their minds the meaning we want or intend to be stimulated. This requires that we adapt our ideas to the background and experiences of our colleagues so that they can adapt to our ideas.

Myth 2: Communication is a verbal process.   When most people, whether they are top management or have just taken an entry-level position, think about communication, they think chiefly about words—written or spoken. They rarely focus on the relevance of the nonverbal aspect of communication. Yet much of communication is nonverbal. In fact, when we talk to someone, our verbal communication is always accompanied by nonverbal messages as well. *How* we say something is as important as *what* we say, and often more important. How we act is as important as what we say, and often more important. Nonverbal actions often contradict verbal messages, and when they do most people believe the nonverbal over the verbal. Thus, *the process of communication is both verbal and nonverbal.*

Myth 3: Telling is communicating.   Many employees and managers feel that if they have "said it to her" or "told him about it," they have communicated. They may have tried to communicate, but that is no guarantee they have communicated. It is very naive to think that this is all there is to communication. *Telling is only part of communication—often a small part.* People who believe that telling people something is equal to communicating with them fail to acknowledge the active role of receivers. Sources have to consider what meaning a receiver might attach to the message, what a receiver's background is, what a receiver thinks and feels. If anything, telling is only half of communicating. To be effective communicators, we have to be sensitive to the other person's views and communication skills. If your boss makes this mistake, you can be assured you will be blamed for the boss's mistake. Consequently, you must take an active role in communicating with your supervisor to be certain you fully understand anything you are told. Although it is not fair to hold you responsible for inadequate communication on the part of the boss, that is the reality with which you must be prepared to deal.

Myth 4: Communication will solve all our problems.   For years, people have tried to convince us that communication will solve all our problems. If the wife and the husband are not getting along, get them to sit down and talk it out—that will solve the problem. If the parent and the child are not getting along, get them to sit down and talk it out—that will solve the problem. If the supervisor and the subordinate cannot get along, get them to sit down and talk it out—that will solve the problem. Unfortunately, it just is not so. *Communication can either create or help overcome problems.*

Remember, there are a lot of ineffective communicators out there, and often they create more problems than they solve by not knowing how to use communication. There are some situations where communication should be decreased, not increased, such as in true conflict situations. The parties should be separated, not forced to communicate. Yet in many organizations, some individuals always think communication can solve problems, so they put two people or two groups together who hate each other. They force them to communicate and cannot understand why matters only get worse. Effective organizational communication may allow us to solve some problems, but it cannot be expected to solve all problems. Communication is no magic elixir. It will not cure cancer, it will not overcome weight problems, and it will not solve all the problems in an organization. But we can, by communicating more effectively, avoid making some things worse.

Myth 5: Communication is a good thing.   Ask 10 people you encounter at work today, "Is communication a good thing?" Probably over half, maybe all 10, will look at you a bit strangely and answer "Certainly," or words to that effect. Since, as we noted above, many people think communication will solve all our problems, it is reasonable they would also think of communication as "good." In reality, communication is neither a good nor a bad thing. *Communication is a tool,* and like any tool, communication can be used for good or bad purposes. The way a person uses communication determines its goodness or badness. For example, take a computer. If we use this tool for its intended purpose—to process information—we can say that it is a good and useful device. Put that computer in the hands of an irate employee and he or she can use it to destroy data and information. Is the computer bad? No, it is simply being used in a bad way. It is the same for communication. We can use our communication for good or evil purposes.

Hopefully, this book will suggest ways in which to use communication as a positive tool to enhance our work environment and our work relationships.

Myth 6: The more communication, the better.   If it is a good thing, and it will solve all our problems, then of course the more of it the better. This myth is tied to the two previous ones. This myth is so prevalent in American society that it has assumed the position of a stereotype. If one meeting is good, two would be better. If one memo is good, two would be better. If one evaluation review conference is good, two would be better. People often do not recognize that *it is the quality of communication that is important, not the pure quantity of it.* In many "white-collar" occupations, meetings are the bane of people's existence. Some people spend more than 75 percent of their working hours in meetings with other employees. Although much of this time no doubt is spent productively, interviews with hundreds of such workers convince us that a very large portion of that time is wasted. It is based on the assumption that the more people talk to one another, the better will be the decision that is made. Not necessarily so. Pooling ignorance does not produce intelligence.

Myth 7: Communication can break down.   When people feel a need to place blame for their poor decisions, their interpersonal incompetence, their failure to consult with wiser persons before taking action, we hear the phrase "communication breakdown." Human communication does not break down, although electronic communication systems can do so. We often communicate unsuccessfully and sometimes we stop talking to someone, but in neither instance has communication broken down. As one learns early in the study of nonverbal communication, one cannot *not* communicate. Although this phrase is the English teacher's nightmare, it expresses very well the nature of communication between human beings. Such communication is ongoing, even if words are not being exchanged. Nonverbal messages are likely to continue and, even in the extreme, silence and the absence of new verbal messages in itself communicates. If your supervisor refuses to talk to you, has communication ended? Hardly, but your employment may be about to do so.

Myth 8: Communication is a natural ability.   Just as Myth 7 is used as a substitute for our failures and foul-ups, this myth is used as an excuse for not trying to be a better communicator. If people are born with or without the ability to communicate, so the thinking goes, how can I be blamed for being a poor communicator? Sorry, no excuse. *Communication is a learned ability.* While our personality and temperament may be primarily determined by our genes, we acquire our communication skills from our experiences and our education. If what we have acquired is inadequate, it is up to us to see to it that we take the initiative to overcome our inadequacy. Communication competence can be learned, and practice can help us improve.

The fact that you have read this far in this book suggests you are taking that initiative. Read on. We will try to be of help in your quest. Our next task will be to make sure we define what you are going to be studying.

ORGANIZATIONAL COMMUNICATION DEFINED

For the purposes of this book, we define organizational communication as *the process by which individuals stimulate meaning in the minds of other individuals by means of verbal or nonverbal messages in the context of a formal organization.* Some portions of this definition may need clarification.

The word *process* indicates that communication is dynamic and ever changing. Communication is much like the river spoken of by the Greek philosopher Heraclitus, who said that you can't step in the same river twice—from the moment you take your foot out of the water until you put it back in, the river changes so much that it really isn't the same river. As we change as individuals over time, and from one organizational event to another, our communication changes in the organizational environment.

The words *stimulate meaning* are intended to suggest that it is through communication with others that we develop, generate, cultivate, shape, and reshape ideas. It is rare that we develop an idea entirely on our own. Many of our ideas are formed or created by meanings that others have stimulated.

Ideas may be stimulated by either verbal or nonverbal messages. By *verbal messages* we mean the language common to the culture and organization. We transmit these language codes or symbols in either spoken or written form. For example, when the manager says to you, "I want this TRR memo handled tomorrow," you have to know the language in order to respond. If you know that TRR stands for Travel Reimbursement Request, you can respond in the appropriate manner. If you do not, you have to ask what the "language" means. By *nonverbal messages* we are referring to messages other than verbal, such as tone of voice, eye behavior, touch, hand gestures, body movements, facial expressions, and so on. When the manager stares at an employee when the employee walks in a few minutes late for the weekly meeting, meaning may be stimulated in the minds of everyone else in the room.

Communication is a complex process, and in order to survive in organizations, you must know what the process is and how it works. To clarify this point, we need first to turn our attention to the components of the communication process.

COMPONENTS OF COMMUNICATION

A number of early writers in the field of communication developed models of the communication process. Most of them included what were considered to be the four essential components of the process: source, message,

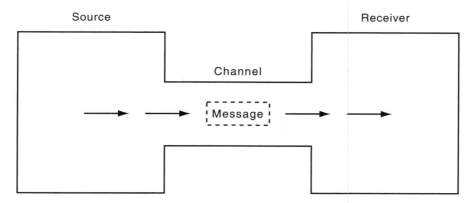

FIGURE 2.1   Basic Communication Model

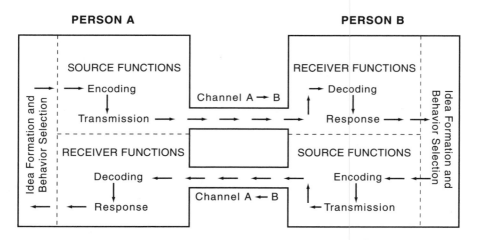

FIGURE 2.2   Interpersonal Communication Model

channel, and receiver. A model representative of those early writings is presented in Figure 2.1. Although the model has some major weaknesses (communication is not presented as a process), it does include what are generally considered the primary components of the communication process.

An expanded version of the early models is represented by the interpersonal communication model (see Figure 2.2). As you can see, this model allows both persons to function as sources or receivers; it also allows for the process nature of communication, for feedback, and for transmission of messages by either party. This model clearly presents human interaction as a process. In the organizational environment, sources are constantly becoming receivers, and the process is ongoing. Communication in the organizational environment is not static; it does not stop or come to a standstill.

People are constantly exchanging ideas and stimulating meaning in the minds of others. Based on a combination of these models, let's take a look at the critical components in the communication process.

The Source.   In the communication process, the source is the person who originates a message. In a broader view, the source could be any individual or collection of individuals—one person, a group, a dyad (twosome), or an entire organization. It could be a group of managers wanting to explain policy changes to employees, it could be a hamburger chain attempting to influence others to buy their hamburgers, or it could be one employee explaining to another employee how to complete a certain task. Whether an organization, group, or individual, the source has three primary functions in communication: (1) determine what specific meaning is to be communicated, (2) encode (translating ideas and information into messages) meaning into one or more messages, and (3) transmit the message(s).

In an organizational environment, one individual may assume all three functions, but it is not uncommon to see each one performed by a different person. For example, a manager wants to communicate certain ideas to his or her employees; he or she may turn to an assistant to ask advice on how best to state the message, and then he or she may select an employee others like and respect and ask that person to carry the message to the rest of the employees. It is therefore very important that as sources we select messages that have mutual meaning for us and the receiver, and that we communicate in a way that will make others want to receive the message.

The Message.   A message is any verbal or nonverbal stimulus that elicits meaning in the receiver. When communicating in any environment, most people use a combination of verbal and nonverbal stimuli to stimulate meaning in another. For simplification, we can think of verbal as employing words and nonverbal as employing other stimuli (gestures, smiles, frowns, groans, nods, yawns, touching others, and so on, see Chapter 3) to stimulate meaning. It is not uncommon for an employee or a manager to use these simultaneously when communicating with each other. It is virtually impossible to monitor all nonverbal behaviors. For example, you can more easily monitor your selection of words, but it is very difficult to monitor every facial movement, body movement, eye movement, leg movement, and so on. Sometimes our nonverbal messages will convey much more meaning than our verbal. Good managers have learned to try to interpret the meaning behind the nonverbal messages of their employees as well as the verbal messages; likewise for employees.

The Channel.   A channel is a means by which a message is carried from one person to another. In live interaction, our senses (sight, sound, touch, smell, and taste) become channels. Channels can also take the form of mediated systems—television, radio, the Internet, the world wide web, film, bill-boards, telephones, etc. In organizations, people often become the most important channels. For example, supervisors function as channels between upper levels of management and lower-level employees. Secretaries often serve as channels between people on different levels and/or in different parts of the organization. People serving as channels make up the informal communication network in organizations.

The Receiver.   Just as the source is the person who originates a message, the receiver is the person who acquires the source's message. Like the source, the receiver can be an individual, a group, or an entire organization. Also like the source, the receiver has three functions: (1) receive the source's message, (2) decode (translation of messages into ideas or information) the message into some meaning, and (3) respond to the message. Again, it is typical for one person to handle all three functions, but not uncommon for more than one person to be involved. For example, a new employee might receive the manager's message, but have an older, more-experienced employee interpret it for her or him and have another employee respond to the interpretation.

For communication to be effective, employees and managers need to consider the backgrounds and experiences of each other. This may require that we "put ourselves in the other person's shoes." A manager needs to know the employees to have effective communication with them; likewise for an employee. One of the primary reasons for problems in the organizational environment is that individuals do not understand what one another is saying because they do not communicate with each other enough to get to know one another's attitudes and feelings. Hence, many employees make major errors in communication—and so do managers. We have to be more effective sources and receivers if we want to improve communication. Even if our supervisor is an incompetent bozo, we will be more effective in communicating with "the bozo" if we go to the effort of getting to know her or him better so we are better able to adapt our messages to take her or his feelings into account.

Feedback.   Feedback is the receiver's observable response(s) to a source's message. Such responses can be either of a verbal nature (for example, I don't agree with you; Yes, that is right!) or a nonverbal nature (for example, a frown, shaking one's head in disagreement, nodding in agreement).

Feedback is extremely critical in all communication situations, but particularly so in interpersonal communication between manager and employee. A manager can carefully observe an employee's response to judge the success or failure of messages being sent. When feedback is negative, new messages can be constructed. Feedback is the method we use to regulate the messages we send and those that are sent to us. Many astute managers have "advisory" groups or boards comprising selected employees whom they use as "sounding boards" for messages and information that is going to be sent to all employees. These "sounding board" groups have ideas bounced off them, and how they respond often determines how the message is sent or whether it is even sent to other employees in the company at all.

Goals. Generally there are three major goals of communication in the organizational environment: developing interpersonal relationships, gaining compliance, and gaining understanding. Let's take a look at each of these goals and its impact on the organization.

Most of us have the need to develop interpersonal relationships with our colleagues in organizations. It is a basic need, much like our needs for food, water, and shelter. We communicate with our colleagues with the idea that good working relationships can be formed. Whether it is in the work environment or in other environments, most of us communicate to develop interpersonal relationships with others. We want friends, colleagues, and companions we can talk with both on a formal and an informal basis.

We also communicate to gain the compliance of others. Communication directed toward gaining compliance seeks to influence others' beliefs and actions. By "gaining compliance" we mean getting another person (manager) to engage in some behavior that is desired by the source (employee). Usually, our desire to get others to comply is influenced by the fact that we want a change of some kind. For example, the employee who wants to change her or his usual vacation time has to communicate with the supervisor in such a way that she or he will comply with the request. The employee might have to persuade the supervisor. She or he might have to promise to do extra work because it is an inconvenience to rearrange vacation schedules. Communicating to get others to comply is a way of life in contemporary organizations.

Finally, we communicate to gain understanding. We all have a need to know and understand what is going on in our environment. To know and understand, we need information. To acquire information, we must communicate with others. Much of the communication in organizations is for this purpose. People will make inquiries and ask for clarification so they can understand how and why the organization operates as it does. Managers and employees talk to each other for many of the same reasons.

Although the three goals can be separate, it is rare when they are achieved independently. In other words, to achieve one of these goals usually requires that one or both of the other two also be achieved. Relationship development in the organization is a good example. When we first meet a new colleague, we often need or want to know how the other person will respond to us. Hence, our desire to know more about the person and how the person will react to us in a given situation creates the need for information, which can be acquired only by communicating with that person.

When we have gained that knowledge, we have reduced some of our uncertainty about the other person, and the goals of relationship development and gaining understanding both have been met. Often when we meet people in the work environment, we establish a relationship and gain some understanding about them. This assists us when we want to gain a person's compliance. For example, employees who know their supervisors well and have a close relationship with them might find it easier to get the supervisor to comply with certain requests. Of course, astute supervisors are aware of this and may avoid allowing many employees to get close to them or know them too well.

Context.   We conclude our discussion of the critical components of the organizational communication process by focusing on the "context" of communication. Generally, we refer to the characteristics of a situation in which communication takes place as the "context." This is an important concern for organizations because people do not communicate in exactly the same way within any two different contexts. Thus, even when we are communicating with a particular individual (for example, a manager), how and what we communicate is likely to change as the context in which we communicate changes.

There are issues we will discuss with our co-workers that we might not discuss with our supervisor. Regardless of our role in the organization, the rules for each interaction will change when we change communication partners. We can easily draw from our own experiences how communication with close friends on the job differs from that with new members in the organization. As our role changes (for example, we get a promotion), so do the rules for communicating with organizational members.

In conclusion, communication is a dynamic, ongoing process. We need to understand the context and the rules for a given context so we can adapt to the "real world" in which we find ourselves. Only by adapting to the context can we be more competent communicators in our organizations.

FUNCTIONS OF COMMUNICATION IN ORGANIZATIONS

Communication serves many functions in organizations. There are six functions that seem to dominate communication in the organizational context. The functions are inform, regulate, integrate, manage, persuade, and socialize.

The *informative* function of communication is fairly self-explanatory. It is the function of providing needed information to personnel so they can do their jobs in an effective and efficient manner. People need to be informed about any changes of procedure or policy that are related to their work. Sometimes this function is accomplished by people at higher levels sending information to people at lower levels, and the reverse. At other times, people needing information must contact people who have the needed information to acquire it.

Much of the informative communication in organizations is conducted in a written format. This way, a whole group of employees can be informed with one message and at one time. On the other hand, managers may decide to call a meeting once each week (or month) which is primarily of an informative nature. Most employees understand that such meetings are for the purpose of disseminating information and can be prepared to inquire about matters about which they feel they need additional information.

The *regulative* function of communication is involved with the communication that is directed toward regulatory policies within the organization or messages about maintenance of the organization. For example, an employee might be informed by the manager that he or she has broken some rule or regulation and is not to break it again. Communication that involves the regulative function is often not pleasant, but it is essential to the smooth operation of the organization.

The *integrative* function of communication is focused on coordination of tasks, work assignments, group coordination, or the fusing of work units toward a common goal. In other words, it is communication directed at getting people to work together and have tasks coordinated so that the "left hand knows what the right hand is doing." It is an attempt to get people to work together and make things run more smoothly. For example, consultants often will find employees duplicating each other's work, whereas if there were more integrative communication, one could do one task and another do a related task.

The *management* function of communication is directed toward the three goals mentioned earlier. It is communication focused on getting personnel to do what is needed, learning information about personnel to know them better, and establishing relationships with personnel. If one can meet the interpersonal relationship goal and the understanding goal, he or she might have a better chance at knowing "how to manage" the employees.

The *persuasive* function of communication is an outgrowth of the management function. Here the supervisor is attempting to influence the employee to do something in particular. Whereas simply issuing an order might accomplish the same function, this approach makes for much better relations between supervisors and subordinates.

Finally, we have the *socialization* function. Although the other functions seem obvious and are rarely missed by either managers or employees, the socialization function is often neglected. This is perhaps the most important function. The socialization function of communication in the organization is the one that can determine whether an individual survives well, or not at all, in an organization. Socialization doesn't mean being "buddies" with everyone. It means being integrated into the communication networks in the organization. It means being told whom one should talk to and what one should talk about. It also means being told whom not to talk to. It means being told what to say in certain situations and what not to say. It means being told how to address others (Ms., Sir, Dr.). It means being told the informal norms of the organization (what social gatherings to attend, what to wear at luncheons, what things others find offensive). It means being told the idiosyncratic behaviors (and pet peeves) of others. It means knowing whom you should associate with and whom you should avoid (who are the "in" people and who are the "out" people). In a nutshell, it means survival! Today, many organizations realize the value of this function and will assign each new employee to an employee who has been with the organization for some time so the experienced person can assist the new-comer in "settling into" the organization the first two or three weeks. These guides help new employees "learn the ropes" without upsetting the system or saying things that could hurt them with the older, more established employees.

In summary, all of the functions are important. However, the function most important and probably most neglected by organizations is the socialization function. Hence, if organizations neglect socializing us, then we have to do it ourselves. The best way is to listen and watch the first few weeks. Then start having what we call CCC (casual conversations with colleagues) to learn what you should or should not say or do in your organization.

ORGANIZATIONAL COMMUNICATION NETWORKS

There are two primary communication networks that exist in any organizational environment. These are the formal communication network and the informal communication network. The *formal* network is communication that follows the hierarchical structure of the organization, or the "chain of command." It follows the formal, established, official lines of contact. In other words, it follows the prescribed path of the hierarchical chart and tends to be explicit in terms of "who should be talking to whom and about what." The formal chart for this network often is provided to new employees the first day they walk in the door. It explains whom they report to and for what. There usually is little confusion about the formal communication network.

The *informal* network involves communication that follows the "grapevine." It carries the "scuttlebutt," the rumors. It is the unofficial network. This is the type of communication that does not follow the hierarchical path or chain of command. It tells you "who is *really* talking to whom and about what." We are not talking about "gossip" here. Gossip can exist in either network. We are referring to informal communication links that have grown out of relationships among employees and management and that have little or no correlation with the formal organizational chart. The informal network is very strong in most organizations. It usually works much faster than the formal network, and often it works with more accuracy. Until you have access to this informal network, you have not really become a part of the system.

An employee needs to be aware of both networks. Management has more control over the formal network than the informal, but employees have more control over the informal network than management does. It usually is relatively easy to learn the formal network, but specific information regarding the informal network may be more elusive. Being properly socialized assists an employee in gaining understanding about the informal system in the particular organization.

It is critical that employees and management remember that the formal network is not the only network functioning in the organization. One needs to remember that the informal network is a very powerful communication avenue and carries information that the formal network doesn't. The informal network tells you "who is playing golf with whom," "who is sleeping with whom," "who has an occasional lunch with whom," "who is distantly related to whom," "who protects or defends whom," "who promoted whom, and why." These all are things the formal network almost never tells an individual, but the informal network usually will when one is properly socialized.

In conclusion, you must learn the formal network, but don't forget to take the time to learn the informal network also. It, too, can make the difference between surviving and not surviving in the organization.

FORMAL COMMUNICATION FLOW AND IMPACT

In this section we review the types of communication flow in organizations and the impact of each type. Communication flows in two directions in the organization: vertically and horizontally. *Vertical* communication is concerned with communication between employees at different hierarchical levels in the organization. It focuses on *downward* and *upward* communication between managers and employees. *Horizontal* communication is concerned with communication between employees at the same level in the organization. It focuses on communication between peers, people at equal or very nearly equal levels in the organization. It is communication that goes across the organization. Let's look at what types of communication flow downward in the organization.

Downward Communication.   The first type of vertical communication is downward communication, that which flows from upper management down to the employees at lower ranks. Downward communication generally is effective when upper levels of management are highly motivated to make it work. There are five different elements that generally flow downward in all organizations. They are job instruction, rationale, ideology, information, and feedback.

Job instruction is the conveying of information to subordinates about what they are expected to do. It can be carried out by a variety of means, such as direct orders, written memos, workshops on how to do the job, and so on. The key here is that job instructions should be precise and applied directly to one's job.

Rationale is the rationalization or explanation of a duty or assignment and how it is compatible with what the personnel are already doing. Again, this can be carried out by various oral or written methods.

Ideology is an extension of rationale. This type of downward communication seeks to obtain the loyalty of the employees. Ideology is the philosophy of the organization. Managers want employees to "buy into" the organizational philosophy. When everyone has the same or similar ideals and goals, communication becomes easier. Many organizations have a written ideology they give to new employees when they walk through the door.

Information is concerned with acquainting employees with general bits of knowledge that they need to know, such as regulations, changes in benefits, and general policies. It usually is of an informative nature and does not require a response from the employee. It is simply to give employees needed information.

Feedback is the manager's way of giving employees information about how they are doing. Feedback can take many forms, such as salary increase or decrease, a pat on the back, a termination notice, a smile, or a frown. Supervisors need to provide feedback on job performance on a regular basis so that subordinates know how to change what they are doing poorly and keep doing what they are doing well. Feedback also needs to be clear, appropriate, and with instructions on how to make any needed changes.

People at the lower levels of the organization are dependent in many ways on the downward communication of management for their own success. However, management controls most of the means by which downward communication occurs. If that control does not permit needed information to flow to you, you must actively prompt the system to get it. It may be management's fault that the downward system is not working, but the person who receives the blame normally will be at the other end of the line. Does this sound familiar?

Upward Communication. Although upward communication is initiated by those at the lower levels of the organization, it can be successful only if those at the higher levels are willing to allow the communication to be effective. There are five factors that are most likely to influence upper levels of the organization to allow the upward communication to be effective. Upward communication should be positive, timely, support current policy, be sent directly to the person who can act on it, and have intuitive appeal in order to go up the system without being stopped, ignored, or sent back down.

Positive communication is more likely to go up the system than negative. Many times employees think the negative will go through the system faster than the positive; however, this is not the case. Supervisors try to prevent negative information from reaching their managers, but forward the positive right up to them. If too much negative reaches a person's immediate supervisor, it looks as if the person is not doing his or her job. Managers try to "keep the noise level down" in their respective units. They don't want negatives going up, so they "filter out" the negative information. They send positive information to their bosses so they are seen as doing their jobs. Hence, if you want something to go up the system, couch it in positive terms.

A message must be sent at the *appropriate time* to be allowed to go on up the system. It should be timely or it may not be acted on. Think of your own situation. When is it a good time to "ask for a raise," "ask about vacation," "ask about different duties," "ask about being absent for a day"? If you do not learn timeliness, you are likely to be asking at the "wrong time" or to be "getting yelled at" for inappropriate behavior. When your boss has a sign on the door that says "Do not disturb," is this the time to go in and ask for help with a problem?

Messages that *support current policy* are much more likely to be given attention than those that are incompatible with current policy. If a message supports current policy, it is easier for management to adapt it to the system. Hence, try to generate messages that are consistent with current policies.

Many times messages are ignored or not acted on because they are sent to people who cannot make a decision about them. It is essential that messages be forwarded to *those people who can act on them*, or else communication will be ineffective. In many organizations if a message is sent to a person who cannot act on it, it is simply discarded. It goes into the ever-popular "File 13." The person who generated the message may never know what happened to it. The best advice is *do not bother to send a message unless you know it is going to the person with authority to act with regard to it.*

Finally, messages that have *intuitive appeal* are much more likely to go up the system than those that don't. "Intuitive appeal" is an idea that "sounds good." For example, messages dealing with ideas about how productivity can be increased quickly, how more profit can be achieved without a great deal of effort, or how major problems can be avoided without a lot of expense are likely to get sent right up the system.

In becoming a more-effective communicator in your organization, you must be aware of what will come down the system and what will go up. Adapt your communication so you can use the system and get messages to the correct sources. Don't expect the system to change because you don't like the communication —it won't. And you cannot force inappropriate messages through the system. At every level there is another person trying to block them.

Horizontal Communication. This is communication that flows across the organization (from peer to peer to peer). There is much more horizontal communication in organizations on a daily basis than there is vertical. This is a function of two things: (1) There are more employees than managers, and (2) employees at the same level feel more comfortable talking with each other than with people at different authority levels.

Horizontal communication often focuses on employee satisfaction and employee morale. Here is where you usually can talk openly and freely about your feelings about the system and can discuss your problems with others who can identify with them. In addition, this is also the channel at which most social interaction takes place within the formal organization. It is through the horizontal channels that you are likely to increase your knowledge, communication skills, and socialization skills. This often is where you can establish long-lasting interpersonal relationships that can assist you in becoming a better employee with a better chance of survival in the organization.

REFERENCES AND RECOMMENDED READINGS

McCroskey, J. C., & Richmond, V. P. (1996). Human communication theory and research: Traditions and models. In M. B. Salwen & D. W. Stacks (Eds.). *An integrated approach to communication theory and research.* Mahwah, NJ: Lawrence Erlbaum Publishers, 233–242.

McCroskey, J. C., & Richmond, V. P. (1997). *Communication in educational organizations.* Acton, MA: Tapestry Press.

McCroskey, J. C. (2001). *An introduction to rhetorical communication.* (8th ed.). Needham Heights, MA: Allyn and Bacon.

Richmond, V. P., & McCroskey, J. C. (1998). *Communication: Apprehension, avoidance, and effectiveness.* (5th ed.). Needham Heights, MA: Allyn and Bacon.

Richmond, V. P., & McCroskey, J. C. (2004). *Nonverbal behavior in interpersonal relations.* (5th ed.). Needham Heights, MA: Allyn and Bacon.

STUDY GUIDE

1. Identify each of the eight myths or misconceptions about communication in organizations. Provide an appropriate alternative view to replace each one.
2. Define "organizational communication." Explain the term *process.*
3. Identify and briefly define the critical components in the communication process.

4. Identify and distinguish among the functions of communication in organizations.
5. What kind of information flows through informal networks? Why?
6. What kind of messages flow top-down through formal networks? Why?
7. What factors increase the likelihood of information's flowing bottom-up through formal networks? Why?
8. Is there more vertical or horizontal communication in most organizations? Why?
9. Explain what is meant by "socialization" and why it is important to peons.

CHAPTER 3

NONVERBAL BEHAVIOR AND COMMUNICATION

Nonverbal behaviors have a significant impact on human communication. In fact, it has been estimated that approximately two-thirds of the perceived meaning in any communication situation is likely to be stimulated by nonverbal messages. Mehrabian and Ferris (1967) estimate that, on an average, 93 percent of meaning in interpersonal communication comes from nonverbal messages. While this estimate may appear somewhat high, scholars and practitioners agree that much of the meaning a person receives from a message comes from the available nonverbal messages. Sometimes, the outcome of communication is entirely the result of nonverbal messages.

Even if a person is not visible to another, (for example, using the phone) the person's voice will send nonverbal cues as to what the person is thinking or feeling. Many people have had the experience of calling an organization for information and getting a person with a voice that is monotone, harsh, and/or unpleasant sounding. Usually, these types of vocal tones result in a negative reaction and do not encourage a person to carry on a conversation or to call back for more information. Our negative reactions (to the person on the phone, and the organization he/she represents) can be entirely produced by the nonverbal messages we receive.

Nonverbal communication is the process of a person or persons (such as a manager) stimulating meaning in the mind of another person or persons (such as an employee) by means of nonverbal messages. Nonverbal communication is that communication produced by all available behaviors and cues other than the words we use. Of course, in talking to people in organizations, using words mandates that we use at least one set of nonverbal messages—vocalic cues, for it is through vocalic cues that words are conveyed to others.

SIGNIFICANCE OF NONVERBAL
COMMUNICATION IN ORGANIZATIONS

There are six reasons why we believe nonverbal communication is extremely important in organizations. Each is a sufficient reason to try to better understand nonverbal communicative messages.

   1. *The first form of human communication was nonverbal communication.* Before the development of formal oral languages, and many additional millennia before such recent developments as writing, sign language, and e-mail, the human species used nonverbal messages as their only form of communication. Gestures, facial expressions, and vocalic noises were used to convey meaning. We see such communication continuing today in our nearest relatives, other primates. Nonverbal communication is a core behavior of humans (as it is in other primates) that surrounds our verbal communication efforts. Our inadequacy to communicate how we feel solely by verbal communication is manifest today even in our most technically advanced communication methods. Who has not been so concerned that they will not be understood, that they have used a happy face in their e-mail? Organizations are made up of human beings (regardless of what we might think some of them descend from). And humans are first and foremost, nonverbal communicators. The receptionist who smiles at us when we enter the door often counts for far more in determining how we feel about the organization than all the lofty slogans the bureaucrats bleat in its name.
   2. *Many people fail at communication because they are nonverbally illiterate.* It is amazing the number of people who disregard the impact of nonverbal communication on relationships in organizations. Quite simply, many managers and employees fail to become effective communicators because they do not understand that nonverbal communication is an integral and critical part of the total communication process. While people work to perfect the verbal, they disregard the impact of the nonverbal. But we are hesitant to place blame on individuals in this regard. Our educational system places almost totally exclusive emphasis on verbal communication, and 99 percent of that on written communication. While every student in primary school and secondary school has been inundated with information about verbal communication (often in multiple languages), less than one percent of college graduates have ever had an opportunity to take a class devoted to the study of nonverbal communication. It is no wonder that the most common and destructive mistakes in communication which are made in organizations are nonverbal ones.
   3. *Nonverbal messages are always present.* Many communication scholars and practitioners realize that nonverbal communication continues even when the verbal communication has ended. The idea that "a person cannot not communicate," refers to the idea that nonverbal messages are ever pres-

ent. People can communicate with each other nonverbally, even when they are not speaking. For example, a severe look or a welcoming gesture may say more than words, and may do so in the complete absence of words.

4. *Verbal and nonverbal messages usually work together.* It is virtually impossible to find a verbal message that does not have a nonverbal component. Even computer language, e-mail, and other nonhuman technologies carry a nonverbal component. The symbols used, size of words, and so on are all nonverbal components of a verbal language. For the most part, as we will discuss in the following pages, verbal and nonverbal messages function together rather than separately.

5. *Nonverbal messages often are more important than the verbal ones.* In some organizational situations the verbal messages can be more important than the nonverbal, but in most situations the nonverbal is more important than the verbal. It is arguable, for example, that in tedious and critical briefings focusing on new information, the verbal messages may be the most important. The verbal messages have their biggest impact in terms of learning content, and this is a content-focused context. However, nonverbal messages better convey the affective component of communication. Consequently, they have their biggest impact on the way people feel about their interaction, and the people with whom they interact.

6. *Nonverbal communication is believed.* In meetings, both managers and employees look for the "true" meaning behind the words. Most importantly, if the nonverbal messages and verbal messages are in conflict, adults overwhelmingly believe what they perceive the nonverbal messages to be communicating. While research indicates that humans are terrible lie-detectors (actually being wrong more often than they would be by flipping a coin in many cases), if a person feels like another person is not telling them the truth (a feeling which usually comes from nonverbal messages), that person will believe the other is not telling the truth—even if they are. The verbal message will be rejected, and the nonverbal message(s) accepted.

FUNCTIONS OF NONVERBAL MESSAGES

There are six primary functions of nonverbal messages. These functions are *complementing, contradicting, accenting, repeating, regulating,* and *substituting.* Some of these functions occur jointly with the verbal or are used in place of verbal communication.

Complementing. Complementing is the nonverbal function of adding to, clarifying, enriching, emphasizing, or supplementing the verbal message. For example, when a manager says to an employee, "This is one of the best proposals I have read," the words alone will probably be well received by the employee. However, if the words are emphasized by a pleasant, warm voice and accompanied by a pat on the back, then the message is even stronger. On the other hand, consider the manager who says to an employee, "This is one of the worst proposals I have read," again, the words alone will probably communicate the meaning to the employee. However, if the words are emphasized by a hard, unpleasant, loud voice and accompanied by a long stare on the part of the manager, then the message is even stronger.

Contradicting.   Contradicting is the use of nonverbal messages that are opposite of the verbal message. In other words, the nonverbal message disclaims or does not support the verbal message. Consider, for example, employees who have been working together on a project for several months. The woman says, "You like my work, don't you?" Another co-worker says "Sure, sure, I like your work." Again, the words alone should be enough to convey the true meaning, but they often are not. The woman needs to listen and watch the nonverbal behaviors of her co-worker. The woman needs to hear the unsure, perhaps even questioning tone, in the co-worker's voice, and observe that while the co-worker is expressing acceptance of her work, the co-worker is still thinking the work could be improved. Whenever the verbal message is contradicted by the nonverbal message, most people tend to believe the nonverbal message.

Accenting.   Nonverbal messages that highlight, stress, or enhance the verbal message serve the function of accenting. These messages can be vocalic behavior, touch, eye contact, body movement, posture, facial expression and so on. For example, when an instructor says, "there will be *five* major points covered on the next exam," students tend to listen better. The word *five* is highlighted by the teacher by vocalic underlining. Usually students will listen and retain more when teachers use accenting as a means to keep attention.

Repeating.   Nonverbal messages that restate, reinforce, duplicate, or reiterate the verbal message serve the function of repeating. Nonverbal messages performing this function can stand alone and still represent a similar message, even if the verbal messages were not present. For example, a manager attempting to get loud employees to quiet down might say, "please be quiet" while putting a finger to her or his lips. An employee requesting help might say, "I need help with this project," while raising a hand. Either gesture (manager signaling quiet or employee raising hand for help) might communicate the intended meaning in absence of the verbal, but when both the verbal and nonverbal are present, the nonverbal gestures perform the repeating function.

Regulating.   Verbal communication is controlled, monitored, coordinated, and managed through the nonverbal function of regulating. Such regulation is accomplished primarily by nonverbal messages. These nonverbal messages can involve most any part of the body and regulate or control the back and forth flow of dialogue. Some of these regulators are as follows: pointing, direct eye contact, raising or lowering voice, looking away, leaning forward, leaning back, sitting silently, pausing, touching on hand, and so on.

Often politicians know how to regulate the back and forth flow of interaction. A politician will pause and look at a newsperson when the politician wants the newsperson to speak. When a politician wants to "keep the floor" or continue talking, he or she will not look directly at the newsperson or pause, but keep a continuous stream of speech and use nonverbal behaviors which do not allow the newsperson to interrupt.

Substituting. Substitution happens when the nonverbal message is delivered in place of a verbal message. Often, a person will replace a verbal message with a nonverbal message because the nonverbal will communicate as effectively, or better than, the verbal message. For example, in a crisis, giving another person a hug may be more reassuring than any words that could be used.

In conclusion, these nonverbal functions do not always occur independently. In fact, many of these nonverbal functions could occur simultaneously. It is possible to complement, repeat, and accent virtually at the same time. Many times one nonverbal function can fulfill the purpose of the source. At other times, several nonverbal functions are necessary to do so. While some verbal messages may be able to stand alone and stimulate the desired meaning, the communication often is enhanced by the interaction of verbal and nonverbal messages.

CATEGORIES OF NONVERBAL MESSAGES

Since the nonverbal component in the human communication process is critical to ongoing, effective communication, several common nonverbal categories need to be mentioned. Each major nonverbal category is listed below and briefly discussed.

Dress and Artifacts. Often, the first message a person sends to another person is generated by our physical appearance. People judge others by physical appearance. If our physical appearance is not acceptable, other persons may elect not to communicate with us. General physical appearance, dress, clothing style and type, and the artifacts or accessories with which a person adorns their body convey messages about the person. For example, if an interviewee wears a tie decorated with vignettes about Bart Simpson, then interviewers may respond differently than if the interviewee wears a more appropriate tie.

In the arena of dress, clothing, and artifacts several ideas need to be taken into consideration by people moving into an organization or moving up in an organizational structure:

- Wear clothing that corresponds with the "formal or informal dress code" of the organization.
- Wear colors of clothing that suggest a business orientation, such as black, grey, navy, or burgundy.
- Keep accessories to a minimum, two for men (a watch, a ring), five for women (watch, ring, earrings, necklace, or bracelet). Women should not wear more than five accessories. Women also should avoid the following mistakes: a flashy scarf, several necklaces, a double-breasted jacket with many gold or silver tone buttons. For both men and women, "less is better" is the basic rule.
- Wear fabrics that are wrinkle-free and do not "scrunch easily" and yet are organizationally appropriate.
- On dress down days or informal days, do not go sloppy, go casual. Check with other more experienced employees about the casual dress code.
- Men and women should try to dress similar to the person who is one level above them, unless that person's dress is completely inappropriate for the organization.
- Managers may be allowed to be more "idiosyncratic" in their dress and clothing choices than their subordinates. *Peons must follow the rules.*

Gestures and Body Movements.   The study of the communicative aspects of gestures and body movements is referred to as kinesics. This area focuses on the movement of hands, arms, legs, torso, limbs, postural cues, walking behavior, head movement, and many other gestures and movements. Even the way in which a person sits can send cues to the other person. If the person sits with legs toward another, this may mean responsiveness. If the person sits with legs away from another, this may mean unresponsiveness. There are many differences between the gestures and movements of high status versus lower status persons. The following movements and gestures send cues in the organizational setting:

- Lower status persons should use appropriate posture (sitting more erect) when speaking with higher status persons, whereas higher status persons are allowed to have a more relaxed body posture when communicating with others.
- Lower status persons should use more positive gestures when speaking with higher status persons, whereas higher status persons can send more negative gestures when speaking with others.

- Lower status persons should use more attentive and interested body posture (for example, lean toward a manager) when communicating with higher status persons, whereas higher status persons can use a less attentive, even casual body posture (for example, feet on the desk) when communicating with others.
- Lower status persons should move or walk as if they are interested and involved in the job. Higher status persons can move more slowly, slouch, and seem less involved in the job.
- The posture of a higher status person may be marked by sideward or backward tilt of the torso, loosely extended legs and fingers or arms extended casually, head resting on back of a chair; lower status persons will sit or stand more erectly, seem more formal, and certainly never rest their head on the back of a chair.
- Persons of higher status are afforded the right to have a more relaxed body position when communicating with employees, whereas persons of lower status are usually expected to have more tense, more adaptive body position when speaking with persons of higher status.

Remember: Peons are lower status persons!

Face and Eye Behavior

The study of the communicative aspects of the face includes all facial cues such as mouth movements, lip movements, nose and cheek reactions, and eyebrow and forehead movement. One element of facial behavior is eye behavior. Many persons in this culture believe that the eyes present more important nonverbal messages than other parts of the face.

Facial behavior can be classified into four major categories of facial management techniques which are often used in the interpersonal and work environment. These categories are: *masking, intensifying, neutralizing,* and *deintensifying*. All four are used in organizational interactions.

Masking is the replacement of one facial expression with another expression. We call this facial technique the "Halloween Effect." Many supervisors and employees will replace one facial expression with another "more appropriate" facial expression. For example, when an employee is given a directive that he or she does not agree with, the employee often will quickly replace an expression of disapproval with one of acceptance.

Intensification is the exaggeration or enhancement of a facial expression. At times, as managers and employees we need to express the external expression of the emotion far beyond what we feel in order to accommodate other persons. For example, when our manager proposes a change in our work unit which we are lukewarm about but we know the change is inevitable then we might exaggerate our "lukewarmness" by facially expressing that "we are very much in agreement with the change."

Neutralization is a "poker-face." Many times in organizational settings it is critical that individuals engage in the facial management technique of neutralization. For example when our manager tells us that all vacations are on hold until a certain project is completed then facial neutralization might be the best expression. Showing displeasure probably will not accomplish anything except irritate the manager.

Deintensification of facial expressions is the "downplaying" or "deemphasizing" of a facial expression. There are circumstances in an organizational setting when downplaying our true feeling is appropriate. For example, an employee might be outraged by a decision made by upper management but the employee would be wise to downplay his or her facial expressions. Usually it is counterproductive for employees to indicate their rage or annoyance about decisions of upper management within the work environment. Of course, letting off some steam to a significant other might be ok!

In communication, people often look to one of three regions of the face for true emotion. These three primary areas are: (1) eyebrows and forehead; (2) eyes and eyelids; and (3) lower face, including cheeks, nose, and mouth. The seven primary facial expressions are: sadness, anger, disgust, fear, interest, surprise, and happiness. It is advisable to control our three primary regions of the face so as to give the appropriate expression in organizational settings. The information a manager receives from any particular area depends a great deal on the emotion being expressed. The following ideas suggest where certain emotions are likely to be found on the face:

- Sadness and fear are best identified from the eyes and eyelids areas.
- Anger is not perceived accurately from any single facial area. At least two areas of the face must be used in order for anger to be judged accurately. For example, anger is usually expressed in cheeks, mouth, brows, and forehead.
- Disgust often blends with surprise. Most often disgust is located in the lower region of the face.
- Fear is often found in the eyes and eyelid region of the face.
- Happiness is often found either in the lower face or eyes and eyelid regions.
- Surprise is found in the brows/forehead's regions, then eyes/eyelid regions, then the lower face.

Our eye behavior functions to establish and define relationships, signal interaction, express emotions, and regulate communication between supervisor and subordinate. There are several considerations related to face and eye behavior between supervisors and subordinates which you should be aware of:

- The supervisor can readily indicate unhappiness, disgust, or displeasure with subordinates' work.
- The subordinate should employ the facial management techniques in order to assure that he or she is communicating appropriately with her or his supervisor.
- Supervisors can stare, avoid, look longer, or use civil inattention with a subordinate. Peons should do none of these things.
- Supervisors often determine by using face and eye behaviors when an interaction will begin and end.
- Subordinates need to learn what their supervisors' face and eye behaviors indicate.
- Employees need to display a "satisfied face" to their supervisors.
- Employees should demonstrate respect by giving their supervisors the appropriate eye contact.

Vocal Behavior.   The study of the vocal aspects of the voice is known as vocalics. The work in this area includes the characteristics of the voice, uses of voice, tone, pitch, resonance, accent, dialect, and silence. A person's voice can convey to others as much information as the body, face, or eyes. For example, the voice of James Earl Jones (the voice of CNN and Verizon) is often equated with power, status, strength, and credibility. Research on vocalics and vocal expressiveness has provided us with some useful ideas:

- Negative vocal expressions are more accurately identified than positive vocal expressions. Therefore, an employee must reduce the negativity in her or his voice when speaking with or about a supervisor.
- Persons who monitor and control their own vocal emotions are better able to identify the vocal emotions of other persons.
- Subtle vocal expressions are difficult to detect. Sarcasm and satire are difficult for some people to understand; therefore, employees may want to avoid subtle, sarcastic, and satirical expressions, but learn to hear their supervisor's subtle expressions.
- Monotone, harshness, and nasality are the most offensive vocal characteristics.
- Subordinates need to modify accents that are stereotyped negatively to avoid discrimination on the job.
- Good vocal delivery consists of reasonable volume, moderate rate of speech, moderate pitch, clear articulation, and fluency (absence of vocalized pauses and expressions like "you know").
- Those persons who speak with good vocal delivery are perceived as more attractive and credible in the organizational setting than others.

Space.   Proxemics is the study of the communicative aspects of space. The study of space usually includes two primary areas—personal space and territoriality. *Personal space* is the expandable bubble people carry with them. This bubble can expand or not based on the closeness of other persons in the environment. *Territoriality* refers to how people manage the space to which they are assigned. For example, how a manager arranges her or his office furniture communicates much about the manager. The following spatial ideas refer to the differences between mangers and employees:

- Managers usually have the better furniture, accommodations (for example, office with a window), and territory.
- Managers can invade or violate the territory or personal space of her or his employees. (However, in today's world excesses in this area could lead to a harassment charge.)
- Managers determine the distance at which employees interact with the manager (such as close versus far).
- As persons move up the organizational structure, the more status and attractiveness their offices and surroundings will display.
- As persons move up the organizational structure, the more privacy they are afforded.
- Lastly, higher status persons not only acquire the better surroundings but are given greater freedom of movement.

Touch.   Haptics is the study of the communicative aspects of touch. Touch has been shown to be one of the more powerful messages transmitted in human interaction. In this culture, many people tend to be touch avoidant either because of an aversion to touch or fear the touch will be misperceived by another person. For example, many managers are hesitant to touch subordinates in a friendly manner because other people in the environment might misperceive the touch. There are a few rules for touch in the organizational setting:

- Generally, managers can touch employees more than employees can touch managers. However, most managers are aware of the possible consequences of touching employees. Therefore, many managers simply do not touch employees, not even in a positive manner.
- Appropriate supervisor touch can be very reinforcing and rewarding for a subordinate (such as a brief pat on the shoulder).
- For both supervisors and subordinates, when in doubt, *don't touch.*

Time.   Chronemics is the study of the communicative aspects of time. The United States is one of the more time conscious cultures in the world. This time orientation determines how a person perceives another person. For example, this culture is unforgiving of the person who is regularly late for events. In fact, people who are consistently late in this culture are stereo-typed as lazy, uncaring, and selfish. This culture is a culture which truly believes, "the early bird catches the worm." Supervisors can be late return-ing work to subordinates but subordinates are not afforded the same in-dulgence. Lastly, upward mobile subordinates should plan to be in the of-fice a little before the supervisor arrives and remain for a while after the supervisor has left.

IMMEDIACY AND ORGANIZATIONAL COMMUNICATION

Immediacy is the degree of perceived physical or psychological closeness between people. The more communicators employ immediate behaviors, the more others will like, evaluate highly, and prefer such communicators; and the less communicators employ immediate behaviors the more others will dis-like, evaluate negatively, and reject them. This behavior/response pattern is known as the "principle of immediate communication" (Richmond & McCroskey, 2004).

Nonverbal Behaviors

We cannot always physically approach people or things we like or move away from things or people we don't like. However, we do communicate our feel-ings most of the time by our nonverbal behaviors. For example, if someone is saying something nice about us, we are likely to stand closer, listen more atten-tively, have more eye contact, perhaps even touch. On the other hand, if some-one is saying something unpleasant about us, we are likely to lean away from that person, have little eye contact, remain silent, and not touch. We use abbre-viated forms of approach or avoidance behavior. These abbreviated forms of nonverbal behavior imply the degree of psychological closeness between peo-ple. The more forms of nonverbal approach behaviors we use, the more we are perceived as nonverbally immediate. The more we use nonverbal avoidance behaviors, the more we are perceived as nonverbally nonimmediate.

Nonverbal behaviors that denote immediacy are those that improve and encourage interpersonal encounters and communication. Scholars sug-gest that some common immediacy behaviors include smiling, touching on the hand, arm, or shoulder, moving close to another, making eye contact, facing another, using warm vocalics, and leaning toward someone.

Outcomes of Immediacy Behaviors

It is clear from the preceding review of immediacy that positive outcomes in relationships can be stimulated by immediacy cues. For example, being verbally immediate, standing close to another, leaning toward another, smiling, having eye contact, facing another, touching, using positive gestures, and spending time with another makes a favorable impression on the other person.

Increased Liking, Affiliation, and Affect.   Considerable research (Mehrabian, 1971; Richmond, 1998; Richmond & McCroskey, 2000) has confirmed that as immediacy increases, so does liking in interpersonal encounters. Mehrabian suggests that "immediacy and liking are two sides of the same coin. That is, liking encourages greater immediacy and immediacy produces more liking" (1971, p. 77). He and others have suggested that people normally communicate with persons for whom they have a positive affect. As they communicate more with people they like, the use of immediacy can improve the affect even more. Research from many areas clearly indicates that the more a person likes another, the more they will use affirmative cues such as leaning closer, touching, mutual gaze, smiling, and nodding—all immediacy cues. On the other side of the coin, Mehrabian (1971) says that "opportunities for increased immediacy can foster greater liking" (p. 77). If one wants to be liked by another, one should use the immediacy behaviors that are likely to increase liking. For example, Mehrabian (1971) states,

> Greater liking is conveyed by standing close instead of far, leaning forward instead of back while seated, facing directly instead of turning to one side, touching, having mutual gaze or eye contact, extending bodily contact as during a handshake, prolonging goodbyes, or using gestures during a greeting that imply a reaching out toward the other person who is at a distance. (p. 42)

He suggests that the above behaviors not only increase liking or affect for another but also increase the approachability of the person.

More Approachable Communication Style.   The person who exhibits immediacy behavior is perceived as having a more approachable communication style than the person who exhibits nonimmediacy behavior. For example, are you more likely to approach someone who is smiling at you or someone who is frowning at you? If the simple distinction between smiling and frowning can make such a big difference in whether one will approach another or not, imagine what a cluster of immediate or nonimmediate behaviors can do. Immediacy cues not only give a person a more approachable communication style, but they also help to decrease uncertainty about the person and the situation. Often we infer how a conversation will go based on the nonverbal cues given by others. Immediacy cues help to decrease uncertainty about communication situations.

More Responsiveness, Understanding, and Assertiveness. Responsiveness is the capacity to be sensitive to the communication of others, to be seen as a good listener, to make others comfortable in communicating, and to recognize the needs and desires of others. Considerable research suggests that people who exhibit immediacy behavior are perceived as more responsive and understanding of others. Ask yourself whether you'd rather communicate with a responsive person or a nonresponsive person. A responsive individual not only knows when and how to listen to another but they know how to respond in a given situation. They know the appropriate nonverbal and verbal communication behavior to use to improve communication. These are immediate behaviors. Assertiveness is the ability to take a stand, defend one's beliefs, and express oneself without attacking or becoming verbally or physically aggressive. Immediate people are perceived as likely to be assertive as well as responsive.

Increased Solidarity between Participants. Solidarity is the perception of "we-ness," of being a team, or members of a common group. As immediacy increases between persons, so does solidarity; as solidarity increases, so does immediacy. We are much more likely to develop a solid relationship with an individual who uses immediate cues with us than someone who uses nonimmediate cues with us. In addition, as we become closer to one another, immediacy tends to increase.

Decreased Anxiety. In most relationships, there is a high degree of anxiety or tension associated with the initial acquaintance stage. However, as the relationship develops, the anxiety lessens. Some of this decrease in anxiety results from verbal communication. Most of it results from nonverbal cues. Immediacy behavior tends to relax and calm another person so he or she can communicate without high anxiety. This does not mean that immediacy is the cure for anxiety; it is simply one method of alleviating tension in relationships.

Decreased Status Differences. Status is the societal level of a person. The higher the difference in status between two people, the less likely the persons will communicate effectively. One proven method of reducing status differences to improve communication is to use immediacy behavior. People of higher status in organizations have learned that to communicate more effectively with subordinates, they must reduce their status without giving up the authority. Immediacy enables them to do this. A supervisor can be friendly and immediate without giving up her or his power.

Increased Perceptions of Communication Competence. Several communication variables emerge from the literature as characteristics normally considered necessary for a competent communicator. The most common of these are assertiveness, responsiveness, and versatility. In order to be perceived as competent, one must be assertive and responsive, and versatile (knowing when to be assertive and when to be responsive). Immediacy behavior can be part of each of these characteristics. People can be assertive while being immediate. People who are responsive are definitely immediate. Lastly, the versatile communicator knows when immediacy is appropriate and when it is not. They also have the option of using it whenever they need to. Many incompetent communicators know what immediacy is, but cannot use the behaviors when they need to. Therefore, immediacy skills help people to be perceived as more competent communicators.

Immediacy behavior is one of the most valuable communication tools an employee can have. However, there are a few drawbacks associated with being immediate. The drawbacks usually are not nearly as serious as those of being a nonimmediate employee.

Drawbacks of Immediacy

The first drawback deals with perceptions. Occasionally, people mistake or misread immediacy cues for intimacy cues. You may have experienced the following scenario. You're in a bar and someone smiles at you and, because you want to seem friendly, you smile back. Before you can count to ten, they are at your side asking if you'd like to go home with them. All you did was smile! There are instances where immediacy is misread for intimacy, and people who mistake immediacy cues for intimacy cues. Over time, as you use immediacy behavior, you will learn when and where you can use it appropriately.

The second drawback deals with anxiety. Some people are not more relaxed or less anxious when another person is being immediate. These people like to avoid communication as much as possible. Communication avoidants can become more anxious, instead of less, when someone is being immediate with them. Immediacy usually increases communication, and communication avoidants want less. Therefore, their anxiety level increases. This is easily recognizable. If you are being immediate and someone else is not responding and seems anxious, the best thing you can do is be less immediate. Let the other person determine the conversational flow.

The last drawback could be interpreted as a positive or negative. Immediacy promotes more communication between people. Sometimes this can be very rewarding. However, occasionally it is not. More communication requires more time. For example, the employee who is immediate with her or his peers might find that this increases communication. This may require that he or she spend more time with peers than is possible in a day and still carry out other duties. Therefore, each employee has to learn how to withdraw gracefully from a communication relationship when they need to move to another one. Many people in sales are very adept at this sort of thing. They can be immediate even as they shake your hand to say goodbye.

In conclusion, the drawbacks to immediacy can create problems. However, the perceptions created in the mind of another person by not being immediate are likely to be even more severe. Nonimmediate people are perceived by others as less friendly, less responsive, less outgoing, less likeable, cold, aloof, and even hostile. Therefore, the advantages of immediacy outweigh the drawbacks.

REFERENCES AND RECOMMENDED READINGS

Birdwhistell, R. (1955). Background to kinesics. *ETC, 13,* 10–18.

Ekman, P. & Friesen, W. V. (1975). *Emotion in the human face: Guidelines for research and an integration of findings.* New York: Pergamon Press.

McCroskey, J. C., & Richmond, V. P. (1992). Increasing teacher influence through immediacy. In V. P. Richmond & J. C. McCroskey (Eds.). *Power in the classroom: Communication, control, and concern.* (Pp. 101–120). Hillsdale, NJ: Lawrence Erlbaum.

Mehrabian, A. (1966). Immediacy: An indicator of attitudes in linguistic communication. *Journal of Personality, 34,* 26–34.

Mehrabian, A. (1967). Attitudes inferred from non-immediacy of verbal communications. *Journal of Verbal Learning and Verbal Behavior, 6,* 294–295.

Mehrabian, A. (1967). Orientation behaviors and nonverbal attitude communication. *Journal of Communication, 17,* 324–332.

Mehrabian, A. (1971). *Silent Messages.* Belmont, CA: Wadsworth.

Mehrabian, A. & Ferris, S. R. (1967). Inference of attitudes from nonverbal communication in two channels. *Journal of Consulting Psychology, 31,* 248–252.

Morris, D. (1985). *Body watching.* New York: Crown.

Richmond, V. P. (1990). Communication in the classroom: Power and motivation. *Communication Education, 39,* 181–195.

Richmond, V. P. (1998). *Nonverbal communication in the classroom.* Acton, MA: Tapestry Press.

Richmond, V. P., & McCroskey, J. C. (1998). *Communication: Apprehension, avoidance and effectiveness.* (5th ed. Needham Heights, MA: Allyn and Bacon.

Richmond, V. P., & McCroskey, J. C. (2004). *Nonverbal behavior in interpersonal relations.* (5th ed.). Needham Heights, MA: Allyn and Bacon.

Richmond, V. P., & McCroskey, J. C. (2000). *The impact of supervisor and subordinate immediacy on relational and organizational outcomes. Communication Monographs, 6,* 85–95.

Richmond, V. P., Gorham, J., & McCroskey, J. C. (1986). The relationship between immediacy behaviors and cognitive learning. In M. L. McLaughlin (Ed.). *Communication Yearbook 10.* (Pp. 574–590). Beverly Hills, CA: Sage.

Thayer, S. (Ed.). (1986). The psychology of touch (special issue). *Journal of Nonverbal Behavior, 10,* 7–80.

STUDY GUIDE

1. List and describe at least five principles of nonverbal communication in organizations.
2. List and give examples of at least four functions of nonverbal communication in organizational settings.

3. List and give two examples of appropriate nonverbal communication in the following categories:

   Dress and artifacts
   Gesture and body movements
   Face and eye behavior
   Vocal behavior
   Space
   Touch
   Time

4. Define immediacy and give two examples of nonverbal immediacy in the organizational environment.
5. Give the outcomes of immediacy behavior between supervisor and subordinate.
6. Give the drawbacks of immediacy behavior between supervisor and subordinate.

CHAPTER 4

ADMINISTRATION, SUPERVISION, AND COMMUNICATION

Mr. Johnson is sitting in his plush office with a window, a recently acquired new desk of his choosing, a new conference table with matching chairs. However, he is not admiring his newly furnished office. He is looking dismally at the stacks of files in the "in box" on his desk, several phone messages given to him by his secretary, the mail that looks like a small mountain, his calendar that seems to have every space filled in with either a meeting with his boss or several of his own clients. He is wondering how he can handle all this work.

In walks Ms. Rogers, one of his subordinates. She indicates that she needs to talk to him about a problem she is having. Mr. Johnson glances at the clock and says, "I'm sorry I don't have time now. You ought to be able to handle that yourself." Ms. Rogers leaves with a chip on her shoulder and wondering how someone like Mr. Johnson ever became a supervisor. "They told me when I was hired that if I ever had a problem, I should go to Mr. Johnson right away. A lot of good that does! All he cares about is his new desk. Well, if he doesn't care, why should I?" She shrugs her shoulders and moves back to her desk.

This example probably sounds like some you have encountered in the work environment. You go in to see your so-called supervisor only to find he or she is unable to work with you, has no time for you, or is not even on the premises. Many subordinates wonder what their supervisors do. They wonder this because they never see them doing anything but issuing instructions or complaining about problems the subordinate has caused. They never see managers providing their subordinates with assistance and guidance. In short, they never seem to be doing anything useful.

SUPERVISORS' DUTIES: SUBORDINATES' VIEWS

Several years ago, we had the opportunity to interview several hundred subordinates to find out what *they* thought their supervisor should be expected to do. Let us take a few moments to outline the 10 roles or duties most commonly mentioned.

First, subordinates feel their supervisor should be trying to improve the general environmental conditions in which they have to work. For example, if the water fountain is not working, they think the supervisor should have it fixed. If the men's room is out of toilet tissue, the supervisor should be making sure the problem is being solved. If parking conditions are not adequate for all personnel, the supervisor should do something about it. If the cafeteria is not serving palatable meals, the supervisor should be certain the problem is solved. In other words, many subordinates hold their supervisor directly responsible for anything that goes wrong in their working conditions and expect him or her to be a "trouble shooter" to make sure such irritants are overcome.

Second, many employees feel their supervisor should resolve any or all personnel disputes. For example, if a secretary tells one of the subordinates to "go to hell," the supervisor must handle the ensuing conflict. If one subordinate cannot work with another, the supervisor should "straighten out" the other employee. If the subordinate is having difficulty with someone in another unit, then the manager must intervene and resolve the problem. If the secretaries are having interpersonal difficulties and cannot seem to work together, the supervisor must resolve these problems. In other words, employees expect their supervisor, in addition to being a trouble shooter, also to be a "go between" or an arbitrator for conflict resolution.

Third, a significant number of subordinates feel their supervisor is directly responsible for the budgets or budgetary concerns of their department or unit. They also feel their salaries are in large part determined by their supervisor, so if their salary needs improvement, it is the supervisor's duty to take care of that. Although these are two separate issues, most subordinates feel their supervisor is largely responsible for any budget problems in the unit. They rarely think circumstances outside the unit might dictate certain budget concerns. For example, subordinates feel their manager should be fighting to get their salaries improved. They also feel that he or she should be fighting to get better facilities, better working conditions, better travel expenditures, and in general should be improving the financial status of the department. In short, in addition to being a trouble shooter and an arbitrator, the supervisor is expected to be a financial wizard.

Fourth, subordinates expect their supervisor to have a sympathetic ear to their individual needs and concerns. They expect their supervisor to open his or her door to their personal problems at home and understand how these things might impact their job performance. For example, an expectant father may go to see the supervisor about his concerns about the birth and the health of his wife. He expects the manager to take the time to listen. If a subordinate is thinking of transferring to another unit or company, he or she might want some advice and support from the supervisor. In other words, in addition to being a trouble shooter, an arbitrator, and a financial wizard, the supervisor is expected to be a counselor.

Fifth, subordinates expect their supervisors to be the "keeper of the standards." In other words, they expect their manager to be responsible for all hiring, firing, employee evaluation, and reprimands. If an employee is smoking in a nonsmoking area, the supervisor is expected to reprimand that person and make certain it does not happen again. If a subordinate is late to work and others are not, the supervisor is responsible for catching the offender and making sure the offense is punished. In addition to being a trouble shooter, an arbitrator, a financial wizard, and a counselor, the supervisor is expected to be the disciplinarian.

Sixth, subordinates feel their supervisors should be responsible for coping with sexual harassment allegations and racial or ethnic tensions that might arise in the work environment. They feel the supervisor should know all the policies concerning these issues and should handle any such problems that occur. For example, if a female employee feels that "dirty jokes" involving females are demeaning to her and are impacting her job performance, then the supervisor is expected to step in and resolve the situation to everyone's satisfaction, including the story teller's. So, in addition to being a trouble shooter, an arbitrator, a financial wizard, a counselor, and a disciplinarian, the supervisor is expected to be the guarantor of social justice.

Seventh, subordinates feel their supervisor is directly responsible for their own personal growth and development in the organization. They feel the supervisor should guide them in their tasks, give them feedback on how they are doing, and assist them in becoming a better, more-productive employee. In addition to being a trouble shooter, an arbitrator, a financial wizard, a counselor, a disciplinarian, and a guarantor of social justice, the supervisor is expected to be a job specialist.

Eighth, supervisors are expected to maintain good working relationships with those above themselves. For example, they must have a good rapport with their boss so "good things come down the system." They should have lunch with the boss, play golf with the boss, go to the conferences the boss schedules, have a drink occasionally with the boss, and if needed take necessary trips with the boss. Thus, in addition to being a trouble shooter, an arbitrator, a financial wizard, a counselor, a disciplinarian, a guarantor of social justice, and a job specialist, the supervisor is expected to be a "kiss-up" artist.

Ninth, subordinates expect managers to be up-to-date on all the innovative methods in the field and particularly innovations that might improve their jobs. They expect the supervisor to bring in the computers they need in their jobs, to find the equipment needed, and to be knowledgeable about all new ideas. In other words, in addition to being a trouble shooter, an arbitrator, a financial wizard, a counselor, a disciplinarian, a guarantor of social justice, a job specialist, and a kiss-up artist, the supervisor is expected to be a scholar.

Tenth, subordinates expect supervisors to maintain a good image and profile with persons outside the organization. They want them to present a good public image and to be a public relations person for the organization and, in particular, their unit. They do not want to read in the morning newspaper that their manager was picked up at 3:00 A.M. under the influence of alcohol with a half-dressed, underage member of the opposite sex in the car. Although some employees might enjoy this, most would feel it hurts the organization and their unit. In conclusion, subordinates not only want their supervisor to be a trouble shooter, an arbitrator, a financial wizard, a counselor, a disciplinarian, a guarantor of social justice, a job specialist, a kiss-up artist, and a scholar, they also expect the supervisor to be a public relations person.

Let us stop here, before this litany becomes a new version of the "Twelve Days of Christmas." If our point is not clear by now, listing more expectations is not likely to clarify it. These 10 roles or duties (and there are many more we have not named) seem reasonable until one begins to realize that only a very special person can perform all the above duties with excellence. It is not that any one of these duties or roles is unreasonable—and none of the people we have interviewed has individually produced such a list as this. The problem comes when many different subordinates have many different expectations, which is what is normal in today's complex organizations.

As one employee we talked with stated, "What we want is Superman or Wonder Woman." Yes, that is what many employees want, and often they are extremely disappointed and disillusioned when they find out that most of their managers either cannot or will not fulfill all these expected roles or duties. But before we cast blame on the "ignorant" subordinates for expecting too much, it is important that we recognize that most people in organizations never learn what the expectations are that subordinates have for their supervisors until they become supervisors. Many schools and colleges have programs to train managers, but there are few opportunities for people to learn how to *be* managed.

WHY AREN'T MANAGERS DOING THEIR JOBS?

In our conversations with both employees and managers, we have found several common reasons that managers aren't doing what we want them to do. Following are the most common reasons managers are not doing their jobs, or at least are not doing them the way those below them in the organization think they should be doing them.

First, it seems both employees and managers are aware of the fact that there is never enough time to perform all the expected roles and duties well. Hence, some duties or roles get shifted to the "back burner." When you are the person getting shifted to the back burner, you do not like it. You at least need to know why this happens so you can better tolerate it, even if you do not like it. The biggest reason is usually that "more pressing matters" have taken precedence. Although managers do not like putting people off, they often have to do so. There simply is not enough time to do everything effectively. Of course, this does not even take into account any unexpected duties managers often get asked to do (be United Way campaign chair, fill in for a person higher in the organization while that person is on vacation, do the work of a subordinate who is absent because of illness, and so on).

Second, some managers are just plain "incompetent" as managers, as communicators, as human beings. They never should have been hired by the organization, much less appointed to a managerial position. The incompetent ones sometimes do not last very long in profit-making organizations, but they may last a lifetime (or at least it seems that long) in nonprofit organizations. Hence, if you truly think they are incompetent and that tends to be the consensus of the unit, you have three choices: (1) Try to have them removed (this usually is difficult, because someone else likes them, such as the person who hired them in the first place), (2) learn to do your job and never depend on them for anything, or (3) find a new position and leave the organization. Do not overlook that third option. Although it may not do anything to get rid of the bad manager, at least *you* do not have to tolerate him or her any more.

Third, although a few managers truly are incompetent, some others are just lazy and settled in their positions. They may realize they do not have to perform a lot of duties in order to maintain the flow of the unit or organization. Again, there is not much you can do. You cannot really prove they are incompetent. They do what "absolutely needs" to be done, at least in the eyes of the people above them. But they will never go beyond the necessary, absolute duties of their position. In this situation, you had better learn to depend on yourself or else leave.

Fourth, some managers are kept busy by their bosses. We do mean *bosses*, not boss. They have too many bosses above them with too many demands. In other words, your supervisor is constantly jumping through hoops trying to CYA and respond to the wishes and needs of the bosses. This often happens in companies where the chain of command is unclear or too much has been delegated to too many persons. One never really knows who is handling which issue, so people spend much of the time "spinning their wheels." If you see your manager consistently going to meetings with various upper-management personnel, this might be a sign that he or she is being kept busy by the people above.

Fifth, some managers are not really busy, but they become very busy whenever you enter the office and need something. This could be a sign they do not like you and want nothing to do with you. If you sense this, you might try to improve your organizational behavior or find out why they dislike you. If not, you may have to transfer or obtain a new position. In addition to disliking certain personnel, some bosses simply hate the overall work environment. This will render them ineffective. They will do only what they have to do to keep their position.

Sixth, it is rare, but there are systems in which daily operations are an utter economic and professional mess. When disaster looms, managers are kept busy just trying to maintain their own unit. They spend an enormous amount of time "trying to rearrange the deck chairs on the Titanic." If the organization is having trouble staying afloat and solid, then this will absorb an incredible amount of a manager's time and he or she will neglect or delegate virtually all other duties.

Seventh, occasionally you will encounter a manager whose personal problems have become so overwhelming that he or she cannot perform his or her duties as well as they should be performed. We know one manager who never missed a meeting, never turned an employee away, never failed to submit a budget on time, and was generally considered a very promising supervisor. At one point in her career, she had a college-age daughter who was killed in an automobile accident. Then her husband had to have triple bypass heart surgery, and her father died. These personal problems were so overwhelming that she was not as effective as she once was. But because she had been so effective before, the employees tried to cover for her and assisted with many of the duties. After a while she was able to resume most of her duties, but it was a long time before she had the zeal for the job she once had had. On occasion, even a very effective supervisor can have problems external to the system that may keep him or her from doing the job.

Eighth, some managers cannot fulfill their roles effectively because they have too many people under them to supervise effectively. This is a significant problem in organizations where the structure is very flat. There are too few bosses for too many employees. The supervisors cannot effectively supervise all the employees. The optimal number of personnel that a manager can supervise effectively is from 8 to 15, depending on the nature of the work involved. When you ask most managers how many people they would like to work with, they usually will say about 10. As the number of subordinates expands, the needs and demands of the subordinates expand. At some point, the supervisor simply cannot perform all the duties effectively. Often this is a problem in growing organizations. Good supervisors are given more and more people to supervise, and eventually they are no longer good supervisors—through no fault of their own.

Ninth, many managers are restrained from performing their roles effectively because they have a conflict of roles. In other words, they are not sure whether they should be administrators or supervisors. Their job contracts usually list a number of roles, some of which are administration,

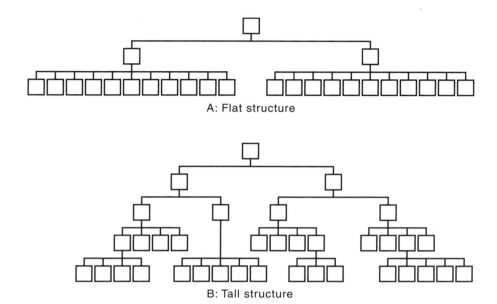

A: Flat structure

B: Tall structure

FIGURE 4.1   Diagrams of Flat and Tall Structures

some of which are more supervision. Once they get into the job, they realize there is "no way" that they can effectively fulfill all the roles assigned to them. So they opt to go the administrative route because this is what will get them into trouble with their boss if it is not fulfilled. We discuss more about this role conflict later in this chapter.

Tenth, some systems inhibit or hinder effective supervision. For example, the structure of the system, tall versus flat, will make a difference. The tall structure has many hierarchical levels. The flat structure has few hierarchical levels (see Figure 4.1). Managers in the tall structure usually have fewer employees to supervise than managers in the flat structure. When you think about it, it makes sense. As we said before, most managers can effectively supervise only 8 to 15 persons effectively. The tall structure chunks people into small units so there are more managers for fewer employees. The flat structure has a large number of personnel under fewer managers. IBM might be a good example of a tall structure; the traditional public school is a good example of a flat structure. At IBM there are many units, with many supervisors, and fewer employees per supervisor in each unit. In the typical public school there is a principal, perhaps an assistant principal or curriculum director and perhaps as many as 40 to 60 teachers, all of whom need supervision. Obviously, effective supervision will not always be possible.

All systems have a certain degree of tallness or flatness. Within systems you can also have different degrees of tallness and flatness in different parts of the system. Generally *the flatter the system, the less effective the supervision.* This does not mean a tall structure is without its problems. In the tall systems it is more difficult for vertical communication to flow, whereas in flat systems vertical communication can flow more effectively. Why? Because in the flat system if one wants to send a message up the system, there are fewer people in the chain of command your message must pass through to the person who can act on it. Hence, tall is better for quality of supervision, but flat is better for vertical communication flow. However, tall is better for horizontal communication flow because there are fewer employees at each level and a message can flow across the organization faster and with more accuracy than in the flat structure.

In conclusion, there are many valid reasons that managers cannot perform all the duties or roles employees think they should. We hope we have clarified these for you and explained the primary reasons that our supervisors cannot always do their jobs to our satisfaction. In the next section of this chapter, we direct attention to the biggest problem our supervisor must face.

TO SUPERVISE OR TO ADMINISTER?
THAT IS THE QUESTION

As suggested earlier, one of the primary reasons many managers seem as if they are not fulfilling their job duties is that often there is a conflict of roles. People hired as managers often are hired to be both administrators and supervisors and they quickly learn they generally cannot do both successfully. Usually they opt for the option that will keep their supervisor off their back—the role of the administrator. What are the typical duties of an administrator?

An *administrator* is the individual who is primarily responsible for facilitating the operation of the organization. This person's roles may include some or all of the following: budget planning, policy planning, hiring, firing, development and maintenance of facilities, delegation of authority, structuring of units or departments, and the maintenance of relationships with individuals and agencies external to the organization. They tend to do a lot of work that deals with "paper pushing" and public relations.

Some scoff at these roles and suggest that an administrative role is insignificant. But when the paper is not pushed to the correct source at the correct time, it can cause havoc in the system. For example, if an administrator forgets to file personnel forms approving salary increases for certain employees, pay checks are wrong. This could cause a lot of extra paperwork, not to mention bad feelings. In addition, who is responsible when things "look bad" in the organization or do not run smoothly? The administrator in charge. Hence, the role of the administrator is very significant, and very time consuming. Much of an administrator's time is spent answering to the persons above about budgeting, policy, hiring, and so forth. Hence, much of administrators' communication is directed to the management above them.

If you have a good administrator you will know it. Your unit will usually get extra "goodies," such as better equipment and a larger budget, and generally be thought of as a good unit. If you have a poor administrator, it will reflect directly on the unit. Reports will not be filed on time, requests will not be acted on when they should, and your unit will miss out on new information and/or needed information. You may not find the good administrator to be particularly open to personal employee relationships, but he or she will do a fine job of getting things you need for your job.

In contrast to an administrator, a *supervisor* is an individual who has frequent, personal contact with subordinates. This contact may include any or all of the following: observation of employees' work, communication of orders or policy, enforcement of policy regarding employees, assistance with subordinates' work, resolution of employees' problems, and generally working with employees to improve their lives in the organization. The supervisor is much more employee-oriented than the administrator. The manager who centers on supervision spends much of the time working with and talking with subordinates. Supervisors are visible and accessible to employees, whereas the administrators may be much less visible and less accessible. Whereas the administrator is working to satisfy those above him or her in the organizational structure, the supervisor is working to satisfy and help those below him or her in that structure. A supervisor's communication is primarily downward and is directed toward the improvement of communication between employees.

If you have a good supervisor, you will know it. Your job will be easier because you know you have someone to go to for advice and assistance in the work environment. You will feel secure that there is someone who supports and believes in you and will assist you with the task at hand. However, having a good supervisor is not always what everyone wants. Some employees want to be "left alone." They do not want any assistance on the job; hence, these employees discourage one from being a supervisor. Fill out the scales in Figure 4.2 and this should give you some feeling about

	As an administrator my manager is:							
Ineffective	1	2	3	4	5	6	7	Effective
Poor	1	2	3	4	5	6	7	Excellent
	As a supervisor my manager is:							
Ineffective	1	2	3	4	5	6	7	Effective
Poor	1	2	3	4	5	6	7	Excellent

FIGURE 4.2   Feelings about Manager Concerning Administration and Supervision

your boss in terms of how good an administrator he or she is and how good a supervisor he or she is.

Remember, it is the rare person in the unusual organization who can be both an effective administrator and an effective supervisor. If you feel you have one of these, count yourself lucky. If your boss is effective on one dimension but less than effective on the other, then you are still doing well. It is the person who says the boss is an ineffective administrator *and* ineffective supervisor who is in real trouble. This person will suffer and so will the organizational unit.

Why is it that most systems do not have people who can be effective at both administration and supervision? Again, there simply is not enough time to do all the duties effectively. The primary reason is that the person assigned the role of manager quickly realizes he or she cannot do both jobs effectively, so he or she must opt for the one that absolutely must be done—administrator. Managers are caught between a rock and a hard place. They become administrators for two reasons. First, they know that if they are not good administrators, they will be fired by the powers above them (those they answer to directly) and second, they know most subordinates will generally do their jobs in a fair manner whether they have any direct supervision or not. Many systems literally force a manager to choose between supervision and administration. This can be costly in terms of both employee satisfaction and productivity.

WHAT KIND OF MANAGER DO YOU HAVE?

The key for subordinate survival is to know when your manager is acting in an administrative capacity and when he or she is acting in a supervisory capacity. The element you must learn to observe is the communication. Observe your manager. If he or she spends most of his or her time behind closed doors and on the telephone, you are working for an administrator. Do not expect that manager to have much time to be a supervisor. If your manager frequently is seen walking through the corridors of the building and talking with employees, then you are working for a supervisor. But many managers at least try to switch back and forth between roles. If your manager puts a do-not-disturb sign on his or her door, it is probably report time (administrator time). If your manager invites someone to join him or her for lunch one day, then it is probably supervisory time. If you want to see your boss and the secretary tells you he or she is on the phone with his or her supervisor, then you know it is administrator time. If you can observe the communication of your boss, then you will know what role is being performed at a given time. In this way you will be learning how (and when) to communicate and survive in the organization.

REFERENCES AND RECOMMENDED READINGS

Koehler, J. W., Anatol, K. W. E., & Applbaum, R. L. (1981). *Organizational communication: Behavioral perspectives.* (2nd ed.). New York: Holt, Rinehart and Winston.

McCroskey, J. C., & Richmond, V. P. (1996). Human communication theory and research: Traditions and models. In M. B. Salwen & D. W. Stacks (Eds.). *An integrated approach to communication theory and research.* (Pp. 233–242). Mahwah, NJ: Lawrence Erlbaum Publishers.

McCroskey, J. C., & Richmond, V. P. (1997). *Communication in educational organizations.* Acton, MA: Tapestry Press.

Richmond, V. P., McCroskey, J. C., & Davis, L. M. (1982). Individual differences among employees, management communication style, and employee satisfaction: Replication and extension. *Human Communication Research, 8,* 170–188.

Richmond, V. P., McCroskey, J. C., Davis, L. M., & Koontz, K. A. (1980). Perceived power as a mediator of management communication style and employee satisfaction: A preliminary investigation. *Communication Quarterly, 28,* 37–46.

STUDY GUIDE

1. Identify some of the most common duties subordinates believe their manager should perform.
2. Why are most managers unable to perform all of these duties?
3. Distinguish between "tall" and "flat" organizational structures. How do such structures impact quality of supervision?
4. Explain what is involved in the "administrator" role. Why is it important?
5. Explain what is involved in the "supervisor" role. Why is it important?
6. Distinguish between administrative and supervisory functions of managers.
7. How can you determine whether your manager is primarily an administrator or primarily a supervisor?

CHAPTER 5

BARRIERS TO EFFECTIVE COMMUNICATION

If you talk with employees in almost any organization, they will tell you there are barriers to effective communication. Several barriers to effective interpersonal working relationships occur in all organizations. We have chosen to discuss what we think are some of the primary communication barriers encountered in both profit and nonprofit organizations. These include the climate of the organization, status within the organization, problems of communication overload, and defensiveness.

CLIMATE CONTROL

The organizational climate established can determine the amount and type of communication between supervisors and subordinates. Following we discuss three types of climate and their impact on communication.

Ralph works in an organization primarily concerned with production—the task—and the managers show little concern for the employees. Most of the communication is top-down with the messages directed toward how to do the job more efficiently and effectively. If an employee attempts to send a message up the system, it usually is stopped by the first-level manager. The system is not concerned about the employees. The attitude is that if people quit, there will be people in line to replace them. Management might sponsor an employee "get together" occasionally, as a token to appease the most disgruntled employees who want attention. There is never any change except that initiated by management.

This climate is generally known as the "Dehumanizing" climate. Employees generally go to work each day with little enthusiasm, do their jobs, and go home. In this climate there is little communication between supervisor and subordinate and the organization does not encourage, or sometimes even allow, communication between subordinates. In fact, the management views communication between subordinates as evil. So they throw roadblocks in the way to prevent that type of communication. They keep employees separated at work, assign them tasks that keep them apart, and try to prevent employees from socializing. The Dehumanizing climate leads to distrust, distortions, dislike, and lower production levels. The employees do not perform at their highest levels because they are unhappy with the communication situation. Both management and employees distrust and dislike each other and are suspicious of the other's motives when change is needed. Overall, this is not a desirable climate in which to work.

Mary goes to work each morning with an optimistic outlook and anticipates socializing with her friends on the job. The managers in her organization have a lot of concern for the employees. In fact, the subordinates vote on whom they want to have for a supervisor. Consequently, managers place employee satisfaction very high on their list of priorities. They give awards to loyal employees and sponsor many social activities. Although they hope that the work gets done, they feel that "people are our most important product." There are many meetings designed to let everyone have a say. Changes are rarely undertaken unless everyone agrees on what should be done.

This is the "Happiness for Lunch Bunch" climate. This climate is primarily concerned with employee welfare and peer communication, and spends little time worrying about change or communication between supervisor and subordinate. The chief concern here is the employee's well-being. Often in this climate you find little time being spent on task and enormous amounts of time being spent on ways to improve the employees' environment.

Sounds great, doesn't it? One might ask, What's wrong with this? Nothing, except it is usually done to the exclusion of the task. The attitude is that the job will get done, and so what if the job is a little late or not quite up to specifications? In this type of climate there often are committees for everything so all employees can have input. In fact, you will often find a "committee on committees" which is to oversee all the other committees and identify any new ones that are "needed." In this type of organization, little work is being performed; most of the communication is through committees, no one is really sure of what he or she should be doing, and everyone is concerned with happiness. This is not an ideal climate for communication either. The communication tends to be narrow and distorted, and often people stifle their real feelings for fear of hurting someone else. Although both of these extreme organizational climates can exist in either profit-making or nonprofit organizations, the Dehumanizing climate tends to represent the excess most often identified with profit-making corporations; the Happiness for Lunch Bunch more often is representative of nonprofit groups.

It is clear that neither the Dehumanizing nor the Happiness for Lunch Bunch climate is desirable. The optimal climate is one that has a concern for both the task and the employee—one that encourages communication up, down, and across the organization concerning both task and employee issues. This climate we call the "Open" climate. This is a climate in which both supervision and administration are needed when the situation calls for them.

In the Open climate, personnel are encouraged to do their jobs, but with assistance from a supervisor. Personnel are encouraged to talk to each other and their supervisor and take problems to their immediate supervisor. This climate is not without its drawbacks, but it is certainly better than the other two. In this climate, the employees, as well as management, are expected to do their jobs well and be open to new ideas and change. This climate is one in which people feel they can express an opinion, be straightforward, and not feel they will be criticized for being honest. This type of climate encourages personal achievement and personal growth—the other two do not. This is a supportive, non-threatening climate in which people feel comfortable and generally enjoy their work. In addition, people are expected to be involved and do more than just "put in time" or "socialize." Hence, this climate may not be for some people. Those who just want to socialize will be happier in the Happiness for Lunch Bunch. Those who just want to do their job and be left alone might be happier in the Dehumanizing climate—at least they know nothing is expected of them.

In conclusion, the Open climate fosters communication between supervisors and subordinates as well as among peers. It encourages change. The Dehumanizing climate does none of these. Management just wants output. The Happiness for Lunch Bunch climate does none of these either. It is concerned with employee happiness to the exclusion of the task. To determine which climate is present in your organization, look to where the concern is and what type of communication is encouraged. You will recognize that the Dehumanizing and Happiness for Lunch Bunch climates represent two ends of a continuum, with the Open climate occupying a section in the middle of that continuum. Sometimes the climate in an organization shifts around between the middle and one of the ends of the continuum, but seldom does it move from one end to the other, unless there is a dramatic change in the personnel at the top of the organization.

STATUS

Status can be a deterrent to effective interpersonal communication between managers and employees. *Status* is defined as one's position in a group or organization. *Status differential* is the distance between one person's status and another person's status. A significant status differential might exist between a supervisor and a subordinate. The higher one's status in an organization, the less likely he or she is to have effective interpersonal relationships with people a few steps removed. The people who have higher status generally receive more communication from others. For example, the president of a college receives more communication than the typical professor, secretary, or student. The president gets messages from external sources as well as internal sources, and the messages come from all directions. The typical employee gets messages from one or two major sources, and less communication overall. Because higher-status persons receive more communication, they often have to limit their interpersonal contacts to those who have a direct impact on them or those who are of equal or higher status. Many high-status persons delegate their communication responsibilities to other persons, such as secretaries, junior employees, and assistants. This does not mean that higher-status persons forget or neglect their employees; it simply means there is less time to spend with them, and others have to handle some of the communication.

Communication between higher-status and lower-status persons tends to be limited, and the higher-status person has control over the communication. In addition, most subordinates (with any common sense) know they should communicate with a higher-status person only when absolutely necessary and should always try to make the communication positive. After all, no subordinate wants a superior to think negative things about him or her. In conclusion, status can be a barrier, but not always a permanent barrier. In a later chapter we review the role of status and discuss more about what you can do to keep it from being a problem.

COMMUNICATION OVERLOAD

> Barbara Jones is hard at work. The phone rings, and it is the public relations office asking if she has time to see a client. She says, "I suppose; send him up." She glances at the pile of morning mail that is still in its box, and the number of phone messages her secretary had given her from the previous day. She remembers she needs to contact the daycare center about her child, who had a slight fever when she dropped her off that morning. She quickly realizes there will be no lunch break for the day and she will probably have to take work home or come in early for several days.

This is a somewhat typical start for the day for many employees across the country. Whether we like it or not, the majority of us have to deal with communication overload on a regular basis. *Communication overload* is when there is more communication or information coming into a unit or system than the system can cope with or handle effectively. It seems many of us (supervisors and subordinates alike) are prone to communication overload. It can greatly interfere with communication and make our communication with others less effective.

Overload occurs when there is too much communication coming from too many directions. We are being bombarded with communication. This is one of the primary reasons many managers have learned to limit their interpersonal contacts to those people who are necessary for them to function. An individual can handle only so much communication effectively. When individuals become overloaded they don't function well. The problem is similar to overload of electronic communication systems. Phone lines can effectively handle only a certain number of calls. On special holidays (for example, Christmas) the phone lines often are bombarded with so many calls they get more than they can handle, and the system ceases to function appropriately. People are the same way when overload becomes too great and unmanageable. Both managers and employees have devised several ways for coping with, managing, or handling overload. Some of these ways are not effective, but they help control the situation. Following is a discussion of the ways people try to handle overload.

Handling Overload

One of the most common ways of handling overload is called *omission*. This is when a manager or an employee simply omits handling some incoming information, omits doing a certain task, or omits communicating with certain people (such as returning phone calls). One employee in one organization told us that he simply omits returning phone messages because he figures "they'll call back" or "they will solve their own problems." Think of how disastrous this could be for his company or unit. Perhaps some people do not mind when messages are left but no call is returned. Others may become outraged and eventually phone his supervisor. Nevertheless, this is one of the most commonly used methods for dealing with overload. Almost everyone who has worked in an organization has purposely omitted devoting time to some task because more pressing matters were at hand. If you have ever found that letter that should have been answered last week, you have employed this method—even if you were not aware you were doing it.

Another method for dealing with communication overload is called *error.* This is not so much a method of dealing with overload as an outcome of trying to deal with it and failing. This "method" is in operation when we fail to correct our errors—not proofreading letters before sending them, not correcting errors on reports, not correcting statements we have made. We are so busy we do not read things carefully and correct mistakes. In other words, we are just too busy to be bothered with checking details in every piece of information. One supervisor in an organization we know had to complete personnel reports on his employees every six months. The reports came at an extremely busy time. He liked a particular employee and wanted to give her an excellent rating in all areas, so he simply checked comments down one side of an employee checklist. He failed to notice which side he checked. He checked the side that said "employee unsatisfactory," so he unintentionally gave the employee unsatisfactory ratings in appearance, work behaviors, written and oral communication, task orientation, and so on. In fact, the rating was so bad an employee in the personnel office could not believe the employee could be that bad and called to check out the rating. The manager had to admit he had "been in a hurry and made an error." Fortunately, this error was caught by someone who was not so hurried. Such mistakes often are not caught in many organizations. That is why some people who have never been late on a bill have poor credit ratings, and other people who are expecting a check to make a payment on their house never receive the check. Overloaded people make errors and do not have time to find and correct all of them.

A third method of handling overload is use of a *filtering* system. When we let things "pile up," some things filter out of the pile by resolving themselves. Deadlines come and go, and we miss them. We might do this type of filtering while we are on vacation, but once we are back at work we will have to handle the remaining messages and apologize for all those we did not handle. Simply letting things "pile up" until a later date and hoping they will go away is no solution. Even though some things do handle themselves or are handled by others, it usually takes longer to make up for what happened than it would have taken to handle the issue on time.

Then there is the ever-popular *priority* system. Here, of course, we attempt to handle input based on some type of "what is important and what is not" system. Obviously, most of us would handle requests from our supervisor before we would handle requests from a subordinate. Life is full of priorities, and most of us have been socialized to prioritize. Even in school we would prioritize which classes were the most important to attend, to get papers turned in for, to do our best work in. Most of us considered our majors the most "important priority" in college and spent more time on courses in them. Some people choose partying over studying, and so on. We do not mind priority systems if we are on the top; it is when we are at the bottom of the list that we dislike priority systems.

There are people who really do try to do it all. They usually end up *approximating,* or doing things "halfway." They do it all, but nothing is done well. At times most of us who try to be conscientious are forced to approximate. But some approximate more than others. For example, some teachers are so overloaded they never really grade any papers or tests well, but they grade them in an acceptable manner. They do not read the answers as thoroughly as they should; they do not read papers as thoroughly as they should; they miss spelling, grammatical, and content errors because they are doing only a halfway job. Some executives are the same way. They do all the work, but it is not in top form.

One of the more-successful methods for handling communication overload is to *delegate* some of the communication and information to another competent person. Many managers have learned they cannot do a successful job with everything, so they have assistance, whether in the form of a person with the title "assistant to" or in the form of a very low-level employee affectionately known as a "gofer." The key to delegation is to delegate to a competent individual. Some things can be handled by a gofer; many things cannot.

Another successful method for coping with communication overload is to *realign resources* so that you are not doing "too much." This is an extension of delegation, but it goes a step farther. You are decentralizing or diffusing some of the decision making to people in the organization who are just as competent as you to handle certain decisions. This is why there are department heads, assistants, middle-level managers, and so on. Sometimes you have too much work or too many duties. If there are competent, willing people in the organization, share the responsibilities with them. They will be better employees for it. They will feel more involved and more useful. You will be less overloaded.

Most successful managers and employees have already learned the next strategy—*plan ahead*. After being in an organization for a number of months or years, one usually knows when the peak overload periods are so one can plan ahead to cope with the potential problems that might arise. If the beginning of the fiscal year is usually a busy time with a lot of calls and people requesting information or needing your time, plan ahead—clear off your desk and be ready to deal with them. If the beginning of each month is busier than usual, plan for it. Procrastinators can never do this. Hence, many procrastinators never make it to levels of responsibility because they are organizational disasters.

Occasionally, you might use the *"no" principle*. This means occasionally simply saying "No, I am already overcommitted." *No* is not a dirty word. Generally, there are some people it is more difficult to say no to than others. But even those people on occasion need to hear you say no. They will get over it. We know one employee who was always asked to take care of her manager's two large dogs when he was on a trip. The employee did not even like pets and often had allergic reactions to the animals, but she did not know how to say no. Finally, a trip the employee wanted to take coincided with a trip the manager wanted to take, and she told the manager it wasn't possible for her to take care of the dogs. The manager was a little peeved and then realized he had been infringing on the employee's good nature and freedom. After that, the manager never asked again. He took his pets to the kennel as everyone else at his level in the organization did.

Finally, there is the *escape* route. When the information and communication become too much, escape. This is more popularly known as the "sick leave," the "mental health day," or the "I need a break day." Occasionally, almost all of us need a day like that. The problem is that the overload does not really go away. It just mounts, and there often are new problems awaiting you when you go back to work. But then again, maybe you are mentally refreshed and ready to deal with the overload. So occasionally you may be better off taking a day off. Some organizations specifically allow employees a certain number of days off per year without the employee's providing the company with any excuse. This allows everyone who feels overloaded to avoid the overload for a day so he or she can come back refreshed and attack it.

As we stated earlier, not all the ways of coping with or handling overload are necessarily positive methods. They all work—some just work better than others. Obviously, priority systems, delegation, realigning resources, planning ahead, and saying no work better than the others. But the other methods clearly are ways we still use. We need to know these in order to realize how overload and the way we deal with it impacts our communication with others.

The question then becomes, Does the system ever have underload? The answer is yes. *Communication underload* is when the communication or information load is below what the system needs to operate effectively. This is not as common as overload, but it sometimes exists. In a way this can be as big a problem as overload. *In underload situations, people do not have enough to do, so they tend to create things to do.* They may create committees to work on useless things, they may get bored and start wanting to make unnecessary changes, and they frequently find fault with the way others are doing their jobs. Often these destructive reactions lead to the sending of memos, often to busy people who are *overloaded!* People with too little communication can become problems, both for themselves and for others.

As we said, underload usually is rare; overload is not. We pointed out a number of viable methods for coping with overload, but we never said how to eliminate overload. Well, you never eliminate overload—it is always there lurking around your desk corner or behind a file cabinet waiting to get you. Systems cannot avoid overload, but they can deal with it better. On days when you have underload, do a little extra so the overload does not get you the next day. Just when you think you have things under control, new problems arise. It does not matter what your job is—teacher, executive, manager, car dealer, whatever. If you are dealing with and communicating with people on a regular basis, you will always have the potential for overload. The more people you have to deal with, the more likely you will have more problems.

DEFENSIVENESS

This section reviews what Gibb (1961) referred to as "the defensive atmosphere." This is when an employee feels threatened or intimidated and doesn't trust others in the organization. While Gibb's observations were made four decades ago, they still deserve consideration today. At that time, much was being made of the so-called humanistic approach to communication. The basic premise of this approach was that if we just treated others better and were open and honest with them, communication would improve and all of our lives would be better. Although the philosophical position is a good one, expecting such things to happen in real, ongoing organizations is a bit overly optimistic.

Gibb's premise was that certain messages create a defensive atmosphere in an organization. This defensive atmosphere, of course, is presumed to create barriers to effective communication. If we feel threatened or intimidated, we must be prepared to defend ourselves; hence, we cannot communicate in an open, honest fashion. Let us look at Gibb's list of six types of messages that he believed would create a defensive climate and defensive reactions.

The first type of message is the one that suggests one is being evaluated. Since Gibb presumed that most people do not think of evaluation as being pleasant, it would follow that such messages would cause one to be defensive.

A second type of message exists when another suggests we should change our behavior. Gibb believed such a controlling message is likely to make us defensive. People often resent others' suggesting that their behavior is inappropriate and should be changed. Hence, they become defensive.

Messages that suggest the presence of some hidden strategy to manipulate another person represent a third type of message said to lead to defensiveness. Most of us prefer not to be manipulated, but to have others tell us directly what we need to know or do.

The fourth type of message that is presumed to stimulate defensiveness is the nonmessage, or message of neutrality. When people in our work environment simply ignore us or are neutral toward us, we may become defensive. We want to be acknowledged for our contributions and ideas, not treated as if we are replaceable objects with little value. Being ignored is seen as being undervalued.

People who behave in a manner viewed as acting as if they are superior are seen as sending the fifth type of message that causes defensiveness. They appear to think they know more than the rest, they are more intelligent, have higher status, and are above others. It is thought to be difficult to work with persons who have a superiority attitude. It presumably makes others feel inadequate and useless.

Finally, people who communicate with messages of certainty when expressing opinions or ideas are seen as creating defensive feelings. For example, people who are quick to answer, are effective in argument, and rarely want to negotiate or compromise because they believe their ideas are the best are seen as causing others to be defensive.

As you can see, these presumably defensiveness-causing messages are seen as barriers to effective communication because they are seen as barriers to feelings of support, trust, and understanding. Instead, these messages are seen as creating hostility and anxiety and causing people to be less willing to communicate.

When Gibb's work was first published, it was so consistent with the popular psychology of the day it was accepted on its face, and continues to be in many books today. Given the current recognition that messages do not possess meaning, however, Gibb's observations may be viewed in a new light. It is not messages of evaluation, control, superiority, and so on that cause defensiveness. In some cases, it is the individual's *perceptions* of messages as connotating such intents that do so. Hence, a more reasonable explanation for defensiveness is that some employees are insecure people with low self-concepts and are likely to feel threatened by others in their organizational environment; and when this happens, such people become defensive and highly unreasonable in their reactions to others. Others, those employees with more secure self-concepts, do not react in the same way. The six types of messages we have discussed (evaluative messages, controlling messages, strategic messages, neutral messages, superior messages, and confident messages) are all necessary for effective managerial communication. Subordinates need to learn to expect these kinds of messages and recognize that these are normal parts of superior/subordinate interaction.

How, then, should we deal with defensive people? The best advice is to ignore them and stay out of their way. Whatever you say to such insecure people is most likely to be taken the wrong way, so it is best to say nothing. The only kinds of communication they can handle are deference and agreement. Since no organization can guarantee that limited type of communication environment, these people are destined to be in a near-constant state of defensive reaction. If one cannot overcome a communication barrier, it is best to avoid that barrier.

REFERENCES AND RECOMMENDED READINGS

Gibb, J. R. (1961). Defensive communication. *Journal of Communication, 11*, 141–148.

Koehler, J. W., Anatol, K.W.E., & Applbaum, R. L. (1981). *Organizational communication: Behavioral perspectives* (2nd ed.). New York: Holt, Rinehart and Winston.

McCroskey, J. C. (2001). *An introduction to rhetorical communication.* (8th ed.). Needham Heights, MA: Allyn and Bacon.

McCroskey, J. C., & Richmond, V. P. (1996). *Fundamentals of human communication: An interpersonal perspective.* Prospect Heights, IL: Waveland Press.

Redding, W. C. (1973). *Communication within the organization.* New York: Industrial Communication Council; Lafayette, IN: Purdue Research Foundation.

STUDY GUIDE

1. Identify and distinguish among the three major types of organizational climate. How does communication operate in each?
2. How does "status differential" impact communication in organizations? Why?

3. Explain what is meant by communication overload. Why is this concept important?
4. What are the common methods people use to cope with such overload?
5. How can people best cope with communication "underload"?
6. What is defensiveness? What communicative elements in the organizational context are thought to make people respond defensively?
7. What is the more contemporary view of the reason defensiveness exists?
8. What is the best way to deal with co-workers who are insecure people with low self-concepts? Why?

CHAPTER 6

PERSONALITY, TEMPERAMENT, AND COMMUNICATION TRAITS

No two people are exactly alike. There are literally thousands of ways people differ from each other, including such obvious characteristics as height, weight, sex, eye color, nose size, skin color, hand size, hair color, vocal quality, bone structure, and facial features. Most of us are well aware that these individual features are a function of the genetic heritage of each individual. Barring cosmetic surgery and/or severe dietary restrictions, there is little one can do about such features. Of course, not all individual differences are so obvious at first sight.

Each person has a unique personality. An individual's personality includes a collection of traits, which are characteristic of that individual. It is these characteristics that distinguish one person from another. Among these characteristic traits are predispositions and tendencies toward communication, which collectively permit us to see how one person is unique from another.

PERSONALITY AND TEMPERAMENT

Over the past seven decades personality psychologists have identified more than 2,000 different personality traits. This massive research effort has made us very aware of how complex human personalities are. It has also made it obvious that we cannot realistically expect to understand all of these personality traits and how they impact individuals with whom we are in contact on a daily basis.

This research has led investigators to study the association of each of these traits with other traits and attempts to identify which are most important. This effort has resulted in the identification of what has been called "Super Traits" or "Temperament" variables. These super traits have been found to be associated with many personality variables and have made it possible to understand how groups of personality traits impact human behavior, including communication behavior. The most prominent classification of super traits was advanced by Hans Eysenck (1990). Eysenck labeled his three temperament variables as extraversion, neuroticism, and psychoticism. Eysenck and his colleagues also reported research that indicates that these temperament variables are genetically based. Other psychobiologists (people who study psychology from a biological perspective) have suggested that there are five temperament variables. Costa and McCrae (1992) labeled their first two variables the same as Eysenck, extraversion and neuroticism. The remaining three variables (a breakdown of psychoticism) were labeled openness to experience, agreeableness, and conscientiousness.

TEMPERAMENT/PERSONALITY AND COMMUNICATION

The association of temperament and personality with communication has been specifically noted by psychobiologists. As Eysenck (1986) put it, temperament represents the "ways in which individuals can interact" (p. 14). As Bates (1989), another leading psychobiologist, put it, "there is general agreement [among psychobiologists] that temperament is manifest largely in the context of social interaction" (p. 4).

Communication scholars have long expressed the view that communication and personality are related. Most have suggested that people communicate the way they do because of their personality. Some, however, have argued that if we change people's communication behavior (generally, through public speaking classes) this will produce changes in their personality as well. Neither view has been established through experimental research, although substantial correlations between personality variables and communication variables have been reported. These correlations confirm the relationship between these variables, but do not establish whether personality causes communication, communication causes personality, or some latent variable causes both.

Most communication research until very recently has been based on the assumption that personality and communication traits are learned. However, this research has provided no substantial support for learning as the cause for communication traits. While it appears that some communication behaviors clearly are learned, such as the language(s) which children speak, and the nonverbal communication behaviors that are unique to particular cultures, communication traits of children (and adults) are often very different than those manifested by their parents, whether the children are raised by their birth parents or adopted.

Recent research reported by communibiologists (people who study communication from a biological perspective) indicates that genetic heritability is the most likely causal factor in communication traits, as it is the primary causal factor in temperament and personality (Beatty & McCroskey, 2001). In short, neither personality nor communication traits cause each other, they are both caused by latent variables. These variables are genetically-based brain systems. These systems produce communication traits, as well the temperaments, which are manifested in communication behaviors.

The importance of this research for communication in organizations should not be underestimated. While organizations develop their own cultures (as we discuss in a later chapter), certain types of communication will be rewarded or punished within that organizational culture. Many people in organizations will not communicate precisely in the way others in the organization (supervisors, subordinates) would prefer. If we recognize that much of our (and our co-workers') communication is genetically based, we will better understand why training, or even threatening, does not produce communication conformance. One can change things that are learned, but changing things that are genetic is much more difficult, and often not possible.

COMMUNICATION TRAITS

Research on many communication traits has been reported. Most of these traits would likely have some impact on communication in the organizational context. We have chosen to discuss the ten traits that we believe might have the most significant impact in this context. In this section, seven traits are discussed: willingness to communicate, shyness, communication apprehension, self-perceived communication competence, compulsive communication, argumentativeness/tolerance for disagreement, and verbal aggression. The remaining three traits, assertiveness, responsiveness, and versatility/flexibility will be discussed in the following section. That section will focus on styles of communication and the communication traits that constitute those styles.

Willingness to Communicate (McCroskey & Richmond, 1987).   The most basic communication trait is willingness to communicate. *The willingness to communicate trait is an individual's predisposition to initiate communication with others.* While most people will respond at least briefly if someone else tries to initiate interaction with them, there is wide variance in the willingness of individuals to initiate communication with other people. Some people are generally willing to communicate with just about anyone, while others will rarely communicate unless someone else initiates communication with them. Most of us fall in between these extremes.

Being willing to communicate is generally considered to be a very positive characteristic in U.S. culture, as it is in many European, Arabic, and African cultures. However, this is not the case in other cultures, particularly some Asian cultures. Modern U.S. organizations generally view people who are willing to communicate more positively than those who are less willing. In many cases decisions on hiring, retention, and promotion are heavily influenced by this trait. People who are willing to communicate are seen as better employees, because they involve themselves more in tasks involving interpersonal and team interactions.

Employees' capabilities in the work environment are often only witnessed through their communication with others. Hence, employees less willing to communicate are often seen as less qualified, less motivated, and less cooperative than their more communicative colleagues. Research has indicated that employees who lack willingness to communicate are often less satisfied with their jobs, less motivated in those jobs, and less likely to choose to stay with their organization. Modern organizations virtually demand communication from their employees. Most positions above the entry level in organizations require that the individual in the position serve as a manager of those in lower-level positions. Management is a communication profession, hence to be an effective manager, one must be willing to communicate. Surveys given to managers indicate that over 90 percent of their time at work involves meetings and interactions with subordinates and supervisors.

Shyness (McCroskey & Richmond, 1982). *Shyness is the tendency to be timid, reserved, and most specifically, talk less.* While willingness to communicate is a trait orientation toward communication, shyness refers to the actual behavior of not communicating. While shyness in young children, particularly little girls, often is seen as "cute" in U.S. culture, it usually is seen in a much more negative light in older children and adults. Particularly in the context of new acquaintances, and people we don't know well, shyness often is perceived as a negative reaction to us, personally. Others see our shy behavior in a similar light. Hence, in important communication contexts in organizations, such as employment interviews, transitory team meetings, interactions with subordinates, and dealings with clients, shy people are often perceived in a very negative way.

However, once people get to know one another well, as is often the case of roommates or interactions between supervisors and subordinates, shyness has a much less negative impact (Cole & McCroskey, 2003). In these situations it appears that receivers do not take the source's shy behavior personally, because they have seen this behavior in the source's communication with others. Shyness in others is taken personally and generates negative responses, unless people know the other person well. Then people tend to be more tolerant of this trait behavior. Unfortunately, in many positions in organizations, people primarily have contact with people they either do not know at all or do not know well. Shyness is seen as rejection, and tends to generate reciprocal responses.

Communication Apprehension (McCroskey & Richmond, 1979). *Communication apprehension is an individual's level of fear or anxiety associated with either real on anticipated communication with another person or persons.*

This communication trait has been the subject of more research than any other. Writings concerning the fear or anxiety associated with communication date back to the ancient Greeks. Some of the earliest quantitative research on communication apprehension was on speech fright or public speaking anxiety. Anxiety about public speaking has been reported by as many as 70 percent of people in the United States in numerous national surveys. Until the 1970s, however, few people realized that many were just as apprehensive, or even more apprehensive, about communication in dyadic or group contexts than public speaking. It is now estimated that between 15 and 20 percent of the U.S. population has high communication apprehension about all communication contexts. More people suffer from the disability produced by communication apprehension than any other disability.

We refer to this communication trait as a disability because of its overwhelmingly negative influence on an individual's communication behavior and success across communication contexts, including the context of organizational communication. The three most common effects of communication apprehension are communication avoidance (avoiding situations where communication might be expected), communication withdrawal (escaping communication by either psychological or physical means), and communication disruption (communicating in a less competent or non-competent manner). All generate negative reactions on the part of others and/or the failure to accomplish outcomes that can be accomplished by less apprehensive individuals. When communication is required to succeed, high communication apprehensive individuals are most likely to fail.

Communication apprehension is negatively related to willingness to communicate and positively related to shyness. Hence, all of the negative outcomes expected from low willingness to communicate and high shyness can be expected from communication apprehension. Unfortunately, these effects may be even more negative. For example, research has found that people who are perceived as high communication apprehensives are seen in very negative ways, even by people who know them well (unlike shyness). Research relating to organizational communication indicates all of the negative outcomes noted previously relating to low willingness to communicate and high shyness are present for high communication apprehensives. Research has been successful in identifying several methods to help people lower their communication apprehension levels. However, the improvement is marginal, only 7–10 percent in most studies. Recent research indicates that the use of anti-depressant drugs may prove to be more effective even though most high communication apprehensives are not suffering from depression.

Self-Perceived Communication Competence (McCroskey & McCroskey, 1988). *An individual's report of her/his own competence in communication across a variety of contexts is described as self-perceived communication* *competence.* It is important to understand that this is a measure of self-perception, not a measure of actual communication competence. One may wonder why we should be concerned with such a perception. The reason is simple. Many decisions about communicating, including whether or not to do so, depend on individuals' self-perception of their competence, and may or may not be impacted by their actual competence. Many incompetent communicators think they are competent, and many competent communicators, as a function of their low self-esteem, think they are not. As with any walk of life, we are more likely to attempt what we think we are good at, and less likely to attempt what we think we are bad at.

Self-reports of communication competence are substantially associated with self-esteem and communication apprehension. In general, people with low self-esteem see themselves as having little potential to do well, to be inadequate in comparison with others around them. People with low self-esteem tend to see themselves as less competent communicators, as do people with high communication apprehension. These traits, of course, are associated with reduced willingness to communicate and increased shyness. This is not to suggest these traits cause one another. Rather, these relationships suggest that they are all influenced by the same genetically-based brain systems.

All of these communication traits are associated with the same temperament variables and self-esteem. Extraversion is positively associated with self-esteem, the willingness to communicate, and self-perceived communication competence, but negatively associated with shyness and communication apprehension. Neuroticism is positively associated with shyness and communication apprehension, but negatively associated with self-esteem, the willingness to communicate, and self-perceived communication competence.

Compulsive Communication (McCroskey & Richmond, 1996). *Some people (about 5 percent of the population) are driven to communicate.* They look at any contact with other humans as an opportunity for communication. This is more than just a high level of willingness to communicate, it is an overwhelming desire to communicate. These compulsive communicators are often referred to as "talkaholics." Their need for communication is as strong as an alcoholic's need for alcohol or a workaholic's need for work. As would be expected, this communication trait is associated with extraversion. However, it is not associated with neuroticism. Hence, this is not a neurotic need, it is just a strong desire to communicate.

Answer this question: "Do you know anyone who talks too much?" If you answered this question, "Yes," you are among the vast majority of people to whom we have posed the question. So, compulsive communicators, talkaholics, are the people who talk too much? Oddly, no. When we contacted people who were identified by others as people "who talk too much," we actually found that fewer of these people (about 2 percent) were scored on the "talkaholic scale" as compulsive communicators in the general population. This indicates that our description of "talks too much" actually references what people are saying or the way they are saying it, rather than the amount they talk. It represents a "quantitative" description of a "qualitative" problem. The people we give this label are either saying things we don't want to hear or communicating so badly that we just wish they would stop. It is the quality of their talk that gives us such a bad impression of them. Most of the people who we say talk too much actually talk no more than the average person. Talkaholics, on the other hand, generally are interesting people who have lots of friends and acquaintances who like to talk with them. Research over the past seven decades has indicated that people who talk more are more positively evaluated than people who talk less, on a wide variety of characteristics. These characteristics include: leadership ability, competence, liking, honesty, caring for others, task attractiveness, and social attractiveness.

Being a compulsive communicator, at least in the general U.S. culture, appears to be good rather than bad. This is confirmed to some extent by research which we did that involved interviews with people identified as talkaholics. These interviews indicated that every individual identified recognized they were a compulsive communicator, thought that being so was a good thing, and had no interest in signing up for a program to help them be less compulsive in their communication behavior. In contrast, in our work with high-communication apprehensives, two-thirds of them immediately volunteered to participate in a program designed to help them reduce their apprehension.

Argumentativeness and Tolerance for Disagreement (Infante & Rancer, 1982). Since these two communication traits are highly similar, and tolerance for disagreement is discussed in detail in a later chapter, we will focus here on the argumentativeness trait. *An argument includes the statement of a position on an issue and the support for that position, including reasons why alternative positions are incorrect.* While some people perceive arguing to be involved with attacking other people and loud verbal exchanges, this is not the kind of communication behavior that we are considering here. We see arguing as involving two or more people in an exchange of ideas stating positions and providing support for those positions. If these exchanges begin to involve personal attacks, rather than exchanges of positions and support, the communication has moved into the category of verbal aggression, which is discussed later in this chapter.

There is wide variance among people in terms of their ability to form and present strong arguments to support their views in contrast to those of others. There also is wide variance in their willingness to argue at all. The argumentative communication trait concerns both of these factors. People scoring higher on this trait generally are good at arguing and enjoy doing so. People scoring lower on this trait generally are not good at arguing and do not enjoy doing so. In the give-and-take of communication in organizations, being able to argue one's views is an important factor in a person's success or failure. High argumentatives are likely to have more influence in the organization, and generally experience less interpersonal conflict in their communication. Low argumentatives, however, are less likely to even introduce their ideas in the organization, much less exhibit skill in supporting them. They also are more likely to misunderstand strong arguments against their ideas, if any are advanced, and perceive them as direct personal attacks (which they are not). This, of course, is highly likely to result in interpersonal conflict with others. Disagreement in organizations is critical to making good decisions and finding better ways to do things. Hence, high argumentatives are likely to be much more valuable employees than those who are low in argumentativeness and prone to initiating verbal aggression toward their colleagues.

While argumentativeness is a communication trait, it also is associated with two temperament variables. Higher argumentativeness is associated with both higher extraversion and higher psychoticism. Tolerance for disagreement also is associated with higher extraversion and higher psychoticism. These relationships suggest that both of these traits are likely to be the result of the same brain systems.

Verbal Aggression (Infante & Wigley, 1986).   Although argumentativeness and tolerance for disagreement are positive communication traits in organizations, verbal aggressiveness usually is considered to be a negative communication trait. *Verbally aggressive communication behavior involves attacking the self-confidence, character, and/or intelligence of another person in addition to, or instead of, their position on an issue.* It takes on the character of "You are a bad person" rather than "Your position is a bad idea." This, of course, personalizes disagreement and is very likely to lead to interpersonal conflict.

People who are low in argumentativeness are more likely to resort to this type of communication because they are less capable of defending their own positions in arguments with others. When their ideas are attacked, they take it as a personal attack and respond with a personal attack on the other communicator. This, of course, is likely to lead to an exchange leading to serious conflict between the people involved.

Verbal aggressiveness is associated with the psychoticism temperament variable, but is not associated with either extraversion or neuroticism. Hence, this type of behavior seems to be the product of only the brain system associated with psychoticism. People higher in psychoticism and verbal aggressiveness traits are likely to use verbal aggression as a strategic weapon against colleagues in the workplace. They may become verbal "bullies" to gain control over others. While this can be a serious problem involving any two people in an organization, it may have its most negative impact when it involves supervisors who are verbally aggressive. Those under such supervisors may perceive that they have no way to deal with such individuals and develop negative attitudes not only toward that supervisor but also toward the organization. It is also likely that people working under such supervisors will be lower in their job satisfaction and motivation to work.

SOCIOCOMMUNICATIVE ORIENTATIONS AND STYLES

Individuals exhibit trait differences in their basic communication styles. While individual communication traits are related to specific kinds of communication behaviors, in this section we will consider three traits and how they interact to produce unique styles of communication behavior. Sociocommunicative orientations reference the way individuals see their own communication behavior in terms of these traits. Sociocommunicative styles reference the way other people perceive those individuals' actual communication behavior.

Assertiveness (Richmond & Martin, 1998). *When people stand up for themselves and do not let others take advantage of them, without taking advantage of others themselves, they are acting assertively.* It is also acting assertively to speak up for one's self, whether that be making a request or expressing a feeling. Assertive communicators also tend to initiate, maintain, and terminate conversations in accordance with their own communication goals. Assertive communicators' nonverbal behavior also is important. They tend to talk faster and louder, use more gestures, make more eye contact, and lean forward more in interactions—they are more nonverbally immediate. Do not confuse assertiveness with verbal aggressiveness. Assertive communicators defend themselves and their ideas, but they do not launch personal attacks on others. Verbally aggressive communicators do launch such attacks.

Assertiveness is most highly correlated (positively) with the extraversion temperament variable, but also has a low negative correlation with neuroticism, and a low positive correlation with psychoticism. Assertive communicators seem to be non-neurotic extraverts who may be slightly psychotic.

Responsiveness (Richmond & Martin, 1998). *When people are other-oriented in their communication, they are being responsive.* Responsive communicators are sensitive to needs, feelings, and communication of others. They are people whom others see as good listeners. Responsive communicators are more nonverbally immediate than most other communicators and are seen by others as being friendly, compassionate, warm, sincere, and helpful. They are able to be empathic with others, hence focusing on the relational aspect of communication. Do not confuse responsiveness with submissiveness. Submissive communicators yield their rights to others, more often going against their own best interests. While responsive communicators are sensitive to the needs of others, they also pay attention to their own needs and goals. The responsive communicator recognizes and considers the other person's needs and rights, but does this without sacrificing their own legitimate rights.

Responsiveness is correlated (positively) with the extraversion temperament variable. However, it has a stronger (negatively) correlation with psychoticism and has no correlation with neuroticism. Responsive communicators appear to be non-psychotic extraverts.

Versatility (McCroskey & Richmond, 1996) **or Flexibility** (Martin & Rubin, 1994). The third element of sociocommunicative orientations and styles has been studied under two different labels, versatility and flexibility, but represents essentially the same trait concept. Because all communication takes place in a given context it is difficult, if not impossible, to identify communication behaviors that are appropriate and effective in all situations. The versatility/flexibility trait deals with one's ability to adapt one's communication behavior to the context, situation, and other person(s) involved in a communication event. Other terms that have been used to describe this kind of communicator include adaptable, rhetorically sensitive, and style-flexing. Communicators at the other end of the continuum are described as rigid, dogmatic, uncompromising, and unyielding.

The key elements of versatility/flexibility are knowing when to be assertive and when not to be, when to be responsive and when not to be, when to be both assertive and responsive, and when to be neither. People who can master these elements are more able to adapt appropriately to the communication of a wide variety of other people. People with little versatility/flexibility are not able to do this, hence they will often be assertive or responsive when they should not be, and not be assertive or responsive when they do need to be.

McCroskey and Richmond (1996) have argued that these three components of socio-communicative orientations and style are the underlying components of communication competence. They suggest that there is no set of communication skills that make for a competent communicator. Rather, true communication competence is based on having a wide variety of communication styles available for use and the proper orientations for when to use which one.

Four basic styles have been advanced as the core styles. They are all based on levels of both assertiveness and responsiveness. No one style is best, each has its strengths and its limitations. While almost everyone's basic style will be one of the following, amiable, analytical, driver, or expressive, the key for communication effectiveness in today's organizations will be to learn how to employ one of the other styles when needed.

Amiable. The amiables are considered relationship specialists and are high on responsiveness and low on assertiveness. The adjectives used to describe the amiables are as follows: conforming, unsure, pliable, dependent, awkward, supportive, respectful, willing, dependable, and agreeable. Merrill and Reid (1981) suggest that amiables seem "to be most comfortable working in environments where they can provide services and be supportive and helpful in their relationships with others" (p. 149). We will often find these people in "careers such as teaching, personnel management, social work, psychology, and other helping professions" (p. 149).

Although amiables are likely to be found in professions such as teaching, that is not to say that all, or even most, people in a given profession will be of a single social style. For example, the special education or kindergarten teacher is likely to be an amiable. The college professor heavily involved in laboratory research is more likely to be an analytical. The teacher who becomes principal and has to be "in charge" of running things may be a driver. The drama teacher or cheerleading coach might be an expressive. You can find the various social styles in all walks of life, but some professions are likely to attract higher numbers of certain social styles than others.

Analytical. The analyticals are considered technical specialists and are low on responsiveness and low on assertiveness. The adjectives used to describe the analyticals are as follows: critical, indecisive, stuffy, picky, moralistic, industrious, persistent, serious, exacting, and orderly. Merrill and Reid (1981) suggest that professions such as science, engineering, construction work, accounting, and certain aspects of law often have a high proportion of this style. Again, there could be other styles in these professions. Some research suggests that analyticals are more likely to be apprehensive about communication and, as a result, be more withdrawn and quiet. Thus, analyticals may be less effective communicators than the other styles and more resistant to attempts to interact with them.

Driver. The drivers are considered control specialists and are low on responsiveness and high on assertiveness. The adjectives used to describe the drivers are as follows: pushy, severe, tough, dominating, harsh, strong willed, independent, practical, decisive, and efficient. These people might be in careers such as small-business owners, top management, production managers, administrative personnel, politics, and other decision-making management positions. "Because of their ability to take responsibility and direct others, top management often puts these individuals into positions of control" (pp. 149–150). Again, there can be drivers in many other professions. The ones listed are only indicators of where drivers are most likely to be found.

Expressive.   The expressives are considered social specialists and are high on responsiveness and high on assertiveness. The adjectives used to describe the expressives are as follows: manipulative, excitable, undisciplined, reacting, ambitious, stimulating, enthusiastic, dramatic, and friendly. "Persons with expressive behavior are often found in sales, entertainment, advertising, art, music, and writing" (p. 150). These people know how to use their communication skills to "gain recognition and attention" and they like being seen and noticed by others. As suggested earlier, you can find expressives in other fields, not just the ones listed previously.

Which style is best? None. There is no best style. They are all different and they all have positive and negative characteristics. In addition, you can be dominant in one style and have the tendencies of another style. For example, one might be an expressive with some driver tendencies or an analytical with some amiable tendencies. The key is that you need to recognize whom you are working with and adjust your style to be compatible with his or hers, particularly if he or she is your boss and you want communication to be successful. Salespersons have known for years that they have to be *versatile* in order to succeed.

The key to much of this success is being versatile, regardless of your style. "Versatility is the dimension of behavior that indicates the extent to which others see us as adaptable, resourceful, and competent; it is behavior that earns their social endorsement of us because it accommodates their preferences" (p. 44). We need to know when to be assertive, when to be responsive, when to push, when to back off, when to listen to others, and when not to listen. As employees we have to understand that working with people who have different styles is going to be required of us, and to be successful we need to see possible conflict areas and adapt. For example, an amiable individual might perceive the driving style as too pushy, impersonal, and dominating. The analytical might see the expressive as too talkative and outgoing.

Merrill and Reid (1981) suggest that no one style is solely associated with success, but if versatility is present, then success is likely even between two potentially conflicting styles. Managers have known for years that they have to be able to deal with many different types of interpersonal relationships. You need to be prepared to do the same.

REFERENCES AND RECOMMENDED READINGS

Bates, J. E. (1989). Concepts and measures of temperament. In G. A. Kohnstamm, J. E. Bates, & M. K. Rothbart (Eds.), *Temperament in childhood*. New York: Wiley, 3–26.

Beatty, M. J., & McCroskey, J. C. (2001). *The biology of communication: A communi-biological perspective*. Cresskill, NJ: Hampton Press.

Cole, J. G., & McCroskey, J. C. (2003). The association of perceived communication apprehension, shyness, and verbal aggression with perceptions of source credibility and affect in organizational and interpersonal contexts. *Communication Quarterly, 51,* 101–110.

Costa, P. T., & McCrae, R. R. (1992). NEO-PI-R: Revised personality inventory. Odessa, FL: Psychological Assessment Resources.

Eysenck, H. J. (1986). Can personality study ever be scientific? *Journal of Social Behavior and Personality, 1,* 3–20.

Eysenck, H. J. (1990). Biological dimensions of personality. In L. A. Pervin (Ed.), *Handbook of personality: Theory and research.* New York: Guilford, 244–276.

Infante, D. A., & Rancer, A. S. (1982). A conceptualization and measure of argumentativeness. *Journal of Personality Assessment, 46,* 72–80.

Infante, D. A., & Wigley, C. J. (1986). Verbal aggression: An interpersonal model and measure. *Communication Monographs, 53,* 61–69.

Martin, M. M., & Rubin, R. B. (1994). Development of a communication flexibility scale. *Southern Communication Journal, 59,* 171–178.

McCroskey, J. C., & McCroskey, L. L. (1988). Self-report as an approach to measuring communication competence. *Communication Research Reports, 5,* 108–113.

McCroskey, J. C., & Richmond, V. P. (1979). The impact of communication apprehension of individuals in organizations. *Communication Quarterly, 27,* 55–61.

McCroskey, J. C., & Richmond, V. P. (1982). Communication apprehension and shyness: Conceptual and operational distinctions. *Central States Speech Journal, 33,* 458–468.

McCroskey, J. C., & Richmond, V. P. (1987). Willingness to communicate. In J. C. McCroskey & J. A. Daly (Eds.), *Personality and interpersonal communication.* Beverly Hills, CA: Sage, 129–156.

McCroskey, J. C., & Richmond, V. P. (1996). *Fundamentals of human communication: An interpersonal perspective* (Ch. 7). Prospect Heights, IL: Waveland Press.

Merrill, D. W., & Reid, R. H. (1981). *Personal styles and effective performance.* Radnor, PA: Chilton Book.

Richmond, V. P., & Martin, M. M. (1998). Sociocommunicative style and sociocommunicative orientation. In J. C. McCroskey, J. A. Daly, M. M. Martin, & M. J. Beatty (Eds.). *Communication and personality: Trait perspectives.* Cresskill, NJ: Hampton Press, 133–148.

STUDY GUIDE

1. Define and distinguish between "personality" and "temperament."
2. Explain how temperament is related to communication behavior.
3. Explain what causes temperament and communication traits.
4. Define and distinguish between WTC and Shyness.
5. Define and distinguish between CA and SPCC.
6. Explain the Talkaholic construct.
7. Define and distinguish between Argumentativeness and Verbal Aggressiveness.
8. Distinguish between SCO and SCS.
9. List the components of SCO/SCS.
10. List the four basic SCO/SCS styles and indicate how they differ from one another.

CHAPTER 7

ORGANIZATIONAL ORIENTATIONS AND COMMUNICATION TRAITS

Koehler, Anatol, and Applbaum (1981) suggest that the personality or culture "of an organization, in many respects, is a composite of the varied behaviors of the people within it" (p. 172). They are absolutely correct. The individual organizational orientations, temperaments, and personalities in each unit influence how people outside view the unit, as well as how the people within the unit see it.

Not all people approach their work in organizations with the same orientation. Some are "organization-friendly." Others are not. Some are organization-friendly only part of the time. Individuals' orientations are a major factor in their success or failure in the work environment. These orientations are associated with both the individual's temperament and their communication traits. All of these are associated with workers' job satisfaction and motivation to work.

ORGANIZATIONAL ORIENTATIONS

Presthus (1962) advanced organizational orientation theory as an explanation of substantial differences in the way employees in organizations approach their jobs. Presthus believed that these orientations result in employees having different orientations toward work itself, motivation toward work, job satisfaction, and ways of dealing with coworkers, supervisors, and subordinates. Presthus viewed his theory as being a theory of organizational behavior. He viewed the behavior of people in organizations as being driven by their traits, which he believed were learned through their experiences while working in organizations.

Presthus identified three organizational orientations which are specifically related to the way people approach their roles in organizations. These reflect the variable orientations different types of people have toward work and the place of work in their lives. These orientations are believed to be traits, that is, people will tend to have these orientations regardless of the organization in which they are employed and the orientations are not expected to change markedly as a person moves from one organization to another. People with high scores on these orientations are known as "upward mobiles," "indifferents," and "ambivalents." All three of these types are found in virtually all organizations. However, it is not common for a person to score highly on more than one of these orientations. Some people do not score highly on any of them.

Upward Mobiles.   Perhaps the most dedicated and most easily recognizable organizational type is the upward mobile. This is the typical "organizational man" or "organizational woman." These people are deeply devoted to the goals and functioning of the organization. They have a strong identification with the organization. These people are self-motivated, believe in the organization's rules and procedures, and expect others to also. Their personal goals are in line with the organization's goals and they strive toward high job satisfaction.

Upward mobiles do not like associating with people they consider to be "losers," people who are not on the same career path that they are. In fact, they might be highly critical of personnel who are not as dedicated or devoted as they are. They thrive on work, decision making, power, and organizational rewards and are ready and willing to "go the extra mile" for the organization. They will openly defend the organization and criticize those who are not dedicated to it. They have high standards and expect others to have the same.

All organizations look to hire potential upward mobiles, and when they have one they are likely to groom her or him for bigger and better positions. Organizations know they can depend on these persons to follow the rules, enforce the rules if necessary, and give "110 percent" support to the organization. These are the people oraganizations are likely to reward and encourage. They represent the future of the organization.

If we work for or with an upward mobile, we will be expected to support the organization and its policies. Communicating with an upward mobile is really quite easy. You know where he or she stands and what is expected of you. Praise him or her and the organization, and rewards will come to you and your unit. However, if he or she thinks you are a "loser," he or she will encourage you to go elsewhere. This person might even say things like "If this is not the job for you, then try some other job," or "In this organization we expect commitment. You don't seem to care, so it is time you move on."

If you want to influence an upward mobile, your suggestions should be couched in terms of how what you want would be good for the organization and, if possible, might help the upward mobile move up in the organization. Such an approach indicates your loyalty to the organization, and also your loyalty to this person. One of the best ways to move up in many organizations is to be "sponsored" by an upward mobile.

Indifferents.   The next orientational type is as easily recognizable as the upward mobile. This person is called the indifferent. These people make up a large portion of the employees in most organizations.

Whereas the upward mobile lives to work, the indifferent works to live. The indifferent is working because he or she has to. People have to make a living, they have to buy groceries, they want to make a better life for their children. Many people are motivated to work beyond their basic needs for survival. However, indifferents work only to satisfy their own very basic needs or the basic needs of their loved ones. This is not to say that they are evil or mean—they are simply not interested in the job or the organization. They are only in it for the paycheck.

These people will avoid participation in the daily organizational routines, they rarely share in the rewards the system has to offer, they are not highly satisfied with their jobs, and they rarely do any extra work without compensation. They would "never" volunteer to do extra work if the only reward was self-satisfaction. These people simply come to work, do their job, and go home.

Much of their communication on the job is about their family or personal life. When encouraged to communicate about organizational matters with colleagues, they generally say nothing, change the topic, or suggest that others should discuss those matters. They are not dedicated or upwardly mobile in any aspect. Hence, if you work with one of these people or have one for a supervisor, depend on yourself. These people will never do more than what is absolutely necessary. Again, they are not evil; they are not a threat to others. They may even be very nice people, but they are in the organization to do their job and be left alone. Every organization needs these people because they can be assigned to do menial, routine tasks that require little thought that others would resent doing. They don't resent these tasks—after all, it is a job and a paycheck—and such tasks do not require a personal commitment.

Getting along with indifferents in the organization usually is not difficult, as long as you do not push them to "give their all" for the organization or your unit in it. They are indifferent to their work, but that does not mean they do not care about anything. They can be very interested in things outside the work environment. Talk with them about their family, what they plan to do over the weekend, where good spots are for fishing, the local team in the sport that is in season, where to go for a vacation—what most people refer to as "small talk." Serious talk about work is not the indifferent's cup of tea.

Ambivalents.   The final organizational type is perhaps the most difficult to work with, because they are unpredictable. Although many of the personality orientations we discuss in this chapter are not necessarily likable, they at least are predictable—this type is not. They are the ambivalents. Koehler et al. (1981) describe the ambivalent as both "creative and anxious."

They go on to state, "The upward mobiles like the status quo and the indifferents accept it, the ambivalents want to change it" (p. 173).

The ambivalents are never truly comfortable in any organization. They may take a position because it seems to be what they want, but within a few months they have found a number of "problem areas" that need changing. They cannot seem to accept organizations or the people within them for what they are. These people can be supportive one day and attacking the next. They are moody, which makes it difficult for people to work with or for them. Chances are they will not stay in any one organization for more than a few years. After a while they feel they have done all they can do and must change positions. Or they get "disgruntled" with the system and change jobs.

Although ambivalents often are quite intelligent and highly skilled verbally, they reject the authority structure and will often try to turn others against the organization and the supervisors within it. They will openly criticize the system. Some of their criticism might be useful, but because of the way it is said, others reject it. Most systems are happy when ambivalents go. These are the people for whom the going-away party is held the day after they leave!

Communicating with ambivalents can be difficult, since you seldom can predict how they will react to ideas. About the only safe topic is criticism of the organization. Gripe sessions get ambivalents' blood churning. However, entering such conversations can be dangerous. You may find yourself quoted the next time the ambivalent decides to take on the organization or the supervisor. The best advice is to stick to small talk with ambivalents.

PERSONALITY TYPES

In the previous section we considered people's orientations which are directly related to organizational life. In this section we turn our attention to the way people are generally—their basic personalities. "Personality" can be defined as the sum of an individual's characteristics that make her or him unique. There are literally thousands of ways people differ from one another. Each person is higher and/or lower than most other people around them on some of these characteristics. This is how we come to distinguish each person from others we know well. Social scientists have identified some of the individual differences which have a distinctive impact on people in organizations as a function of their influence on communication behaviors. We will consider several of these below.

Authoritarianism.   This personality type has highly predictable patterns of behavior. Authoritarians, if they are anything, are consistent. The authoritarian personality type is very structured and rule-oriented. Often authoritarians are stern, unhumorous, conventional, suspicious, and at times hostile. Authoritarians respect authority. They are obedient to those above them, and they expect those below them to be obedient to their demands.

Authoritarians intensely dislike it when others do not show proper respect and obedience to their authority. They may become very vindictive when treated in a disrespectful manner by those below them in the hierarchy. It might seem that this is one type an organization surely could do without, but some organizations want this type of person in certain jobs. They will get people to "toe the line" and keep order and make sure things run smoothly.

Since they firmly believe power and status should be recognized and that some people should have a lot of it, whereas others should obey those who have the power and status, authoritarians often become the favorites of supervisors, particularly if the supervisor also is an authoritarian. As supervisors, high authoritarians make their subordinates feel as if they should "salute" each time they pass one another in the hallway. They usually manifest conservative attitudes, rarely find things funny at work, want others to be submissive and show deference to them, and become hostile when others ignore rules and policies.

In one organization with which we worked there was such an authoritarian individual who was not a supervisor. Many of her peers went out of their way to torment her. They quickly learned that she truly had little control over them, since she was not well liked by her supervisor, so they would do things that would "drive her up the wall." If she felt someone was not dressed properly and commented on it, the next day the person would show up even less properly dressed and watch this person fuss and fume. If she would suggest there is "too much fun in the office," then there would be more of it the next day, and it would be directed at her. If she would comment on the music people played in their offices, they would play it more loudly and obnoxiously. Because high authoritarians are so demanding of others and expect others to always obey their wishes, they can become targets, particularly if they are not in a supervisory position.

If you work under a high authoritarian, you need to understand his or her need for authority and obedience. If you choose not to conform, he or she is likely to make your life miserable. If you cannot accept doing what you need to do to be able to work with this type of person, you probably should leave your position. In many ways, authoritarians are easy to work for because you know what you need to do to stay out of trouble. But if you are not willing to do what is necessary, leave.

Communicating with highly authoritarian people is easy. Agree with them. "Yes" is the word they most enjoy hearing. "No" is not often acceptable. It is quite acceptable for you to ask them for explanations concerning how to do what they have instructed you to do. It is not acceptable of you to question why that should be done. Challenging a highly authoritarian person is like stamping on a dog's tail. If you do it, you can expect to be bitten.

While dealing with high authoritarians is not particularly difficult, if you are willing to do it, dealing with people who are unusually low in authoritarianism may be even more difficult. These are people who have no respect for authority. They do not respect the rules, and their behavior may be seen as aberrant in the organization. Being seen allied with such a person does not make one popular in an organization. Communication with these people should be handled very carefully, and kept to a minimum at least in the presence of other organization members.

Machiavellianism. People with the next personality orientation can be useful to the organization, if they are working with and for the organization, not against it. These people are Machiavellians. Nicoli Machiavelli wrote the book *The Prince,* in which he described what a prince would need to do to be an effective leader and rise to greater control of a society. The book was long on tactics and short on morality. Since that time, people who are highly manipulative have come to be known as "Machiavellians."

People high in Machiavellian tendencies are willing to manipulate others, enjoy manipulating others, and are good at it. Usually they get what they want, either for themselves or for their organization. This is not to suggest that Machiavellians necessarily are evil or that manipulation is wrong. Although Machiavellians do not typically subscribe to traditional high moral principles, that does not mean they are immoral. They view their manipulative skills as amoral tools. Morals simply are not an issue. If people are manipulated into doing something against their best interests, others might be appalled, but the high Machiavellian would more likely be amused.

How do you know a high Machiavellian when you see one? Usually, you don't unless you go out of your way to look. It is rare that high Machiavellians are widely recognized in an organization. In fact, it is more likely that people who are moderately high in Machiavellian tendencies will be thought to be high, since their attempts at manipulation will be more obvious. However, Machiavellians can be identified. Look for the following: They seem to get what they want without being pushy, they get people to do things for them that those people would not do for others, they rarely look as if they are manipulating, they generally are well liked by others in the organization, and they usually do well in the organizational environment.

Machiavellians typically do well in the "people professions." That is, they succeed when influencing people is necessary for success. Some typical occupations with a large proportion of high Machiavellians include education, law, religion, politics, fund raising, and many forms of sales. Most people that rise to the top, or near the top, in most organizations have high Machiavellian tendencies. High Machiavellians will manipulate to help themselves or others. Hence, they can be very good friends—or dreadful enemies.

How should one communicate with high Machiavellians? Very carefully! Remember, they get their way by being nice to others. They do not steal your money or power, they get you to give it to them! When communicating with a high Machiavellian, you need to be careful to have everything spelled out in detail. Do not consent to anything unless you are absolutely certain you know what you are doing and that it is in your best interests. Even then, you should delay for as long as possible. There are plenty of easy targets for high Machiavellians to manipulate. If you can manage to delay, there usually is little reason for Machiavellians to persist in trying to take advantage of you. If they are just doing it for fun, your delaying takes the fun out of it. If they really are after some benefit, they quickly recognize their time would be better spent by going after another target.

While high Machiavellians provide a challenge to other people in the organization, low Machiavellians present a different picture. These are the people who are manipulated by others in the organization. They are particularly easy to manipulate. Hence, they are unreliable colleagues and/or friends. Whoever has the last word, has these people on their side. This is a particularly serious problem if you have such a person for a supervisor. Who knows what others will convince this person to do that will not be in your best interests? The only advice we can give you, and it is easier said than done, is to be sure you get the last opportunity to influence this person before they have to make a decision important to you. Low Machiavellians often are the spineless wonders you find in middle-management positions who, in good faith, promise you one thing and then do the opposite—because someone else persuaded them to change their mind.

Achievment Orientation. Organizations are particularly thankful for the next personality orientation. These people are the high achievers, sometimes overachievers. Money is not the main motivator behind the high achiever. These people work because they want to achieve certain goals for themselves. They are often overcommitted, overextended, and overworked. They will often take on more duties than they can handle, but they will work overtime to make sure things get done. They are the "work horses" in most organizations.

You can spot them: They seem frazzled at times, have more work than most, more responsibility than most, and love it. They will often let others know how much they do by complaining about being overworked. They thrive on sympathy and praise. They are likely to volunteer for extra duties a minute after they have complained about being overworked. They are the people who validate the old maxim that "if you want something done fast, give it to a busy person."

High achievers have a tendency to blame themselves when things they are responsible for do not work out. They tend to be harder on and more critical of themselves than others would be, and often get overwrought when others show a streak of laziness. These people also need some praise from their co-workers or supervisors for jobs well done. If you praise high achievers, they will work, and work, and work, and work. The biggest drawback to this personality type is that they might take on more work than they are capable of handling effectively. Hence, an astute supervisor should be happy to have a high achiever, but must be careful that the person does not insist on more work than he or she is capable of handling. It is easy for systems to abuse these people, because they are willing to do more than others. Hence, if you are a high achiever, be careful.

High achievers are easy to communicate with. They will try to assist you with your problems and make your job easier. In fact, they will rarely expect you to do what they don't. However, they do expect you to work hard. The key to interacting with high achievers is the appropriate use of praise. These people need to know that you respect what they do. If you like their work, they like you.

Dogmatism.　People of the next personality type often are considered "difficult." These are the people in organizations who have a narrow view of issues and expect others to see their point of view. These are the highly dogmatic persons. They are rigid in their beliefs and do not tolerate viewpoints that disagree with theirs. They tend to be narrow in their thinking and will either avoid those that do not think as they do, or simply get rid of them if they can. Dogmatics see things as right or wrong, black or white—there are no gray areas or compromises. The classic example of a highly dogmatic was Archie Bunker on the TV show "All in the Family." On the same show there was another highly dogmatic person—Michael Stivik, Archie's son-in-law. They were equally hard headed and dogmatic. They each had their views, and neither was willing to see or even listen to the other's viewpoint. Their confrontations were hilarious to the millions of viewers who watched this show regularly, and still are funny today, decades after they were originally shown, to a whole new generation of viewers. Unfortunately, we find dogmatics in our organizations to be much less entertaining.

It is virtually useless to argue with a highly dogmatic peer, much less one who is your supervisor. He or she will simply discount your arguments as wrong, frivolous, or just plain stupid—and develop similar views about you. Hence, communication with a highly dogmatic individual is not easy. You have to determine what his or her views are, fit your ideas into his or her viewpoints, and even let him or her think he or she generated the idea, and you might be successful in communicating with a dogmatic person.

If you cannot do this and the dogmatic is your supervisor, you might have to leave the system. Think of what it would be like if your supervisor were a combination of a high authoritarian and a high dogmatic. Communication will be restricted to only views on issues with which he or she agrees. Even unemployment might look attractive in comparison.

Self-Esteem.   Many people in contemporary organizations have constant feelings of inadequacy. These feelings dominate their entire personalities. They have low self-esteem. We refer to these people as "inadequates" because that is the way they see themselves. They worry that they cannot perform their work well. They fear that others will not like them. They worry that they might be promoted, because they know they could not succeed at a higher level. They are insecure about their marriage, their children, life in general.

The first thing we should recognize is that a person who has low self-esteem can be right. That person may really be inadequate. But many people who have these perceptions are incorrect in the way they see themselves. Nevertheless, we must deal with these people every day in our organizational lives. Most of us have the common response of trying to tell these people they are more adequate than they think they are (even if they are not). That response will be met with rejection, as will praise for something the person does well.

As we noted in Chapter 5, these insecure people also tend to see attacks coming from all sides. Thus, to be on the safe side, we can simply accept an inadequate's claims of inadequacy, and move on to some other topic. Avoid praising their work, since they will not believe you anyway, and be extremely careful to avoid anything that would sound like criticism. Anything of that type is likely to prompt a highly defensive reaction (such as aggressive denial) or an emotional acceptance of blame. Either will be unpleasant. Fortunately, these people seldom are promoted to supervisory positions, since others recognize they are not likely to succeed in such positions. Consequently, most of the inadequates we will encounter will be peers or subordinates.

ORGANIZATIONAL ORIENTATIONS AND TEMPERAMENT

Although the early work with organizational orientations was based on the assumption that these orientations are learned, this view has come into question. Recent research (McCroskey, McCroskey, & Richmond, 2004) has determined that the three organizational orientations have substantial associations with temperament. Higher levels of both ambivalence and indifference are associated with both higher levels of neuroticism and higher levels of psychoticism. In contrast, higher levels of extraversion are associated with higher levels of upward mobile orientations. Because temperament has been determined to have a strong genetic base, it may well be that organizational orientations do too.

ORGANIZATIONAL ORIENTATIONS, TEMPERAMENT, AND COMMUNICATION TRAITS

Research has determined that communication traits are substantially related to both temperament and organizational orientations (McCroskey, Richmond, Johnson, & Smith 2003; McCroskey, McCroskey, & Richmond, 2004). Assertiveness has been found to be positively associated with extraversion, and upward mobility. Responsiveness has been found to be negatively associated with psychoticism, ambivalence, and indifference. Nonverbal immediacy has been found to be positively associated with extraversion, but negatively associated with psychoticism, ambivalence, and indifference. Clearly these three sets of orientations are highly interrelated.

ORGANIZATIONAL ORIENTATIONS, TEMPERAMENT, AND ORGANIZATIONAL OUTCOMES

Two major outcomes for employees in organizations, as well as for the organization itself, are employee job satisfaction and employee work motivation. Research has indicated that both temperament and organizational orientations are substantially associated with these outcomes (McCroskey, McCroskey, & Richmond, 2004). Upward mobility and, to a lesser extent, extraversion are positively associated with both job satisfaction and motivation. Ambivalence, indifference, neuroticism, and psychoticism are all negatively associated with both job satisfaction and motivation. Clearly, both individually and collectively, these employee traits are very important predictors of success in organizations.

For many years scholars believed that the kinds of trait orientations we describe in this chapter were learned by individuals as a function of contact with their parents, teachers, peers, siblings, and the general culture in which they live. The two studies referenced provide some support for this belief. The participants in the first study were upper-division college students (average age 20), who had comparatively little experience in full-time employment. The participants in the second study were older people with many years of experience working in organizations. The mean scores on both indifference and ambivalence were much higher for the younger group than the older group. It seems likely that the older group modified their indifference and ambivalence as a function of their work experience. It would be difficult to explain how genetic factors would produce such a major change.

Nevertheless, given the research findings discussed previously, it is clear that there are genetic factors influencing the relationships among these groups of trait orientations and their impact on organizational outcomes. Even if learning is a meaningful influence in establishing organizational orientation traits, they still are traits. That is, they remain generally consistent across organizations and across time.

This, of course, does not mean that people are totally unable to change their trait orientations. However, it does suggest that even if one really wants to change, change may be difficult, and the amount of change which can be made may be comparatively small. We need to keep this in mind so that we recognize how unrealistic it is to expect our supervisors and colleagues to change just because we want them to. Alternatively, we must learn to adapt (as much as our own traits will let us) our communication to the way other people really are rather than the way we wish they were. This is the only realistic path to effective communication in organizations.

In conclusion, an organization is as good as its personnel. We have reviewed a number of personality orientations that exist in all organizations. Some are easier to work with than others. Of course, some people may exhibit characteristics of two or more personalities. For example, a person could be an upward mobile with high achiever tendencies. What we must learn to do is recognize the personalities we work with. Then we must communicate with them in ways that will not go against their personality predispositions. If we can do so, we are likely to be pleased with the outcomes of our communication. If things do not work out right, we might wonder if our own personality orientations got in the way. Could it be that your personality fits into one or more of the types we have discussed in this chapter?

REFERENCES AND RECOMMENDED READINGS

Adorno, T., Frenkel-Brunswik, E., Levinson, D., & Sanford R. (1950). *The authoritarian personality.* New York: Harper and Row.

Argyris, C. (1957). *Personality and organization.* New York: Harper and Row.

Christie, R., & Geis, F. (1970). *Studies in Machiavellianism.* New York: Academic Press.

Ghiselli, E. (1963). *The concept of role and theoretical basis for understanding organizations.* Bologna: University of Bologna Press.

Infante, D. A., & Rancer, A. S. (1982). Aconceptualization and measure of argumentativeness. *Journal of Personality Assessment, 45,* 72–80.

Koehler, J. W., Anatol, K. W. E., & Applbaum, R. L. (1981). *Organizational communication: Behavioral perspectives.* (2nd ed.). New York: Holt, Rinehart and Winston.

McClelland, J. (1961). *The achieving society.* New York: Van Nostrand Reinhold.

McCroskey, J. C., & Daly, J. A. (1987). *Personality and interpersonal communication.* Beverly Hills, CA: Sage.

McCroskey, J. C., Daly, J. A., Martin, M. M., & Beatty, M. J. (1998). *Communication and personality: Trait perspectives.* Cresskill, NJ: Hampton Press.

McCroskey, J. C., Richmond, V. P., Johnson, A. D., & Smith, H. T. (May, 2003). Organizational orientations theory and measurement: Development of measures and preliminary investigations. Paper presented at the annual convention of the International Communication Association, San Diego, CA.

McCroskey, L. L., McCroskey, J. C., & Richmond, V. P. (April, 2004). Applying organizational orientations theory to employees in profit and non-profit organizations. Paper presented at the annual convention of the Eastern Communication Association, Boston, MA.

Presthus, R. (1962). *The Organizational Society.* New York: Alfred A. Knopf.

Richmond, V. P., & McCroskey, J. C. (1990). Reliability and separation of factors on the assertiveness-responsiveness measure. *Psychological Reports, 67,* 449–450.

Rokeach, M. (1960). *The open and closed mind.* New York: Basic Books.

STUDY GUIDE

1. List and explain the three organizational orientations.
2. List and explain the five types of personality that are related to organizational communication.
3. Explain the relationships between organizational orientations and temperament.
4. Explain the relationships of organizational orientations and temperament with the communication traits of assertiveness, responsiveness, and nonverbal immediacy.
5. Explain the relationships of organizational orientation and temperament with organizational outcomes.
6. List the possible causes of organizational orientations and communication traits.
7. Explain what workers should do to deal with the traits of their supervisors and subordinates.

PERCEPTIONS OF PEOPLE IN ORGANIZATIONS

In the previous two chapters we discussed how people in organizations exhibit a wide variety of personalities. Most likely you thought first about how these various personalities applied to you—on which ones you thought of yourself as being low or high, and maybe which ones didn't seem to apply to you at all. Then you may have thought about your current supervisor (or a past one) and thought how well that person seemed to fit one or more of the personalities described. If you engaged in either of these activities, you were involved in "person perception."

Person perception is a normal activity in which we engage whenever we come in contact with another person. It may range from a very intense activity (such as when you are interviewing someone you might want to hire) where you consciously focus on that person and carefully try to figure out what makes her or him "tick." Or, it may range all the way down to a fleeting notice of the other person where you simply record in your memory how that person appeared or was behaving at that moment. Over time, with sufficient contact, we form fairly stable ways of perceiving other people in our environment. We come to expect those people to behave consistently with our perceptions, and we adapt our own behavior in accordance with those expectations. The other people engage in the same person-perception process with us as the target. I develop an image of you, you develop an image of me. In addition, each of us develop an image of our selves. Would it surprise you if you saw your supervisor differently than he/she saw her/himself? Would it surprise you if your supervisor saw you differently than you see yourself? Many people actually are surprised when these differences come to light. However, we should not be. With the possible exceptions of people in our immediate family, we usually spend only a small portion of each 24-hour day in the presence of any other given individual. Similarly, our supervisor spends the majority of her/his day outside our presence. Hence, few people are around any other person for a large enough portion of the time to really get a good opportunity to see how that other person behaves, much less thinks, most of the time.

Another element which leads supervisors and subordinates to misperceive each other is a very common human reaction which sometimes is referred to as "basic attribution error." Basic attribution error occurs when we attribute the causes of our own behavior, particularly our bad behavior, to external factors and the causes of another person's behavior to internal factors. This is referred to as an "error" because we exaggerate the impact of other people's personalities on their behaviors and exaggerate the impact of situations on our own behaviors. You did it because you are bad person; I did it because everyone else was doing it. You are late because you didn't get up early enough to get here on time (you are delinquent); I am late because of unusually heavy traffic (I was unfortunately detained). It is just the way you are; I was a victim of circumstances.

It should not be surprising, therefore, that people see themselves differently than others see them. It is a normal aspect of human contact. It is very difficult to see others as they see themselves, or to get them to see us as we see ourselves. It is even more difficult to get others to see us as *more nearly perfect* than we really are, which is the way we usually want our colleagues and supervisors to see us.

One of the cold, hard facts confronting people who hope to communicate effectively in organizations (or anywhere else, for that matter) is that *messages are interpreted through the receiver's impression of the source.* Messages do not generally speak for themselves (even epitaphs on tombstones!). As we have indicated previously, meanings are in people, not messages. In order to interpret messages, we strive to understand what its source meant by it. How about the simple phrase, "Nice job!" What would you take this to mean if your supervisor said that to you? If an incompetent coworker said it? If a coworker who can't stand you said it? It is unlikely that the same meaning came through to you from these varied sources.

No message is interpreted by a receiver apart from its source. Almost 2,500 years ago, this point was made by Aristotle when writing about the "ethos" or image of the communicator. It is not just a modern phenomenon. The source/message relationship is so strong that if the receiver doesn't know who the source is, it is likely the receiver will create a source in her/his mind (McCroskey & Dunham, 1966). Political candidates have long understood this and have used well-liked and respected people to introduce them at political gatherings. In that way the "sponsorship effect" of these positively perceived people "rubs off" on the unknown or little known candidates.

If your supervisor thinks you are a slacker, whatever you say or do, verbally or nonverbally, will be interpreted as a message coming from a slacker. If we want to communicate effectively with our supervisors and coworkers, therefore, it is critical that we create positive perceptions of ourselves in their minds. It is also critical that we develop realistic perceptions of our supervisors so that we do not generate distorted interpretations of her/his messages. There are a wide variety of person perceptions which have been found to be important in organizational communication. Several of these will be outlined in the following sections.

SOURCE CREDIBILITY

Source credibility refers to how *believable* a source is perceived to be. If we see a person as highly credible, we will tend to believe what they say. Often, we will take what the person says at face value, without seeking other information or opinions. If we see a person as less credible, however, we may question virtually everything the person says, and look to other sources to verify or challenge what that person says. Aristotle suggested that there are three dimensions or components of source credibility (which he called *ethos*). Contemporary social science has confirmed these dimensions to be appropriate within the organizational context today (McCroskey & Teven, 1999). These are labeled *competence, trustworthiness,* and *goodwill.* All of these dimensions are interrelated, but each deals with a separate element of credibility.

Competence.   This dimension of credibility refers to the degree to which a person is perceived to be knowledgeable or expert in a given subject. We judge the person on a continuum ranging from being completely competent to being completely incompetent. While sometimes competence is perceived on an absolute basis (Is this person an expert or not?) often it is viewed as a relative matter (Is this person more competent than I am?). For more important concerns we tend to move to the more absolute position, but in everyday matters we are more likely to use the comparative approach. In many circumstances competence is the first credibility judgment we make, for if we deem the person to not be knowledgeable about the issue, we may care little about the other two dimensions.

Trustworthiness.   This dimension of credibility is concerned with the honesty of the individual. It is a character issue. We may see the person as an expert, but if we feel that we cannot trust the person to tell the truth about what he or she knows, we are likely to perceive the person as having little credibility. Perceptions of trustworthiness exist along a continuum similar to that of competence, our judgments of a person may range from being totally trustworthy to totally untrustworthy. This perception, however, is not often mediated by our perception of our own trustworthiness. Even a person who is totally dishonest will perceive little credibility for a person they perceive also to be dishonest.

Goodwill.   This may be the most important element in source credibility, particularly in contexts where people must come in contact and work with each other on a daily basis. Another term for goodwill is *caring*. In short, do we perceive this other person as caring about our well-being? Is he/she concerned about our welfare, or is this person motivated primarily by selfish concerns? Even highly competent people may fail to tell us what we need to know. Even highly honest people may not look at the issue from our perspective and what the impact may be on us. People may be seen on a continuum with a range from highly concerned about our well-being to totally unconcerned with whether we even live or die. If we perceive our supervisor is working extremely hard to help us get ahead, we may overlook the fact that he/she is less competent than we are, or even that he/she sometimes exaggerates or twists the truth. We write this not to suggest that goodwill is more important than competence or trustworthiness in all contexts. Rather, it is to stress that caring really counts, whether it is a subordinate perceiving a supervisor or a supervisor perceiving a subordinate. If we don't believe another person has our best interests at heart, we are highly unlikely to believe what he/she says to us.

Competence, trustworthiness, and goodwill have long been known to be important factors in creating the impression of believability. If we can establish these perceptions of ourselves in relationships with others, our influence with those others is likely to be substantial. Even peons in an organization can generate these perceptions over time. Establishing good relationships with peers is the initial step to generating these perceptions. Achieving this step usually is helpful to taking the next step as well. That step is establishing these perceptions in the mind of one's supervisor, and ultimately, those higher in the organization.

INTERPERSONAL ATTRACTIVENESS

Interpersonal attractiveness refers to the degree to which we are drawn toward another person. If there are five strangers in a room, which one do we feel we want to be near? If five coworkers are available to help us, which one do we feel we want to go to? If five acquaintances are at a social gathering, which one do we want to talk with? People are drawn to some people, but are repulsed by others. This is the phenomenon of interpersonal attraction. Like credibility, interpersonal attractiveness is multi-dimensional. There are three dimensions: *physical, social,* and *task* (McCroskey & McCain, 1974). All of these forms of interpersonal attraction may be related. However, each has a unique component which may function separately from the other two.

Physical Attractiveness.   Whenever attractiveness is mentioned, most people think of physical attractiveness first. And, indeed, this is the dimension of attractiveness which typically has the most impact on initial human relationships. In fact, it may determine whether there is any human relationship at all.

Physical attractiveness is a perception, a perception which may or may not be shared by people with different backgrounds, cultures, or experiences. It is a matter of taste and preference. This is why two people may see the same person at the same time and report very different levels of physical attraction. Generally, however, within a culture and to an extent even across cultures, there is substantial agreement on the physical appearance characteristics which result in people seeing an individual as physically attractive. Most of these characteristics have to do with bone and facial structure (about which we can do little), weight (over which we usually can have some control), and stylishness, cleanliness, carriage, and neatness (over which we typically can have a great deal of control).

Perceptions of physical attractiveness have their greatest importance during the initial phases of human relationships, particularly within organizations. Humans often prevent contact with people they see as interpersonally unattractive. That is, if we see someone we perceive as physically unattractive, we are likely to take extra effort not to have any additional contact with them, while we will go out of our way to make contact with people we perceive as physically attractive. The implications of this for job interviews are obvious. In addition, presuming the person can overcome that obstacle and get the job, lack of physical attractiveness also may be a major obstacle to gaining acceptance of other people in the work group. Simply put, for humans physically attractive means good. All kinds of positive characteristics are commonly attributed to people who are seen as physically attractive—intelligence, honesty, experience, insight, wealth, credibility, and sexuality.

Thus, it is obvious that the more physically attractive we are seen, the better. Almost, but not quite. There are two reservations to this presumably obvious conclusion. First, people who are extremely physically attractive often are rejected by those less endowed. They are not seen as approachable. They are seen as having a superiority complex. They are seen as getting a lot of advantages they haven't earned. Often they are deeply disliked by others of the same gender (particularly true for females). Yes, these are responses generated by envy and resentment.

However, the second reservation probably is more important. That is, the impact of physical attractiveness has a short life. If we interact with the physically attractive individual and find a lack of other positive qualities, we tend to see the person as less attractive on the other attractiveness dimensions. Over time, we even reevaluate their physical attractiveness downward. Thus, physical attractiveness has a major (mostly positive) impact in organizations during initial encounters, but that impact tends to lessen for the more attractive individuals as more interaction occurs. In contrast, people seen initially as unattractive, may actually be seen as more attractive over time. This comes as a function of the way they are perceived on the other attractiveness dimensions. Most of us have friends who are considered by others as somewhat physically unattractive, although they may not be seen that way by us. We perceive their social and/or task attractiveness as high and generalize that perception in part to their physical attractiveness.

Within organizations, physical attractiveness is particularly important for people who apply for (or hold) positions which call for direct contact with the public—such as positions in hospitality, direct sales, and public relations. Much of the communication in these positions is conducted within the context of initial encounters—precisely where physical attractiveness has its strongest and most positive or negative impact. Where more long-term contact is mandated, the other dimensions of attractiveness come into play more strongly.

Social Attractiveness. This dimension of attractiveness represents the degree to which a person is seen as one with whom other people would like to spend time at a social level. A socially attractive person is one with whom we would like to go get a cup of coffee, have lunch, or get together outside the work environment. We might invite this person to our home. This type of attractiveness is not based on physical appearance (although that can make a contribution), but rather how friendly and likeable the person is perceived to be. While we might initially be socially attracted to a person because of their physical appearance, this attraction will disappear unless the person is also socially desirable. If we find someone socially attractive, it is likely that we will desire a relationship with them that continues for an extended period.

In contemporary society, many people spend more time with their coworkers in an organization than they do with any other people—including family. It is no longer unusual for a person's social friends to also be their coworkers. Hence, when people move to new organizations, it is quite common that they will find new people to be socially attractive, and hence they will develop new friendships. The line between coworker and friend has become finer in recent decades. This, of course, does not mean that we will develop friendships with all of our coworkers. This will be true only with those coworkers we find socially attractive and who also see us as socially attractive.

Task Attractiveness. This dimension of attraction is the one which is most relevant in the organizational context. We see people who we believe (or know) to be easy and pleasant to work with to be task attractive. Also contributing to perceptions of task attractiveness on the part of achievement-oriented workers is competence in performing work-related tasks, a willingness to share responsibility and workload, a commitment to successfully completing tasks, and a willingness to engage in goal-directed communication. Of course, not everyone is highly interested in work. Some employees find people who are lazy and shiftless to be task attractive—since they don't want to work either.

Task attractiveness, then, is based on what one desires as a work partner. Generally, but not universally, we want pleasant, hard-working, competent people as coworkers. We want people who will do their share, if not more, and do it in such a way that the work environment is a pleasant place to be.

It is quite possible that we have people in our environment who we find to be attractive on all three dimensions—they are pleasant to look at, be with, and work with. But that certainly is not the typical situation. Think back to when you were in high school and had to do a team project. You probably were pleased to learn that the class nerd was assigned to your team—but probably you didn't want her/him to join your social group or be your date for the prom! While it is quite possible that a person can be perceived as attractive on more than one dimension, that is not necessarily the case. There are people we want to work with, and people we want to socialize with. There may be some overlap in the two groups, but it is rare if the groups are identical.

Attractiveness, particularly social and task attractiveness, is in the eye of the beholder. Attractiveness is a perception, not a possession of the person we find attractive. Just as was the case of source credibility, attractive is something we are seen to be, not necessarily something we actually are.

HOMOPHILY

First, to avoid distraction, let's make one thing clear: homophily has nothing to do with sexual orientation. The term roughly means "coming from the same category." It has to do with actual or perceived similarities. There is a "principle of homophily" which explains why homophily has such a major impact on communication in organizations. This principle holds that "the more similar two people are, the more likely they are to attempt to communicate with one another, the more likely their communication will be successful, and the more similar they are likely to become." By extension, the more we see another person to be like our self, the more we are attracted (task/social) to that person, the more we talk with that person, and the more influence that person is likely to have on us. The reverse is also true—when others see us as similar to them in important ways, we are likely to be more influential with them. Research indicates that this principle is pancultural—that is, it operates in much the same way in all cultures. Consequently, this is one of the most powerful principles related to communication that has been established. The three types of homophily which appear to be most important are *demographic, background, and attitude* (Mc-Croskey, Richmond, & Daly, 1975).

Before we consider these individual types of homophily, it is important that we distinguish between "objective" and "perceived" homophily.

"Objective" homophily involves similarities which actually can be observed and noted by outside observers. Most of the early research focused on this type of homophily. In contrast, "perceived" homophily is like perceived trustworthiness or perceived social attractiveness. It exists in the mind of the perceiver, and may have no objective reality for other people. While source credibility and interpersonal attractiveness are perceptions of others, and not rooted firmly in reality, homophily has an objective base as well as a perceptual base. This distinction will become more clear as we examine the different types of homophily.

Demographic Homophily.   Demographics are physical or social characteristics of an individual that are objectively identifiable: age, sex, height, religion, culture, ethnicity, socioeconomic status, educational level, etc. These are real characteristics. They are observable and knowable by others. This is the most objective type of homophily, which probably is why most of the early research was focused on this type. Such work found a consistent pattern of results. For example, communication between people from the same age group is more effective than cross-generational communication. Communication between people from the same ethnic group is more effective than inter-ethnic communication. Communication between people with similar socioeconomic status is more effective than communication between people from different status levels. The effect of demographic homophily is very strong. In organizations this is manifest when supervisors and subordinates have substantial demographic similarities. The communication between supervisors and subordinates is much more effective under such circumstances than when they lack demographic similarities. Of course, the same is true for coworkers with high demographic homophily.

Of course, other people do not always know that they have a demographic pattern similar to our own. Hence, it is often advantageous for us to let them know that is the case. Even though we have demographic homophily with someone else, if they and we do not perceive it, the potential positive impact of that homophily may not be realized. Often, in the earliest stages of interaction between new acquaintances, demographic information is the primary type of information exchanged. This represents attempts by both people to try to find demographic similarities upon which they can base an initial relationship. This pattern manifests itself in most initial interviews of potential new employees.

Background Homophily.   This type of homophily is composed of both objective and perceived elements. It deals essentially with similarity of life experiences. Furthermore, such homophily is relative to the context. For example, if two people meet in Paris and find that they were both raised in Wyoming, that might be a very important similarity for them. If, however, these people first meet in Wyoming, where just about everyone else around them grew up in Wyoming, this similarity may be so trivial as not to be noted. If it is noted, the attention probably will shift quickly to "What part of Wyoming?" and then move on to other demographic elements.

If people have similar life experiences (both been to college, both been in the military, both had jobs as sales persons, etc.), it is more likely they will have more similar interests and see things in more similar ways. Of course, the life experiences may have not been all that similar. Just the fact that they are somewhat similar may result in either or both people perceiving much more homophily than what objectively exists.

Attitude Homophily.   This type of homophily is primarily perceptual. It is the degree to which a person perceives another person to share her/his attitudes, beliefs, and values. In other words, do we think alike? While levels of demographic and background homophily are perceived quickly by new acquaintances, and usually become stable in a relatively short period of time, it may take longer for perceptions of attitude homophily to develop and mature. During the early weeks or even years of acquaintance, this perception may be subject to substantial fluctuations as a function of discovering new attitudes, beliefs, and values of the other.

Attitude homophily ordinarily is far more important in organizational communication than either demographic or background homophily. It provides the foundation upon which strong work relationships are built. When such relationships are built between supervisors and subordinates, as well as among coworkers, this makes interpersonal trust, effective teamwork, and collaboration possible. Effective organizations frequently are based on high perceptions of attitude homophily among the employees.

Generally, homophily is a good thing. However, homophily is the natural enemy of diversity—a major problem we will consider in Chapter 12. Also, we must consider the problems associated with *"fabricated homophily."* People who understand the homophily principle, as well as others who intuitively sense that similarity seems to be good and/or is an important part of a good image, are likely to present an image of themselves which reflects what they believe others want to them to be.

For many of us, our first attempt at fabricating an image was associated with our first dating experiences. Most young people have this experience. We want to look and act as good as we can—but that isn't the real person. While this may get us through a few dates (and if we are extremely unlucky, even into a marriage), over time the real person begins to show through. We may be willing to attend the opera (in spite of hating the experience) because our date is an opera fan. At some point, we may just not be able to live the lie any longer. The fiction of our "opera homophily" becomes obvious, and the relationship may well be over.

The same sort of thing may exist in the organizational environment. Even though we hate the job, we may be able to present a positive front, at least for a while. Over time, however, it may become clear to others—including our supervisor—that we are not happy with the job. The homophily that was built on this fictitious foundation will disappear like a whiff of smoke, and so will many of our working relationships which were built on it. Bottom line: it is not a good idea to build an image on false homophily in an organization. When (not if) this is recognized by coworkers, whatever trust you have built with them will disappear—and you won't be able to get it back. While you need not ever disclose your deep, dark secrets, it is not wise to present yourself in a way that is not consistent with the real you. One thing is absolute about the work environment, if people don't want you as you really are, you don't want to be there. Effective long term communication cannot be maintained if it is based on false homophily.

One final item relating to homophily needs to be addressed. How much is good? This is a difficult question to answer. Probably the best way to address this concern is by examining opinion leadership. An opinion leader is someone others turn to for advice and information. Opinion leaders are extremely influential in organizations, as we will emphasize in Chapter 13 when we examine the impact of informal communication channels in organizations. Opinion leaders have been found to be very similar to their followers, except that they are perceived to know more about a given topic or topics than their followers. People tend to reject people who might be opinion leaders if they perceive them as knowing a great deal more than they do on the topic. Such competence is intimidating to them. Such people are seen as not similar to themselves. For opinion leaders we want people we can trust (read "people like us"), but who know more than we do.

We have dedicated a lot of space in this chapter to perceptions. Are these really this important? Yes. In communication, *perceptions are reality* for the people who have those perceptions. All decisions are made about communication on the basis of these perceptions. If a source of communication is an expert genius, but the receiver doesn't think he/she is competent, the source is not competent for that receiver. It is as simple as that. Perceptions count, and in many cases, that is all that counts. Power in organizations is based on perceptions. That is the focus of the next chapter.

REFERENCES AND RECOMMENDED READINGS

Beatty, M. J., McCroskey, J. C., & Heisel, A. D. (1998). Communication apprehension as temperamental expression: A communibiological paradigm. *Communication Monographs, 65,* 197–219.

McCroskey, J. C. (1966). Scales for the measurement of ethos. *Speech Monographs, 33,* 65–72.

McCroskey, J. C. (2001). *An introduction to rhetorical communication.* (8th ed.). Needham Heights, MA: Allyn and Bacon.

McCroskey, J. C., & Dunham, R. E. (1966). Ethos: A confounding element in communication research. *Speech Monographs, 33,* 456–463.

McCroskey, J. C., & McCain, T. A. (1974). The measurement of interpersonal attraction. *Speech Monographs, 41,* 261–266.

McCroskey, J. C., Richmond, V. P., & Daly, J. A. (1975). The measurement of perceived homophily in interpersonal communication. *Human Communication Research, 1,* 323–332.

McCroskey, J. C., & Teven, J. J. (1999). Goodwill: A reexamination of the construct and its measurement. *Communication Monographs, 66,* 90–103.

McCroskey, J. C., & Young, T. J. (1981). Ethos and credibility: The construct and its measurement after three decades. *Central State Speech Journal, 32,* 24–34.

STUDY GUIDE

1. Why are interpersonal perceptions important in organizational communication?
2. What is source credibility? Ethos? How do they differ?
3. What is the "sponsorship effect"?
4. List and explain the three dimensions of source credibility.
5. List and explain the three dimensions of interpersonal attraction.
6. List and explain the three types of homophily.
7. Explain the "principle of homophily."
8. Explain what opinion leadership is and how it is related to homophily.
9. Which dimension of source credibility is most important in organizations. Why?
10. Which dimension of interpersonal attraction is most important in organizations. Why?

CHAPTER 9

APPROACHES TO MANAGEMENT

Which of the following would you like to have for your supervisor?

First we have Mr. or Ms. "Do It My Way or Else." This type of manager typically expects employees to do exactly what the manager wants and when he or she wants it. He or she never allows any time for creativity or thinking on the job. He or she believes he or she knows the best way to do the job and does not want input from employees about how the job should be done. This manager will often go out of the way to impede the process of change and does not like those who disagree with his or her ideas.

Next we have Mr. or Ms. "I Want to Be Nice to Everyone." This manager typically is overly concerned about the employees' welfare. He or she is constantly checking with employees to see if there is anything that can be done to improve the work environment. In fact, he or she reminds one of a mother hen. Employees like this person for awhile, but then begin to realize that this manager generally cannot deliver on all of his or her promises to improve the work environment. In addition, this manager has little concern for getting the work done.

Finally we have Mr. or Ms. "Slave Driver." This type of manager expects employees to put aside all their personal feelings and problems and constantly concentrate on the task. Managers like this expect 100 percent commitment from their employees and expect them to adhere to all organizational policies and rules. He or she is highly critical of employees who do not conform to the organizational policies and will even take steps to get rid of them. He or she is insensitive to employees' needs and is seen as a heartless, sterile individual who cares only about the work to be done.

Agreed. Choosing among these three is like making the proverbial choice between being shot and being hanged. You are dead no matter what choice you make.

Although none of these alternatives may seem desirable, they are all characterizations of managers who do exist in organizations. None of these are people for whom we might want to work, but they are people for whom we might have to work unless we are willing to leave an organization and look for a new position. Not only do managers like these exist, they often survive for years in an organization in spite of all the complaints registered by their subordinates.

These are examples of managers who will generate employees who are not satisfied with their jobs and who have little commitment to the organization beyond the minimum expected of them. If they were not indifferent to the organization when they were hired, they become so to tolerate working in this atmosphere. Although there are other, more functional approaches to management, these three represent common extremes. This chapter reviews these and various other orientations toward management, the relationship between management and communication, and the results of each in the organization.

EARLY ORIENTATIONS

Scientific Management.   Scientific management has perhaps received the most recognition and study. It has been used for so many years in the United States that today aspects of this approach can be found in most organizations. It was the dominant orientation in the preunion (1900–1940s) industrialization era. The dominant writers on the scientific management approach were persons such as Taylor, Fayol, Gulick, Urwick, and Weber. Their writings are still central in the early training of contemporary managers.

The basic orientation of scientific management is that "people are replaceable" and should be treated as if "they are parts in a machine." It is, as Rogers and Agarwala-Rogers (1976) describe it, a "mechanistic view of behavior" (p. 30). The ultimate scientific manager, therefore, is the skilled efficiency expert.

Scientific managers believe the best way to manage people is to assume they are like machines. People should be pushed or driven like machines, it is argued, and if they wear out they can be replaced. This sounds cruel and insensitive, and it hardly can be described in any other way. But we must remember the historical circumstances in the work environment of the early 1900s. There was no history of decent treatment for workers in the industrialization process. The value for human life, which is taken as a given today, was at best an idealistic hope at that time. The most brutal and life-threatening conditions we can find today are better than the norm for that period. However, most people were happy to have a job, even if it meant long hours, hard work, and little reward. There were no laws to protect employees from grueling hours and brutal bosses. Even children were subject to brutalizing and life-threatening conditions. The child-labor laws we have now were barely hoped for in the early 1900s.

It was the post–World War I and pre–World War II period when many of the scientific management organizations sprang into existence. Unemployment was high, employee-protection laws were nonexistent, and people needed jobs to live. Hence, the mechanistic view worked. Most people were treated as if they were cogs in a machine that could be replaced if the job was not done well. Indeed, hundreds of thousands were used up and replaced. And the replacements were used up and replaced. This was not a glorious period for the common worker. Only during the period before slavery was abolished were people treated as badly in America as they were during this period. The common worker was, for all intents and purposes, the economic slave for the industrial master.

As you probably can imagine, if managers do not care whether employees live or die, the communication between managers and employees will not flow smoothly. Scientific management exists today, but circumstances certainly are not as brutal as they once were. Nevertheless, employee-to-supervisor communication still is limited and controlled. Scientific managers still are not interested in a lot of upward communication, and when they send a command down the system, they expect it to be followed. Vertical communication follows a command-and-report pattern. Horizontal communication often is restricted. Employees are not encouraged and may even be punished if they spend time talking with another employee at the same level while "on the clock."

Under scientific management, people are seen as being in organizations to work—not to communicate. The presumption is that the people at the top know how things should be done, and it is the duty of those at the bottom to do as they are told. The emphasis is on written or oral formal communication that follows the channels of the top-down chain of command. Most personnel learn to do their jobs, work hard, and stay out of the way of management. If they get into trouble or try to change the system, they are likely to be replaced. Unemployment still is feared by many workers.

The difference today is that few large firms operate under the scientific management orientation. The existence of unions and labor laws reduces the abuses of those that do. Scientific management is common, however, among small firms with a limited number of employees. Thus, it is likely you have worked under the modern version of scientific management at some point. So if you think the description of scientific management seems familiar, it well may be.

In conclusion, the scientific approach is a mechanistic, driving type of management style. The management tolerates little change, allows limited communication, and expects people to work, work, work. Although it is less popular than it once was, it still exists in many organizations. Most people employed in such organizations simply accept the conditions management requires and do their job. They are not necessarily pleased with the conditions, but they need their job. Fortunately, not everyone has to work under this form of management.

Human Relations. Mayo, Barnard, and others led the way for the *human relations* approach to management. Mayo is still considered by many to be the founder of the Human Relations School. Mayo, Roethlisberger, Dickson, and many others were asked to complete a series of studies between the 1920s and 1940s which became known as the "Hawthorne Studies." Although these studies originally were designed as part of the scientific management approach, they proved to be the foundations of the human relations approach.

This approach evolved from such famous studies as the industrial lighting series at the Western Electric Hawthorne plant in Cicero, Illinois, the relay assembly room test, and the bank wiring observation room experiment conducted by Mayo, and others. These studies, and several others during that time period, were designed to determine what variables could improve employee production. In these studies and many others, the researchers found that if employees were treated like human beings—not like cogs in a machine—were given some time to have informal communication among themselves, and could communicate with management and make some changes in the environment, then production would increase, regardless of the working conditions. The researchers manipulated the working conditions and inadvertently manipulated the communication between employees and management. They "stumbled" into the discovery that communication on the informal and formal levels will improve production even when working conditions are less than desirable. When this was done on purpose, it became known as the human relations approach.

The human relations approach takes a more sensitive view of the employee. The developers of this approach did not believe the employee was replaceable; in fact, they tried to integrate the goals of the organization with the goals of the individual. The human relations advocates were aware that employee participation in decision making, employee communication with management, affect toward work, job satisfaction, and some fulfillment of social needs—all of these—would increase worker productivity and increase the profitability of organizations. One should not look at this approach as an "altruistic" or "humanistic" one. It was simply an alternative way to make management more effective.

Human relations managers encourage both formal and informal communication. In fact, the "suggestion box" was originally introduced by such a manager. There is emphasis on communication at all levels, and good human relations managers realize that rumor mills exist. Finally, much of the communication is directly related to concern for employees' welfare.

This type of management approach worked well when first introduced. Then, people started abusing the system. Sometimes the task would become lost and communication was mostly about employee concerns. The "Happiness for Lunch Bunch" was born.

Both of the early approaches to management were acceptable for the times in which they were developed. Neither was perfect. They both had positive aspects and they both had drawbacks. Either extreme today is unacceptable. Too much of a scientific approach can restrict communication so severely that employees become deeply dissatisfied and even try to sabbo-tage the organization. Too much of the human relations approach can focus so much communication on employee needs and so little communication on the task that the organization could be in danger of collapsing. Hence, both worked, both were successful for their times; however, neither in the extreme would be desirable today. Today, both exist in modified forms. However, both are being replaced in many organizations by a new ap-proach—human resources management.

Human Resources.   The human resources approach includes contribu-tions from both scientific and human relations approaches. However, it fo-cuses more on the intellectual contribution which may be made by workers. In short, in this approach employees are expected to do their assigned work, but it is also anticipated that they can contribute by sharing their ideas related to that work. While in many ways the behaviors of human re-sources managers are like the behaviors of human relations managers, the big difference is the former are not likely to accept all the assumptions un-derlying human relations management. They have a more realistic view of their workers. Employees may be placed in work teams, not to make them "feel good" about participating, but because the group of workers may be able to share ideas and come to better decisions than could distant supervi-sors and managers, or individual workers by themselves. The focus of man-agers in this approach is on using the intellectual expertise of workers and, of course, often this results in expanded training for workers so as to im-prove those intellectual skills. Like the earlier approaches, some of these human resources efforts (such as self-management teams) have been more successful than others (such as Total Quality Management). While many workers like working in groups, others hate it—particularly shy and/or high communication apprehensive workers. Assuming that all workers like to participate is equally as bad an over-generalization as the assumptions made by scientific or human relations managers.

The key to understanding the human resources approach is the recog-nition by managers of the intrinsic value of a good employee. Organizations that foster human resources management recognize that investments in training and improved working conditions (high-quality benefits included) are likely to result in more loyal employees and less employee turn-over. Turn-over has become a serious problem for many organizations that de-pend on educated and skilled employees for their success. Such people are needed in a wide variety of organizations, hence may leave for another job if they do not feel satisfied in their current position. As the owner and chief executive officer of one high-tech company, a leader in its field, put it, "Most of my employees will leave the parking lot at about 5 o'clock this evening. I believe my most important role in this organization is to get them to come back to work tomorrow morning." While he acknowledges that it costs several million dollars every year to invest in his workers' skills and job satisfaction, he notes that to do otherwise would cost even more than this investment in terms of turnover costs alone.

While not all organizations that attempt to employ the human resources approach to management are as successful as this organization has been, it is important to recognize that just having a "human resources division" in an organization is not always an indication of the use of human resources management. In many cases, organizations with such divisions are, in reality, simply using the same old human relations approach. A critical component in making the human resources approach work is management's total commitment to believing that their employees are valuable assets of the organization and then treating them in that way.

LEADERSHIP APPROACHES

McGregor (1960, 1967) developed a seemingly dichotomous theory of management behavior that closely paralleled the scientific and human relations approaches to management. He titled his approaches *Theory X* and *Theory Y*.

His Theory X orientation assumed that most people had little capacity for creativity in problem solving, most personnel needed to be closely controlled and often coerced to achieve goals, work was inherently distasteful to most people, most people were not ambitious and had little desire for responsibility, and most people preferred to be directed. Finally, motivation only occurred at the physiological and security levels.

Under Theory X the communication would be mostly downward in direction with orders from the top. Decision making would be concentrated in the hands of a few near the top. Upward communication would be limited to spy systems. For example, employees would inform on other employees to the managers. Most interaction between employees would take place in a climate of fear and distrust, and vertical communication would be limited to announcements, with little encouragement for upward communication.

McGregor's Theory Y orientation assumed that work could be as natural as play if conditions were right, people could be self-directed and creative if allowed, the capacity for creativity in solving organizational problems was widely distributed and employees should have input in some decision making, and self-control was often indispensable in achieving organizational goals. Finally, it assumed that motivation could occur at the social, esteem, and self-actualization levels, as well as physiological and security levels.

Under Theory Y the communicative messages could travel up, down, and across the organization. Decision making would be distributed throughout the organization, with people being involved from all levels who had knowledge in the area. Feedback would be encouraged, and frequent, honest interactions could take place in a climate of trust. The flow of downward communication would be sufficient to meet the needs of the employees. Finally, because of the up, down, and across communication and participative decision making, the quality of decisions would be improved.

Although these theories seem dichotomous, McGregor suggested that a manager might use aspects of each theory or shift from one to the other, depending on the circumstances and employees involved. He suggested that some situations and personnel required the Theory X approach and some circumstances required the Theory Y approach. At times a manager has to be hard and at times he or she has to be softer. These theories would allow a manager some options on how to deal with personnel.

In many organizations there is a constant pull and tug between the X and Y orientations. Generally, employees much prefer the Y orientation. However, if it is followed too far, everyone will be happy, but the organization may fail. Thus, managers are under pressure to move toward the X orientation. The problem is that both theories are right, but they apply to different people. It is the difficult task of the manager to apply the right theory to the right people. Often it is an impossible task.

The two extremely different managerial orientations represented by McGregor's theories, then, do not represent the only options open to a manager. Rather, most managers employ a combination of these orientations. There are two concerns to which every manager must attend: (1) a concern for production or the work itself and (2) a concern for workers—the people doing the work (Blake & Mouton, 1964). These have been referred to as "task concerns" and "people concerns." Figure 9.1 presents these concerns graphically with regard to each being represented by a five-point continuum. Theoretically, there could be 25 different leadership styles. We discuss only the five most prominent leadership styles, which often are viewed as approaches to management.

The *Social Leader* (1, 5) management style has a high concern for people and a low concern for task. This person strives to maintain a happy, sociable organizational climate and keep people from feeling distressed or disgruntled. They could be called the "Happiness for Lunch Bunch leaders." This manager likes to have a friendly, comfortable organizational environment. Of course, the biggest drawback to this style is that the task might be neglected because when issues or disagreements arise concerning the task, the manager will tend to resolve them in a way that makes the most people happy. He or she does not always consider the impact on production when making the decision; the employee is foremost in his or her mind, and hence production could suffer. Communication with this manager is generally at a light, superficial level. This person does not like to discuss serious, task-demanding issues and might often delegate that responsibility.

Some people cannot work for Social Leaders. These people are so friendly and easygoing that task concerns are seen as inappropriate. Communication is restricted to the social level. If you work for someone like this and

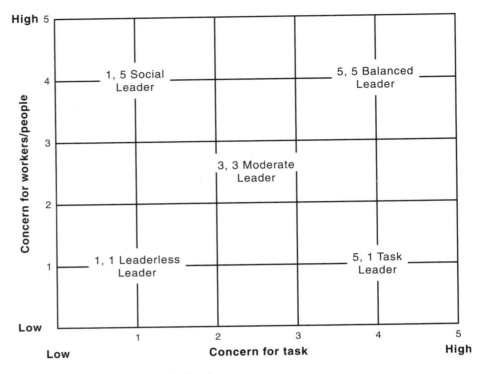

FIGURE 9.1   Leadership Style Options

you are motivated to be a good worker, you will have to adapt and try to communicate your ideas and concerns in such a way that they fit into the orientation of the Social Leader style. That may be a lot easier said than done.

The *Task Leader* (5, 1) management style has a high concern for task and a low concern for people. This person strives to maintain an efficiently operating machine-like environment. Of course, the biggest drawback to this style is that the personal concerns of employees might be neglected because of concern for the task. In fact, this manager really dislikes it when personal concerns interfere with work. He or she is not likely to want to listen to your personal problems and certainly is not fond of discussing such topics as your children, your pets, your garden, your vacation, your home movies—and these issues never should interfere with work. Task Leaders are often seen as insensitive, cruel, and demanding. Hence, if you work for someone like this, you will have to adapt and try to communicate your ideas and concerns in such a way that they fit into the task-oriented leadership style. However, it would be best to keep your personal life just that—personal.

The *Balanced Leader* (5, 5) management style has a high concern for task and a high concern for people. This person strives to maintain an efficiently operating organization while at the same time showing commitment to meeting employees' needs and concerns. Such managers are few and far between. The Balanced Leader works to see that organizational goals and employee goals are integrated. He or she tries to create an environment of trust and friendship while at the same time encouraging employees to do a good job. He or she encourages communication at all levels and is generally open to communication or change.

Balanced Leaders are almost too good to be true. One of the reasons these managers are few and far between is that they often are your typical "workaholic types" who usually burn out after a few years of trying to maintain both task and personnel concerns at such high levels. If you work for one of these persons you are very fortunate, unless you are an indifferent who just wants to be left alone. Communication with a Balanced Leader is likely to be effective and rewarding for most people in the organization.

The *Leaderless Leader* (1, 1) management style has a low concern for task and a low concern for people. This person is primarily concerned with "sustaining the organization." He or she is concerned with minimum work to get the job done and keep employees from openly rebelling. An atmosphere is created where "don't rock the boat" might become the group's motto. This manager will avoid decision making, change, disagreements, and will act only when his or her immediate supervisor makes him or her do something. He or she generally likes to be left alone and will leave you alone if you do the same. If you are working for this person, do not depend on him or her; depend on yourself. Never assume the Leaderless Leader will support you, because when push comes to shove he or she will take the route of least resistance. This leader does not want to be disturbed and will generally avoid most communication about task or personal problems. Often, he or she will just let the organization maintain itself. You often find these managers in nonprofit organizations because they can survive more easily and longer there than they can in most profit-making organizations. If you have an urge to communicate with the Leaderless Leader type of manager, suppress it. It would be a waste of your time.

The *Moderate Leader* (3, 3) management style has a moderate concern for task and a moderate concern for people. This person is concerned with adequate output and will have adequate concern for personal issues. He or she falls short of being a Balanced Leader, but is not a Leaderless Leader. He or she tries to balance task and personal concerns. He or she will try to be fair and will often try to compromise rather than insisting on a high-task or a high-personal-concern decision. Although you might prefer to have a Balanced Leader, the best most people can realistically hope for is the Moderate Leader. Such leaders generally are open to communication with subordinates, and have concern for their needs as well as the organization's. Decisions that are made may not be the most ideal, but they will not be the worst available either.

In conclusion, the preceding leadership styles are the ones that dominate contemporary organizations. They have been and still are styles that can be spotted every day in almost any large organization. The key to working with each style is being able to recognize the style and dealing with it as it is rather than trying to make it what it is not.

THE IDEAL LEADER?

There have been volumes written on the most-desirable characteristics of leaders. But what are the critical characteristics: competence? honesty? intelligence? aggressive and bold? able to take charge? vigorous and youthful? mature and older? respectful and respectable? an initiator? sensitivity? tall, dark, and handsome? blonde and petite? Take your pick. Someone will agree with you.

We suggest that regardless of the leadership style or social style employed by your supervisor, he or she needs to have two major characteristics: versatility and consistency. In other words, for you to be able to work with him or her, he or she must be able to adapt to the needs of others while at the same time making predictable, consistent decisions regardless of the persons involved. For example, on the versatile dimension, there is a need to realize when to be an expressive and when not to. On the consistency dimension, the supervisor needs to be predictable and consistent in his or her communication and decision making so employees know how to communicate with him or her. There is nothing worse than trying to communicate with a moody person—one who is unpredictable or inconsistent. You might be reading this and saying, "One cannot be both *versatile* and *consistent*—that seems like an oxymoron." No, it isn't. One can be adaptable to situations and people while at the same time being firm and predictable on decisions. As employees we also have to do the same for our managers. We need to be more versatile and predictable so they know what to expect from us and how to communicate with us.

REFERENCES AND RECOMMENDED READINGS

Barnard, C. I. (1938). *The functions of the executive.* Cambridge, MA: Harvard University Press.
Blake, R., & Mouton, J. (1964). *The managerial grid.* Houston: Gulf Publishing.
Fayol, H. (1949). *General and industrial management.* London: Pitman.
Gulick, L., & Urwick, L. (1937). *Papers on the science of administration.* New York: Columbia University, Institute of Public Administration.
McGregor, D. (1960). *The human side of enterprise.* New York: McGraw-Hill.
McGregor, D. (1967). *The professional manager.* New York: McGraw-Hill.
Mayo, E. (1933). *The human problems of an industrial civilization.* New York: Macmillan.

Rogers, E. M., & Agarwala-Rogers, R. (1976). *Communication in organizations.* New York: The Free Press.

Taylor, F. (1911). *Scientific management.* New York: Harper and Row.

STUDY GUIDE

1. Explain what is meant by "scientific management." What is the communication like in such an environment?

2. Explain what is meant by "human relations management." What is the communication like in such an environment?

3. What is Theory X leadership? What are the types of communication under this style of leadership?

4. What is Theory Y leadership? What are the types of communication under this style of leadership?

5. What are the five primary types of leaders? How does communication function with each type?

6. What are the essential characteristics of an idealized leader? Why?

CHAPTER 10

MANAGEMENT COMMUNICATION STYLES AND DECISION MAKING

Two of the most significant questions subordinates have are "How do I know when to communicate with my supervisor?" and "What should I communicate to my supervisor?" Often problems are created in organizations because people simply do not know when or what to communicate. Their timing is bad. Things are said that should not be. Things are not said that should be.

These problems often occur because people have taken communication for granted or have not become sensitive to the communication signals of others. For example, when a manager posts a sign on the office door that says "Do not disturb," there always seems to be someone who ignores the sign and interrupts and then wonders what is wrong with the manager. People are constantly sending communication signals, but others either are not aware of them or simply disregard them. Hence, communication problems occur between supervisors and employees. Of course, the better one knows his or her supervisor, the better he or she will be at predicting the supervisor. This knowledge, too, comes through communication. In this chapter we discuss management styles of communicating in relation to decision making and demonstrate that if one can predict a supervisor's style, then one will also know when and what he or she should communicate.

Considerable interest in the notion of communicator style has been generated among researchers concerned with interpersonal communication as a result of the work of Norton and his colleagues (Norton, 1978). As we noted in the previous chapter, each person has a basic socio-communicative style. This style is strongly associated with one's basic temperament and personality. Like temperament, one's basic communication style is heavily influenced by genetic factors (Horvath, 1998). As a consequence, these styles are hard to change and have a major impact on the individual's decision-making and leadership styles as well.

Prior to the development of an interest in communication style, the work of Tannenbaum and Schmidt (1958) on decision-making styles and leadership had considerable influence on the study of leadership in organizations. Tannenbaum and Schmidt postulated a seven-step continuum of leadership orientations within an organization, ranging from the extreme "boss-centered" to the extreme "subordinate-centered." As one moves from the first extreme to the latter, the use of authority by the manager decreases and the freedom for subordinates to participate in decision making increases. The original seven-step continuum included the following steps: (1) Manager makes decision and announces it; (2) manager sells decision; (3) manager gives ideas and invites questions; (4) manager gives tentative decision which is subject to comment or change; (5) manager presents problem, invites suggestions, and makes decision; (6) manager sets limits and asks group of subordinates to make decision; (7) manager allows employees to function within parameters defined by him or her and to make decisions. As you can see, the use of management authority diminishes as the area of freedom for subordinates increases. Subsequently, close or overlapping steps were merged to form a four-step continuum with the labels Tell, Sell, Consult, and Join.

Corollary to the preceding research is that of Likert's (1961, 1967) participative decision management (PDM) theory. He suggested that most management styles could be categorized into four systems (Systems 1, 2, 3, and 4). System 1 was very similar to McGregor's Theory X orientation and System 4 was very similar to McGregor's Theory Y orientation. Likert felt management styles fell on a continuum somewhere between System 1 and System 4. He also felt that all organizations could be described in terms of eight operating characteristics: leadership, motivation, communication, interaction, decision making, goal setting, control, and performance. Likert would have people respond to these characteristics of organizations, and eventually they could be classified into one of the four systems.

System 1 is called the *exploitive authoritative*. In this system management does not trust employees, and, hence, the employees are rarely involved in any decision making. The atmosphere is usually one of fear and mistrust, and most employees avoid communication with supervisors.

System 2 is called the *benevolent authoritative*. In this system management still makes the majority of the decisions, but a few are passed along for subordinate input. Management has some faith in the employees but not much. The atmosphere is one in which employees know that if they misbehave they will be punished and the benevolent authoritative will turn into the exploitive authoritative.

System 3 is called the *consultative*. In this system management has substantial trust and faith in employees, but many of the major decisions are still reserved to be made at the top. However, many decisions that directly impact subordinates are made at the lower levels. The atmosphere is one in which employees feel some confidence in management and themselves and there is a feeling of responsibility at both levels.

System 4 is called the *participative*. In this system management has complete confidence in employees and, as in Theory Y, decision making is

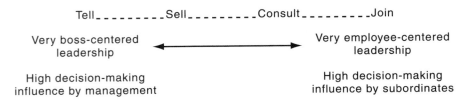

FIGURE 10.1   Continuum of Tell, Sell, Consult, and Join

widespread throughout the organization. The atmosphere is one of trust, friendship, and mutual respect. The personnel also feel they can communicate openly about decisions and ask for input from all levels.

A quick comparison between the revised Tannenbaum and Schmidt approach and the Likert approach indicates strong similarities. Both conceive styles of leadership and decision making ranging from highly authoritarian to highly participative with similar steps in between. After an examination of these approaches, and the presumed relationship between management style and communication style, we advanced the concept of Management Communication Style (MCS). "The communication style of a supervisor within an organization, we believe, is a function of both the management style imposed on the supervisor by the organization (or chosen by the supervisor within the parameters permitted by the organization) and the communication style of the individual supervisor which that individual brings to the organizational context—hence our term MCS" (Richmond and McCroskey, 1979, p. 361).

A manager's MCS is probably relatively constant across time within a given orgnization, but it may change sharply if the individual moves into the context of another organization or his or her own supervisor is changed. We also believe that a supervisor's MCS directly impacts employees' perceptions of both the supervisor and the organization and, as a consequence, is a major determinant of employee satisfaction. Hence, based on the works cited and our assumptions, we took the Tell, Sell, Consult, and Join (see Figure 10.1) framework and expanded the definitional structure of each to accommodate our definition of MCS. This framework is explained next.

DECISION MAKING AND COMMUNICATION

Tell

Decision Making.   The manager who employs this style habitually makes decisions (or receives them from above) and announces them to subordinates, with the expectation that they will be carried out without challenge.

Communication.   Primarily downward, unidirectional, and noninteractive. Questions generally are accepted if they are concerned with clarification of how the job is to be done. Inquiries questioning the desirability of the decision are discouraged or even forbidden. Expressed concern for employees' satisfaction is rare.

Sell

Decision Making.   The manager employing this style also makes the decisions (or receives them from above), but rather than simply announcing them to subordinates, the manager tries to persuade the subordinates of the desirability of the decisions.

Communication.   Primarily, but not exclusively, downward; sometimes bidirectional, and generally interactive. Questions usually are actively encouraged and challenges often are met openly with persuasive counterarguments. Concern for employee satisfaction with decisions often is explicit.

Consult

Decision Making.   The manager employing this style also makes the ultimate decisions, but not until the problem has been presented to the subordinates and their advice, information, and suggestions have been obtained. Although the problem may emanate from above the manager, the decision does not.

Communication.   Primarily upward, bi-directional, and interactive. No adversary relationship is established; subordinates communicate with the manager to help make the best decision and explore advantages and disadvantages of various options based on the needs of both the employees and the organization. Employee well-being is a specific criterion for discussion.

Join

Decision Making.   The manager employing this style does not make the decision; rather, the authority to make the decision is delegated to the subordinates, either in cooperation with the manager or in his or her absence. The manager defines the problem and indicates the limits within which the decision must be made. Typically, majority opinion will determine the decision after open discussion.

Communication.   Primarily horizontal, some bi-directional, highly interactive. Manager and subordinates communicate as equals or near equals. Employee desires become a primary criterion for decision making and discussion.

Although these approaches may appear to be categorical, it should be stressed that they reflect points on a continuum, and few managers would be likely to operate at all times at only one point. Most likely there would be a general tendency to operate at one point, but to have some variability around that point.

An important implication of these management communication styles is that communication styles are imposed by the management style chosen in the organization. Clearly, if all decisions are made above a manager, he or she can only select a Tell or Sell style, which would restrict the communication styles available for use. However, if a manager is given a great deal of autonomy, suggesting a Consult or Join style above, he or she has great flexibility in selecting an MCS for interface with employees. Thus, as we noted previously, MCS is a function both of a decision-making and a communication style preference of a manager and the management style imposed on the manager from above.

MCS is directly and meaningfully linked to employee satisfaction. As MCS becomes more employee centered and interactive, employee satisfaction increases. Since the original study, many employees have suggested that their favorite MCS type would be the Consult because, as one employee stated, "I have input and get to give advice and experience satisfaction, but in the end I am not responsible for the final decision." In the Join MCS, the employees are totally and completely responsible for the decision. In the Consult, they can always say, "I advised my manager against doing that. He [she] chose to ignore my advice." We must remember that in the Tell, Sell, and Consult styles, the manager ultimately makes the decision and is responsible for it. In the Join, the subordinates designated to make the decision are ultimately responsible for any outcomes (Table 10.1).

WHY MANAGERS SELECT ONE MCS
OVER ANOTHER

As we noted previously, the management communication style of an individual manager is impacted by both the MCS of the person immediately above him or her and his or her own personal preference. Although these two factors most often determine which style a manager will employ, there are numerous other reasons that a manager might select or avoid a given MCS in a particular situation. This section reviews various factors that influence the selection or avoidance of a certain style.

A number of persons we have interviewed suggest that managers select a certain style based on the time constraints under which the decision is

TABLE 10.1 **Management Communication Style, Who Makes Decision, and Communication Employed**

MCS	WHO MAKES DECISION	COMMUNICATION EMPLOYED
Tell	Manager makes or receives decision from above to announce to subordinates	Primarily ↓ Unidirectional Noninteractive
Sell	Manager makes or receives decision from above and persuades subordinates of desirability of decision	Primarily ↓ Some bi-directional Somewhat interactive
Consult	Manager makes ultimate decision but gets advice and suggestions from subordinates first	Primarily ↑ Bi-directional Interactive
Join	Decision making delegated to subordinates—manager does *not* make decision; manager sets parameters and lets subordinates make decision	Primarily ↔ Some bi-directional Highly interactive

being made. For example, if an organizational unit must make a decision about the distribution of travel funds within 48 hours, the manager may simply have to make the decision her/himself, or consult with only a few select personnel, and then make the decision. Many times supervisors ask managers below them to make immediate decisions, which leaves them no choice but to use a tell or a sell. They must make the decision, based on limited information, and give the decision to their boss. It is not unusual in organizations to regularly have decisions that must be made within a few hours. This leaves the manager no time to consult. One of these decisions might be the appointment of personnel to organizational committees, the appointment of people to represent the organization at meetings, or the distribution of funds. Democracy and participation take time. When decisions must be made quickly, there is no time for the communication required to make this approach work. Hence, immediate decisions rarely can involve subordinate input.

Managers who are new to the organization or the position have a tendency to go one of two directions—they either make all decisions or they delegate all decisions. Many novice managers feel insecure and unsure of their personnel, so they will make all critical decisions or else they delegate so they will not offend their personnel. Either direction can cause problems in the long run. The new manager who delegates all decisions is perceived as a pushover or an abdicator. However, our suggestion to new managers is that until you know to whom you can safely delegate some decisions, do not delegate. It is easier to move from being a tyrant than to move from being a pushover.

We had one manager tell us that when he interviews all potential new employees, he makes it clear who is the boss and who is the subordinate. Then, if applicants accept job offers, they know what to expect. Later, if the new employees can adapt to the system and pay their dues, he is willing to allow them a voice in the decision-making process. His view is that opportunities for participation are earned, not obtained by "divine right."

We have also had managers who initially used the delegation model and found that employees got angry with them later when they had no choice but to use a tell approach. They wished they had used more of a tell orientation in the beginning of their appointment.

Again, the orientation of the system influences what a manager can do. Some systems are more authoritarian and some are more democratic than others. In highly authoritarian organizations, much of the MCS will be of a tell or sell nature. There will be little consult or join. Usually, in authoritarian systems, if there is a consult or join used, it is on decisions that have little impact on the organization. More democratic organizations will allow for delegation of decisions and trust managers to select personnel who can make good, solid decisions.

Some managers will make many of the decisions when they feel their personnel are either untrained, unknowledgeable, or incompetent in the areas being discussed. Remember, the person who ultimately suffers because of poor decision making is the head of the unit (the manager). Hence, if a manager has new, untrained employees or employees who are simply incompetent in certain areas, he or she cannot delegate because the employees might make a poor decision that the supervisor might have to live with. For example, we talked with one department chair at a major university who had just hired seven new people. His department was literally being rebuilt by hiring almost half of its allotted members in a single year. He ultimately was the person who would be held responsible for the outcome. So he made all of the critical decisions. When he felt he could benefit from consulting, particularly with older faculty members, he did. But he had to be cautious. He had 22 years of experience in the department head position, whereas most of the new employees had never even taught at a major university before. In fact, for most of them, this was their first "real" job. They simply were untrained and unprepared to make most of the important decisions.

In conjunction with the preceding, a manager will make decisions if he or she feels some of the employees are truly incompetent (ignorant). Some employees (including, of course, some managers) are just plain dumb. It is not that they are inexperienced and need to be taught—they are too dumb to learn. How these people get hired in organizations is open to speculation, but the fact is they are hired and then managers or subordinates have to deal with them. A smart manager will recognize these persons, exclude them from the decision-making process, or make them feel like they contributed, but will never delegate critical decisions to them.

The manager will generally use a tell or sell approach when he or she has been exposed to the information needed to make the decision and the employees have not. Alternatively, he or she can inform the employees about the information and allow them to make the decision if he or she feels comfortable doing this. Often, when a person knows he or she has the needed information, he or she will simply make the decision and inform others. This is a legitimate reason for making decisions, and it saves a lot of time and effort.

Managers sometimes will select a certain MCS because it is what employees expect and want them to do. Some employees do not want to be involved in decision making, so they will make statements such as "Just tell me what to do and I'll do it." If one is working with a group of indifferents, they generally will not want to participate in decision making; they simply want to be told what to do and be left alone. On the other hand, some outgoing, creative, and upward mobile, high-achieving employees want input and will often ask if they can be involved in decision making or, more likely, complain if they are not involved.

Managers sometimes will select one style over another based on what they think the persons above them want. This is a form of CYA. If a manager has an idea about what upper management truly wants, then he or she will try to manipulate circumstances and the decision process so that he or she can give upper management what they want.

In some cases, managers will select the style that seems easiest to use. Sometimes it is easiest just to tell or sell people. Often this takes less time, presents less controversy, and can be done in written form. If the situation calls for a consult approach, then the manager might simply consult those directly impacted by the decision. This is perfectly legitimate, too. An effective manager can determine when to use what style in most cases. The selection of an MCS is often determined by the situation in which the manager finds her/himself.

The management communication style of a supervisor is impacted by many factors—some personal, some situational, and some personality based. However, a truly effective manager knows when to use a style and how. In other words, he or she knows when to be versatile while at the same time being consistent in decision making. The basic premise is that there are many styles open to managers, but each manager has to select a style and understand the consequences that come with each style. In a tell style employees have no input and can come to feel ignored and neglected. But it is quick and avoids wasting the time of a lot of people. In a sell style employees have limited input but may feel a little more satisfied. However, they may feel that they are being conned into supporting what the manager wants. In a consult style employees have input but the supervisor makes the final decision, so the employees are not totally responsible for the final decision. But if their advice is not taken, the subordinates may feel their advice was ignored and resent the supervisor. In a join style the employees bear the burden of the decision and the supervisor generally has to live with their decision. This is a time-consuming process with no guarantee people will like the decision finally accepted or that the decision will be the best one.

Managers and employees alike must understand the impact decision making has on the organization. They also must know what style is being used so they know how to communicate with one another.

IDENTIFYING THE MCS

How can an employee determine which management communication style is being used? Simple. Observe the communication being employed and you will know what MCS is being employed. Here is a test. The manager invites a select group of subordinates to give advice and suggestions, but says the ultimate decision still rests in his or her hands. What is being used? A consult, of course. The manager announces to subordinates that there have been changes in the sick leave policy and informs the employees they will have to follow the new policy. What is being used? A tell, of course. The manager presents arguments that support a new policy on parking assignments and demonstrates how the new policy will benefit all and answers questions with arguments in favor of the new policy. What is being used? A sell, of course. Next test. The manager defines the problem, sets parameters, and selects a group of employees to make the decision. What is being used? A join, of course. Is it really this easy to identify the MCS in everyday life? Yes, it is. In each case, if you observe the communication or lack of it, you will know the MCS in operation and be prepared to decide how to react to your manager.

Much of the time in most organizations, a tell MCS is being employed. With a tell MCS in operation, communication is limited and often discouraged. Hence, if you know you are working with a tell orientation and the decision is made and communication is limited to clarification on how the job is to be done, accept that decision and the accompanying limitations on communication. Do not try to change a tell MCS into a join MCS, or vice versa. If you try to fight the system, you are the kind of employee that most systems will want to eliminate. You will look like an ambivalent or a troublemaker, and most systems want those people gone. Successful employees (this includes managers) know what management communication style is being employed; they understand and accept it and generally do not try to dispute it. Success in the organization is highly correlated with one's understanding and acceptance of the management communication styles being used. If you feel you cannot live with the type of MCS your supervisor uses, don't live with it. Seek a new position. Whether higher managers have decided it or your manager has determined the MCS under which you are working, this is not a decision that ordinarily is up for review. As a subordinate who hopes to survive in the organization, you need to do two things: Recognize the MCS that is being used, and adapt to it.

REFERENCES AND RECOMMENDED READINGS

Horvath, C. W. (1998). Biological origins of communicator style. In J. C. McCroskey, J. A. Daly, M. M. Martin, & M. J. Beatty (Eds.), *Communication and Personality: Trait Perspectives* (pp. 69–94). Cresskill, NJ: Hampton Press, Inc.

Likert, R. (1961). *New patterns of management.* New York: McGraw-Hill.

Likert, R. (1967). *The human organization.* New York: McGraw-Hill.

McCroskey, J. C., & Richmond, V. P. (1996). *Fundamentals of human communication: An interpersonal perspective.* Prospect Heights, IL: Waveland Press.

McGregor, D. (1960). *The human side of enterprise.* New York: McGraw-Hill.

Norton, R. W. (1978). Foundation of a communicator style construct. *Human Communication Research, 4,* 99–112.

Richmond, V. P., & McCroskey, J. C. (1979). Management communication style, tolerance for disagreement, and innovativeness as predictors of employee satisfaction: A comparison of single-factor, two-factor, and multiple-factor approaches. In D. Nimmo (ed.), *Communication Yearbook, 3.* New Brunswick, NJ: Transaction Books, 359–373.

Sadler, P. J. (1970). Leadership style, confidence in management, and job satisfaction. *Journal of Applied Behavioral Science, 6,* 3–19.

Styles of leadership. (1962). 16mm. film. Beverly Hills, CA: Roundtable Productions.

Tannenbaum, R., & Schmidt, W. H. (1958). How to choose a leadership pattern. *Harvard Business Review, 36,* 95–101.

STUDY GUIDE

1. Likert identified four systems of management. Identify and describe each.
2. There are four types of management communication styles (MCS). Identify each and describe how decisions are made for each.
3. Explain the nature of the communication that exists under each MCS.
4. Identify and discuss why managers select a certain MCS as opposed to the other options.
5. What type of MCS do employees prefer? Why?
6. How can a subordinate determine the MCS type under which he or she is working?

CHAPTER 11

POWER AND STATUS

Janet Smith has finally made it! She has a secretary outside her office to screen people and calls. Her secretary's office is plush, comfortable, and has a window. Her secretary is pleased with the office. Janet's office has a work area and a conversation area. Her desk is made of the finest mahogany and her chair is a plush swivel model. Her office is color coordinated and at one end of the room she has windows that enable her to have a view of the city. She clearly has status.

Status is the thing many employees strive for more than pay. To be perceived better than someone else or have higher status than someone else can make otherwise fairly decent people lie, cheat, and steal. They want "things," status symbols that say they are *somebody.*

NATURE OF STATUS

Status is a person's role or position within a group or an organization. Status can be earned or awarded to us by our position in the organization. Because people quickly learn that status is something to work toward, everyone wants a slice of the pie. For example, attending some schools carries higher status than attending others (for example, Harvard University versus South Dakota State University). To be associated with certain groups is to gain a certain amount of the status associated with them (for example, to be a member of the football team, even a bench warmer). Wearing certain clothing connotes more status than wearing other clothing. Why did Izod, Guess, and Calvin Klein become so popular? Was it because of the quality of the clothing? Hardly. It was because of the status associated with them. If you wore Calvins you seemed to have money, power, and status. Some jobs carry higher status than other jobs. White-collar jobs are usually ranked higher than blue-collar jobs in terms of status. Being a corporate lawyer usually carries more status than being a sanitation engineer, but being a sanitation engineer has far more status than being a janitor. Which would you rather be, a meteorologist or a weather girl? How about weather *boy?*

We must remember that status affects how some people respond to their jobs and how people interact with others who have status, as opposed to those who do not have status, in organizations. People think that with status comes power and authority. That is not necessarily true. One can be of high status in terms of material items, but command little respect or have little power over others. However, because employees *think* status gives them power, they work very hard for status.

STATUS SYMBOLS

In the previous section we said status could be earned or sometimes it is afforded us by the position we hold in an organization. For example, corporate executives often are granted certain status symbols with their jobs. Many organizations feel that status is a means of rewarding an individual for a job well done. They also feel that their employees should have an image that is compatible with the company's image, so they provide status symbols (plush offices, parking spaces, company cars, company credit cards, expense accounts, and so on). Then again, some of us bring status symbols with us into our organization.

Some status symbols employees typically bring into organizations are age, ethnic background, religion, gender, parentage, competence, education, seniority, previous associates, skills, and experience. Although all employees might bring sources of status with them, a particular individual might have a higher social rank or status because he or she came from a better, more established school than the others. It is said that an MBA from the Harvard Business School is worth the money, time, and effort because the status it brings practically guarantees a good position with a good firm. Of course, today many organizations are attempting to meet affirmative action guidelines with qualified candidates, hence, ethnic background and gender can play a role in status.

Aside from the rather obvious status symbols that employees bring into organizations, there are many symbols we are given or can earn. The following is a typical list of status symbols people want in organizations: good salary, job title, size and location of office, type of office furniture, furnishings, window, location of parking space, secretary, privacy, key to the building or office, clothing, company car, privileges, car phone, possessions, computer, up-to-date equipment, longer lunches, vacation, time off if needed, flexible hours, type of briefcase, plants in office, and answering machine. Most of these status symbols are visible, tangible symbols, but there are some forms of status that are not tangible or visible but can be earned. Some of these are respect of supervisors and peers, others come to you for advice, and you are generally trusted by others to do your job—people are not constantly checking on you. However, these generally take years of hard work and dedication to earn.

Most organizations attempt to motivate employees by using tangible status symbols as a means of motivation. This can work for only awhile because eventually the available symbols will be exhausted. The biggest drawback with using tangible, visible symbols of status to motivate people is that there is never "enough for everyone." Even massive, well-funded organizations have employees who feel there is not enough status for them or that some people have too much status while others have too little.

What are the ramifications of either too much or too little status in organizations? First, too much or too little status can inhibit communication. If there is too much of a status differential between employees, they do not feel they can communicate with each other. If there is too little status differential, the supervisor is virtually like one of the subordinates and may not command their respect. When communication between employees and supervisors is inhibited, other problems follow. Second, employees do not develop solidarity or closeness to each other. They are constantly trying to earn what little status is available and cannot develop a solid relationship with others. Or there is so much status available they are all busy competing for it. Third, too much or too little status interferes with work. People spend too much time thinking about how to get the status that is available rather than working. Fourth, too little or too much status can cause resentment or conflict. In a system where there is too little status, people resent those who have it. Everything is relative. In a system where there is too much status, people will battle tooth and nail over it. This is not healthy competition—it is a battle.

In conclusion, status differences are always going to exist in organizations, but if we let status become a barrier between us and our peers or supervisors, then the communication flow will be inhibited and problems with solidarity and with the work may arise and resentment can occur.

COMMUNICATION AND STATUS

We are not trying to suggest that status symbols are not important. We realize status can be important in motivating people, helping personnel establish their role in an organization, giving employees an identity, and giving people a sense of inclusion. We are suggesting that when status gets out of control, communication can be affected negatively.

More communication in organizations is directed to higher-status persons than to those of lower status. Hence, higher-status persons may become overloaded so they have to learn to screen their messages. This can cause some resentment at the lower levels. People who get to talk with the higher-status person are automatically granted status themselves, whereas those who get ignored are automatically assigned lower status. However, employees must realize that many, many messages are directed at higher-status persons, and sometimes they simply cannot process all of them effectively.

In addition, there is always a risk for the lower-status person when communicating with the higher-status person. The lower-status person might get rewarded for communicating with the higher-status person; on the other hand, he or she might get rebuked. This can cause a lot of inhibition by the lower-status person. If he or she gets rebuked for communicating with the higher-status person, this reaffirms the person's lowly position and makes him or her feel even less capable and somewhat helpless. This rebuke is felt many times more painfully if it occurs in the presence of peers.

Also, many employees when communicating with higher-status persons will attempt to say what they think the higher-status person wants to hear. They may send only positive messages and generally try to communicate what they think their supervisor wants to hear. Hence, supervisors are often making decisions without having all the information because employees are too inhibited by the status barrier to give the truth or report all the information.

We can see that perceived status barriers have a real impact on communication. We might conclude by suggesting that *as the perceived status differential increases between supervisor and subordinate, the quality of communication decreases* (see Figure 11.1). By this we mean that as status differences go up, communication goes down. There is less communication and it is probably less likely to be honest communication when it occurs. People become intimidated by extremes in status. We might also conclude that *as the perceived status difference decreases between supervisor and subordinate, the quality of communication increases.* By this we mean that as status differences go down, communication goes up. There is more communication and it is probably more honest.

The most effective way of reducing status differential without giving up one's status is to build solidarity. *Building solidarity* means building a solid, close, trustworthy relationship, one in which people know they can "be open and honest" and not be punished for it. We might conclude that *as perceived solidarity increases between supervisor and subordinate, the perceived status differential decreases.* This allows for more open and honest communication without fear of being rebuked or punished. Hence, *as perceived solidarity increases between supervisor and subordinate, quality of communication will increase.* How does one build a solid relationship with one's supervisor? One must work hard, do one's job well, and be reliable. It is not accomplished overnight. It takes time, hard work, and commitment.

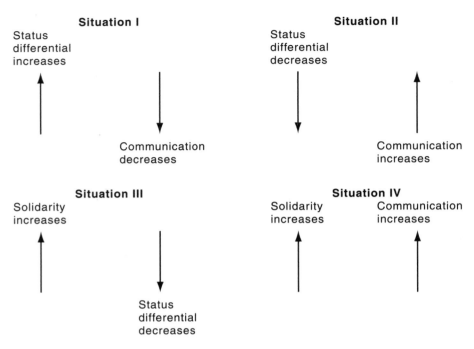

Situation I

Status differential increases

Communication decreases

Situation II

Status differential decreases

Communication increases

Situation III

Solidarity increases

Status differential decreases

Situation IV

Solidarity increases   Communication increases

FIGURE 11.1   **Impact of Status and Solidarity on Communication**

POWER

One of the primary reasons we communicate is to influence others. Some sources are better at influencing than others. Why is it that some supervisors can get their employees to do so much while others are barely tolerated by their employees? Much of it has to do with the type of influence used in organizations. Much of it depends on the appropriate power strategy effectively used to change another's behavior.

In this section we define an individual's power as the ability to have an effect on the behavior of another person or group. More specifically, this broader view sees power as *the capacity to influence another person to do something he or she would not have done without having been influenced.* A useful model of power is the one developed by French and Raven (1968) in which they explained the five bases of social power: coercive, reward, legitimate, referent, and expert. We have added two more.

French and Raven describe *coercive power* as being based on an individual's expectations that he or she will be punished by another if he or she does not conform to that person's influence attempt. Thus, in terms of an organization, supervisors who are perceived as communicating with coercive power are those supervisors who communicate messages of threat or force in an attempt to influence subordinates. The strength of coercive power is contingent on the probability of punishment for not complying minus the probability of punishment for complying. For example, a manager's coercive power is contingent on the employee's perceptions of how probable it is that the manager will exact some punishment for nonconformance and the degree of negative consequences such punishment would entail, minus the probability of punishment from other sources (other employees) if the employee does comply. The use of coercive power will gain only compliance on the part of an individual; it will never create motivation.

Another way of looking at coercive power is referring to it as "negative KITA" (KITA is an acronym advanced by Herzberg in 1968. It means "kick in the behind." Herzberg's theories are better than his spelling.) Managers can threaten to dock pay, make people work overtime, give them poor schedules, give them the bad clients, and a number of other things—none of which are pleasant.

Reward power, on the other hand, is based on an individual's perception of another's ability to mediate rewards for him or her. This ability involves the ability both to administer positive things someone wants, and to remove or decrease negative things someone doesn't want. Thus, within the organization, persons who are perceived as communicating with reward power are not only those individuals who can grant pay raises and promotions, but also those individuals who can eliminate menial tasks and other negative aspects of the system. The strength of reward power is contingent on an individual's perception of the probability that another can mediate a reward. Managers mediate rewards just as they mediate punishments.

Another way of looking at reward power is "positive KITA." The question becomes, "Would you rather have the carrot or the stick?" The stick is coercive power and the carrot is reward power. Reward power is only the flip side of coercive power. It does not get motivation, only compliance and movement, in most cases. Although coercion and reward are the flip sides of the same coin, only the jaded among us would prefer the coercive side. For this reason, reward power is thought to be much more effective than it actually usually is. Usually the rewards available are limited. Hence, managers will soon run out of rewards to influence workers' behaviors. Granted, some corporations seem to have almost unlimited rewards at their disposal, but most of us do not work in such corporations.

Power that gives a person the "right" to direct, evaluate, reward, and punish others within certain, usually well-defined limits, is referred to as *legitimate* or *assigned power.* In brief, use of legitimate power is based on an individual's perceptions of another's right to influence or prescribe behavior for him or her. Generally, legitimate power is characterized by positions in an organization's formal hierarchy (manager, principal, supervisor, and so on). It is sometimes referred to as "positional power." This type of power usually does not lead to motivation, only movement. For example, the employee will respond but will never do the task again without being asked to do so again.

The fourth base of power is *expert power*. Expert power is based on an individual's perceptions of another's competence and knowledge in specific areas. Consequently, the strength of expert power depends on an individual's perception of another's competence or expertise in a given area. For example, many managers are well educated and have expertise in many areas that can benefit both the employees and the organizations. Hence, through expert power, managers and employees can gain respect and be willing to change behaviors and perform duties for the other that they ordinarily would not perform, because they believe the other person knows better what should be done than they do themselves.

The fifth base of power, according to French and Raven (1968) is *referent power*. Referent power comes as a function of one person wanting to be like another person. When subordinates have a high respect for their supervisor, and want to model themselves on that supervisor, this grants the supervisor considerable power. The supervisor no longer needs to tell the subordinate what to do, in many cases, but only do it her/himself and the subordinate will imitate that behavior.

The first power base we add to this list is known as *relational power*. The existence of relational power is based on the personal relationships between people in the organization. When someone desires to please another person, they grant that other person relational power. It is very possible, even typical, for supervisors and subordinates to develop relational power with each other. Similarly, coworkers develop such relationships. The stronger the relationship between people, the more each one wishes to please the other, and the stronger the likelihood that they will behave in ways they believe the other would like them to behave.

The final base of power is *moral responsibility*. This base rests on an individual's perceptions of responsibility to others—the organization, the supervisor, coworkers, subordinates, etc. Everyone is expected to do their share, help their colleagues, meet the norms, not foul up the system, and cooperate. People will do a lot to avoid others thinking badly of them—to save face and be a part of the group. Often these things get done because someone feels responsible for doing them, and often they feel that way because of what someone else has suggested to them.

It is clear that the area of power has many options for influencing people. The question is, "Which types of power will motivate people and which types of power will not?" Before this can be answered, we have to review the three levels of influence (Kelman, 1961) that can be achieved. Employees can comply with, identify with, or internalize the thinking of another.

Compliance occurs when a person accepts another's request because he or she can see either potential reward for complying or potential punishment for not complying. For example, an employee might comply with the requests of his or her boss to gain a reward (a day off) or to avoid punishment (lose a day's pay). Compliance is when people just "do something." They do not necessarily agree that it should be done, or care about it, or identify with it—they just do it to get a reward or avoid punishment. Hence, any satisfaction gained from compliance is mainly superficial and there is no motivation to do the act again unless a reward is attached or force is threatened again. Compliance leads to movement—a temporary change in behavior—on the part of the employee to avoid punishment or receive a reward. Managers who operate within the framework of Theory X presume that employees work best under the compliance model.

To be certain a subordinate will comply in the face of potential punishments or rewards, the manager must be able to illustrate concern, control, and scrutiny. For example, the law-enforcement agencies of this country have shown their concern about speeding by having speed restrictions in certain areas. They have shown that they can control speeding with road monitors and that they can scrutinize or watch for offenders by the use of radar. When all of these methods are available, compliance with speed laws probably will occur. However, when any one of them is missing, compliance may not occur. For example, if the radar is turned off for a day, offenders know they are not being scrutinized and they will speed even if concern and control are present. Managers who say they want employees to do certain distasteful tasks, but then leave the work area, have told the employees they are not *really* concerned about the task. The employees probably will do only a halfway job of it, if that much.

Compliance only gets people to conform, not to identify with or internalize a specific idea. *Identification* occurs when an individual accepts the influence of another person or group because he or she identifies with and wants to establish a relationship with that particular person or group. Identification with the person (a manager) or group (an organization) is paramount, and often the employee will even model the behaviors and dress of the person or organization. When new employees identify with an organization, they will start conforming to the ideas and requests of the organization. The amount of change and motivation achieved by the identification mode is much higher than in the compliance mode. Changes tend to be long term, at least in the sense that the person can identify with the group's goals and values. This type of change can also lead to motivation, not just movement, on the part of employees. They are likely to perform desired behaviors even when no supervisor is present and when no special reward or punishment is likely to be given.

Internalization occurs when an employee adopts a way of thinking or behaving because it is intrinsically rewarding and is similar to that person's value system. When an idea or behavior is internalized, it is integrated into the individual's existing value system and is a part of the way the person thinks or behaves. It is undistinguishable from the person's already existing

TABLE 11.1   Types of Power and Impact on Levels of Influence

	LEVELS OF INFLUENCE		
Five Types of Power	*Compliance*	*Identification*	*Internalization*
Coercive	✓		
Reward	✓		
Legitimate or Assigned	✓		
Referent	✓	✓	✓
Expert	✓	✓	✓
Moral Responsibility	✓		
Relational	✓		

behaviors in the same area. For example, if we do not believe in cheating, then it would be difficult for us to cheat on corporate expenses. We automatically comply, identify with, and internalize into our system the behavior of not cheating on expenses.

When internalization is achieved, the employee is induced to perform the behaviors regardless of the scrutiny of his or her boss. He or she has become internally motivated to perform and feels this is the right or good thing to do. The employee believes in what he or she is doing and often will perform tasks without even being asked to do them. In effective organizational relationships, when internalization is present, employees will do tasks for others without even being asked to do so. They will do tasks because they believe they need to be done. They not only comply and identify with those behaviors, but also have internalized the behaviors and will perform whether scrutiny is present or not. People who are internally motivated are close to being classified as the organizational man or woman.

As we can see, compliance leads to movement (temporary changes in behavior), not motivation (long-term changes in behavior). Identification and internalization do lead to motivation. However, if the compliant behavior is reinforced and rewarded, it may pave the way for identification to occur at some point. Any of the previously mentioned levels of influence is dependent on the type of power employed by a manager (see Table 11.1).

It is clear that the type of power employed by a manager affects the level of influence over an employee. All types of power will lead to compliance. But only two types of power will lead to identification and internalization—referent and expert. Remember, with compliance there is minimal commitment and the employee will do the job well only as long as he or she is being scrutinized. With identification there is understanding and motivation to do tasks. With internalization there is understanding, commitment, dedication, and motivation to do tasks without even being asked to do them. Hence, the selection of power strategies is obvious—the supervisor should use referent and expert power when at all possible. Most organizations grant managers the first three types of power: coercive, reward, and legitimate. Relational and moral responsibility will develop as supervisors and subordinates work together. But managers must earn referent and expert power. This is not as easy as it may seem. Many managers have never learned to develop a personal rewarding relationship with employees. Hence, many managers are not comfortable with referent and expert power. They do not have any, and thus they must resort to punishment, rewards, or legitimate authority.

Power can be influential only when an employee is willing to acknowledge that the manager has any power. If an employee is not concerned about being punished or threatened with job loss, then the manager has no influence—not even compliance. In addition, systems quickly "run out" of ways to punish and reward personnel. Hence, working from a punishment or reward model will work for only awhile. Even to work that long, one has to know what punishes a person and what rewards a person. If you threaten to send someone home, he or she might not find this as punishment; it might be seen as a reward. If you promise to promote employees if they do well, some might see this as punishment, not reward. The power bases of coercion and reward are imperfect because some people simply cannot be threatened and others may not be rewarded. And worse yet, we may not be able to distinguish the rewards from the punishments for others.

FROM THE PEON'S PERSPECTIVE

As employees, what power bases do we have? We clearly do not have coercion, reward, or legitimate, at least not when we are first hired. As we become more experienced we develop some of each, and we are very likely to develop some relational and moral responsibility power as well. We are even more likely to develop referent and expert power as we display our competence at our work. But we must exercise the power we develop with care. Generally, you should avoid threatening to punish your supervisor—you might lose. For example, one employee we know threatened her boss with leaving the system if he did not give her what she wanted. What she did not realize was that by leaving she was rewarding him, so he made sure he did not grant her request. She left. Hence, employees have to be cautious about trying to use coercion or reward to influence their supervisors. It might backfire.

No one has power over anyone who does not grant him or her that power. We grant someone reward power over us when we decide we want the reward. We grant someone coercive power over us when we decide we want to avoid a punishment. We grant someone legitimate power over us when we decide he or she has the right to make certain demands of us. We grant someone expert power over us when we decide he or she knows more about something than we do. And we grant referent power to someone when we decide we like and respect him or her and would like to be more like that person. In a free society power is granted, not taken. Remember, you can always quit. If you decide you are not going to quit, then you are granting another person power over you.

Most power is relationally defined. Thus, you can develop power to control your supervisor's behavior to some degree, just as he or she receives from you some power to control your behavior. These powers are negotiated between supervisors and subordinates as a function of the relationships they build with each other. If you want to build a strong relationship with your supervisor, in all likelihood you can do so. Do what you were hired to do—your job. And do it well. This is the way to build the expert power base. When the supervisor asks your opinion about something concerning the job, respond in a positive manner. Let your supervisor "know you know your job." This will help build your credibility while at the same time building some power.

Next, build your referent base. This is built by communicating liking and respect for your supervisor. Demonstrate to your supervisor that you respect him or her and the organization. We don't mean "brown-nose." We mean be honestly dedicated and committed to the job as well as letting your supervisor know you are dependable. How might an employee build referent and expert power? First, do your job well without whining. Let's face it. All jobs have tasks people do not like. Do them and go on. No one likes a whiner. In addition, avoid associating with whiners. They will want you to start whining too. Second, if your supervisor asks your advice, give the best answer you have or admit you are not sure, but would be willing to try and find an answer. Third, spend time observing and learning the right norms and behaviors to make you a more dedicated employee—one who looks as if he or she belongs in the organization. Fourth, avoid special-interest groups or groups that want to create tension in the organization. Many a good employee has been ruined by getting in with the perpetual protestors in the organization. Fifth, communicate with your supervisor in a positive verbal and nonverbal manner.

The main results of this approach will be that your communication with your supervisor will be improved, you will have established an influence base for yourself, and you will be a more satisfied, motivated employee. You will be able to influence your supervisor on occasion, and perhaps have input on some major decisions in the future. True, some of your peers may see you as a bit of a "kiss up." Smile all the way to the promotion, and do not be late for their going-away parties!

REFERENCES AND RECOMMENDED READINGS

French, J. R. P., Jr., & Raven, B. (1968). The bases for social power. In D. Cartwright (ed.), *Studies in social power*. Ann Arbor: University of Michigan Press.

Herzberg, F. (Jan.–Feb. 1968). One more time: How do you motivate employees? *Harvard Business Review, 46,* 53–62.

Kelman, H. C. (1961). Processes of opinion change. *Public Opinion Quarterly, 25,* 58–78.

McCroskey, J. C., & Richmond, V. P. (1996). *Fundamentals of human communication: An interpersonal perspective*. Prospect Heights, IL: Waveland Press.

McCroskey, J. C., & Wheeless, L. R. (1976). *An introduction to human communication*. Boston: Allyn & Bacon.

Richmond, V. P., Davis, L. M., Saylor, K., & McCroskey, J. C. (1984). Power in organizations: Communication techniques and messages. *Human Communication Research, 11,* 85–108.

Richmond, V. P., McCroskey, J. C., & Davis, L. M. (1982). Individual differences among employees, management communication style, and employee satisfaction: Replication and extension. *Human Communication Research, 8,* 170–188.

Richmond, V. P., McCroskey, J. C., & Davis, L. M. (1986). The relationship of supervisor use of power and affinity-seeking strategies with subordinate satisfaction. *Communication Quarterly, 34,* 178–193.

Richmond, V. P., McCroskey, J. C., Davis, L. M., & Koontz, K. A. (1980). Perceived power as a mediator of management communication style and employee satisfaction: A preliminary investigation. *Communication Quarterly, 28,* 37–46.

Richmond, V. P., Wagner, J. P., & McCroskey, J. C. (1983). The impact of perceptions of leadership style, use of power, and conflict management style on organizational outcomes. *Communication Quarterly, 31,* 27–36.

STUDY GUIDE

1. What is "status"? Give examples of "status symbols" in organizations.
2. What is the relationship between status and solidarity? How is each related to communication in an organization?
3. Identify and describe the seven primary types of power. Which ones are likely to enhance superior–subordinate communication? Which ones are likely to detract from it? Why?
4. Identify and describe the three levels of influence.
5. Identify and describe the three conditions necessary for people to engage in compliant behavior as a result of threatened punishment or promised reward.
6. Who determines how much power a manager has in an organization? Explain.
7. Explain what *you* can do to increase your power in an organization.

CHAPTER 12

ORGANIZATIONAL CULTURE

We are all "cultured." Those who believe it is necessary to have an appreciation for German funeral dirges, Italian operatic sopranos, Shakespearean theater, and abstract French paintings to be cultured will not agree with this statement. That is because they equate the terms "cultured" and "refined," and reserve for themselves the right to prescribe what those terms mean. It is unfortunate that the term "culture" has been abused in this way for so long in North America. It has resulted in many people rejecting "culture" as an area of interest, and feeling like they are not a part of their own North American culture.

While many of us are not particularly "refined," especially in the way some American cultural elitists choose to define that term, we repeat: *We are all cultured.* Everyone is a part of some culture. Culture surrounds us, and everything we do. Culture simply cannot be avoided in contemporary society.

DEFINING CULTURE

Culture is "an accumulated pattern of values, beliefs, and behaviors shared by an identifiable group of people with a common history and a verbal and nonverbal symbol system" (Neuliep, 2000, p. 26). More simply, a culture is a group of people with similar backgrounds who think, act, and communicate a lot alike.

Most discussions of culture are directed toward national groups, hence we hear about Japanese culture, Brazilian culture, Irish culture, Mexican culture, Turkish culture, and American (usually meaning U.S.) culture. As this suggests, a culture can include an entire nation, or even more than one nation. It also can include only a portion of a nation (such as Texas culture). Most importantly here, it may include only the people in a given organization. We will return to this concern shortly.

CULTURE AND COMMUNICATION

A major characteristic of a culture is that the people within the culture communicate frequently with one another. Most often, the majority of the people in a given culture will speak the same language and share the usage of nonverbal emblems. As a result, the people have regular patterns of communication behavior that may be different than people from other cultures.

The role of culture is critical in the communication development of children, as well as other "newcomers" to a culture. While humans are genetically programmed to learn language, what language (or languages) they learn is a function of what one(s) they are exposed to. Not only will children learn the language(s) they hear, they will learn to speak the language with the accent they hear and employ the dialect to which they are exposed. As we noted in Chapter 3, most of the nonverbal behavior patterns that we learn are those to which we are exposed as children. In addition, most of the social skills of communication are learned via modeling of others in our environment. Since communication is a central aspect of being human, communication is primarily responsible for sustaining the values, beliefs, and behaviors common to the culture.

Cultures pressure their members to communicate in very similar ways. However, we all know that there are major differences in communication behaviors among people in our own culture. The same is true of other cultures. The reason for this is that each individual, regardless of culture, is born with temperamental and personality orientations which makes her/him distinguishable from others. Temperamental and personality orientations, while they may be shaped by cultural influences, have a strong genetic base. In the absence of the genetic differences, cultural influences would likely be much more successful in their persistent attempts to get all of the culture's members to think and act alike.

CULTURAL TERMINOLOGY

There are a variety of terms that are used to describe cultures and contacts among people from different cultures. Most of these are relatively easy to understand, but it is important that we clarify how people commonly use them to avoid confusion.

Subculture.   While there are many cultures which are composed of hundreds of thousands or even millions of people, most of these have smaller cultures within them. These are commonly called "subcultures," meaning they are subdivisions of a larger culture whose members have a variety of shared differences between themselves and the larger culture. Some refer to these as "co-cultures," to suggest their equality with regard to the larger culture. Within the larger U.S. culture, for example, we have subcultures based on region (Northeast, Midwest, Southern California, Texas, etc.), ethnicity (African American, Japanese American, Mexican American, Italian American, Irish American, Cuban American, etc.), and religion (Catholic, Jewish, Baptist, Islamic, etc.). The people in each of these groups share with each other characteristics, beliefs, attitudes, and/or behaviors which mark them as different from the larger culture. However, they still share a great number of similarities with members of the larger culture (and other subgroups) which mark them as members of the larger culture as opposed to a different large culture. For example, African Americans compose a distinct subculture within the United States, but generally are more similar to other members of the general U.S. culture than they are to any of the cultures of Africa. Similarly, Irish Americans are culturally much more like people in the general U.S. culture than they are like people living in Ireland. Living as a member of a subculture does not remove one as a member of the larger culture. It merely means that one may have closer ties to the subculture than to the larger culture. We will consider this later in terms of working in larger organizations, for the implications of this for organizational success are substantial.

Communication between Cultures.   There are a variety of terms employed to describe various communication contexts for communication. "Intracultural" refers to communication between people of the same culture. "Intercultural" describes communication between people of two different cultures or, in some cases, two different subcultures. "Cross cultural" sometimes is used interchangeably with intercultural. However, it most often is used to describe references to comparisons between or across cultures.

"International" most commonly refers to communication between people from different countries. They may be from highly different or very similar cultures, but the fact of being of different nationalities is a central characteristic of the communication. Government to government communication, for example, is international communication. "Interethnic" refers to communication between members of more than one ethnic subculture. "Interracial" refers to communication between members of more than one racial subculture. This term is declining in usage due to the difficulty in making clear distinctions among racial groups.

Special Terms.   There are several terms which are used in discussions of culture and communication which are not generally used in the same way in other contexts. It is important that we clarify their common usage within this context.

"Pancultural" refers to something that holds true over all (or nearly all) cultures. That which is characteristic of all humans is pancultural. Our basic anatomy and biological functions, for example, are pancultural. How we adjust to these characteristics, however, is not. The human smile is pancultural, but what produces it is not, and how we should interpret it is not. Very little in communication is pancultural.

"Diversity" suggests differences. Cultures influence their members in ways that reduce diversity and make differences among people less acceptable. Nevertheless, international commerce and tourism have brought a high degree of diversity to areas which used to be extremely homogeneous. This is true of the United States generally and organizations in the United States in particular. Diversity is a fact of life in most organizations today. It has many positive, as well as negative, impacts on organizational life.

"Gender" is considered in most dictionaries to be equivalent to "biological sex." However, in discussions of culture, these two concepts are separated, for good reason. "Female" and "male" and their linguistic translations refer to biological sex in all cultures, and they are referencing the same biological qualities. "Gender" is taken to refer to the concepts of "femininity" and "masculinity." These concepts are *not* referencing the same characteristics across culture. What is feminine in one culture may not be in another, and the same holds true for masculine. For example, male friends holding hands while walking or sitting and talking is very masculine in many cultures. It typically isn't in the general U.S. culture.

ORGANIZATIONS AND CULTURES

Organizations exist within cultural environments. Within each organization there is a culture unique to that organization. These are the contexts within which organizational communication occurs. To say that these cultures have an influence on communication in organizations is an understatement. They virtually determine that communication.

The Organization within a Culture. All organizations have a home base, even internet organizations. The vast majority have workers who live reasonably close to a central location where they all come together to work each day. Many of these workers are hired because they live in that area. Others move to that area after they are hired. That area provides the culture in which the organization lives. The organization depends not only on their own employees who live in that culture, but also on other people living in that culture for what it needs to survive—water, gas, electricity, roads, airports, telephones, food service, etc. The governmental policies, schools, churches, and recreational opportunities provided by the area directly impact the organization. The organization is never "free to be what it can be." In some cultures it may not even be allowed to operate on Sundays!

If an organization is based in New York City, it likely will be dramatically different than one located Birmingham, Alabama, San Diego, California, or Sioux Falls, South Dakota. The people in it are likely to differ on the accent and dialect they speak, their religion, a general attitude toward life, what is good food and what time of the day it should be eaten, work habits, ethnic background, and a wide variety of other things which are culturally relevant. All of these external cultural elements work to shape the nature of the organization. Whatever area the organization chooses for its home base, the people from that area will serve as a significant proportion of the organization's work force. That work force will expect (or demand) that the organization will operate in ways that are consistent with the local culture. The bottom line is: Cultures shape organizations.

The Culture within an Organization.   Over time, organizations create their own cultures. While, as we have just noted, the culture of an area impacts an organization, there are other forces at work as well. The culture of the organization is impacted by the kind of work that is done in the organization—blue collar and white collar organizations tend to have very different cultures. The leadership of the organization has a major impact on the organization—the kinds of people who are at the top tend to define what kinds of people the organization values, and often what kinds of people are hired and retained (remember our earlier discussion of the impact of homophily). Over time (usually only a few years) an oral history of the organization develops. In this way myths about great and terrible things that have happened become real, and current and former employees become the rogues and heros of the organization. Traditions are built, and acceptable (as well as unacceptable) behavior patterns are determined. Most everyone learns "how we do it around here." Diversity, at least in terms of values, beliefs, and attitudes, declines. Individuals begin to identify with the organization and an "in-group" is identified (the organization becomes "we") and other competing organizations are increasingly seen as evil and not nearly as good as "we" are, hence "out-groups" are formed ("they"). Expectations for new employees become more elaborate and more rigid—and more programs designed to mentor, train, and socialize new employees are developed.

The bottom line is: Organizations shape cultures. Organizations are a lot like people. Where they grow up makes a big difference in how they are acculturated. Nevertheless, each one develops its own personality. However, organizations which have multiple work sites, even if they are all within a close geographic area, are likely to develop different cultures. And if organizations physically move from one area to another area, the impact is much like moving a person from one area to another. They go into "culture shock" and have an extremely hard time dealing with the culture of the new area. If they get past that, and many do not, they develop a new culture, one that has some of the old and much of the new. Imagine, if you can, what happened to the people in American Airlines as well as the organization itself. They had been solidly lodged in New York City for decades. Then they moved to Dallas, Texas. As the Texas tourist bureau puts it: "Texas, A Whole Other Country!" While this may be thought of as an amusing slogan and good attention getter for the tourist business, never doubt whether it is the actual orientation of a very large proportion of "real Texans," as well as long-term immigrants from elsewhere!

Global Organizations.   Until quite recently, most organizations had their home base in one country and conducted most of their business in that country. Many are still like that but others have become multi-national or global organizations. Some of these have accomplished this by creating branch organizations in countries beyond their home country. Others have accomplished this through mergers with or acquisitions of other organizations. At one time many products had a "Made in the U.S.A." identification on them. That was taken to mean that the product was made from U.S. materials by U.S. workers in a U.S. located plant owned by U.S. people. Being "Made in Japan" meant the same thing, except substitute Japan for U.S. Today, being made in the "U.S.A." (or any other country) is hard to define. Today we buy a product which was designed by a German-owned firm in Canada, put together by U.S. workers in a plant in California owned by a Dutch conglomerate, from parts imported from 35 other countries. There are so-called "American" cars that have less U.S.-made parts than so-called "Japanese" cars, and vice versa. And we can buy blouses made in Indonesia in Dutch-owned factories with material made in Mexico in Canadian owned factories according to specifications of U.S.-based designers. And they have the designer's label on them!

Organizations aren't what they once were. They are much, much more complex. When multiple large cultures come together, within a single organization, we would assume that the cultures merge into some blended culture. Many people who have looked at this phenomenon suggest this often is not the case. Rather, there often is a culture clash where people from the different cultures actively seek to get rid of one another—and, ultimately one group wins, and the other loses. This can be very costly on all dimensions for the organization. Similarly, sometimes organizations branch into new cultures and try to make things work the way they do in their home culture. They virtually always fail. Both of these patterns are commonly based on the same basic cause: The organization is highly ethnocentric.

ETHNOCENTRISM

When children are born they are virtually helpless. Their parents lay them in a crib and after a while they are able to see around them in their environment. Everything that exists to the child is what is in that environment. People come in and out. Some talk, some touch, some hold, and all go away.

When cultures developed originally, they were created by groups of people whose worlds were almost as restricted as the typical child's. They didn't know much about the world which was over the next hill or across the river. While they may have known that there were some other people over the hill or across the river, they knew little about them—except that they definitely were not like themselves. Their world was what they could see around them. It is no wonder that little children see themselves as the center of the world (as early cultures did).

Egocentrism.   To understand ethnocentrism, we must first understand egocentrism. All children (and most adults) are egocentric. That is, they see themselves as central to everything that goes on in their world. Since little children have been waited on "hand and foot" by their parents and others their whole lives, does it not make sense that they would think that way? It is not hard for them to learn that if they scream loud enough, long enough, someone will come wait on them and do their bidding. As they grow older, they become aware of the community in which they live. That place is the center of the Earth, of course, because they are not aware of anywhere else yet. Now they begin to sort out people in their community. There are those who seem to agree that they are the center of the universe and should be catered to (good people), and those who don't behave that way (bad people). Others begin to call them names—"spoiled" often comes first. Then they move on to "self-centered." The subsequent list of names are probably best left to the imagination. What they all really mean is "egocentric."

Ethnocentrism Defined.   Klopf (1998) notes that the term "ethnocentrism" is derived from the Greek words "ethnos," which refers to "nation," and "kentron" which refers to "center." Literally, then, this term refers to the view that one's country is the center of the universe. Hofstede (1991) has argued that ethnocentrism is to a people what egocentrism is to an individual. It is important that we recognize that "a people" is not necessarily restricted to a large number of people, like a country. It can also apply to any group that forms a subculture within a larger culture. It can also apply to the people in a given organization. Most importantly, it can even apply to a relatively small but identifiable subgroup within an organization. This can be a branch of the larger organization, or even a division or department within the organization or the branch. The production division is the central unit of the organization—to people in the production division. The marketing division is the central unit of the organization—to the people in the marketing division. If these two ethnocentric divisions cannot learn to work together, the organization is in trouble.

In-groups and Out-groups.   An important aspect of ethnocentrism is the creation of in-groups and out-groups. When we become ethnocentric there must be a "we" and a "they." We are the good people, of course; and everyone who is in our group is good. Hence, "in-groups" are good and it naturally follows that other people compose "out-groups" and "they" are the bad people. All cultures are ethnocentric (including subcultures) and, hence, identify people in their culture as the in-group and people in all other cultures (and subcultures) as the out-group. This, of course, provides the basis for dislike, hate, discrimination, conflict, and even war between cultural groups. In the presence of too much ethnocentrism, friendly competition between people of different organizational cultures can evolve into hatred and sabotage of each group by the other. Hence, a major function of managers in organizations is controlling the ethnocentric (as well as egocentric) tendencies of the various subgroups (and individuals) within the organization. Since it exists in all cultures (is pancultural), it is reasonable to conclude that ethnocentrism is a naturally occurring phenomenon in human societies. The key to dealing with it is understanding its various levels.

Levels of Ethnocentrism.   There are five levels of ethnocentrism. From the least to the most extreme, they are equality, sensitivity, indifference, avoidance, and disparagement.

Equality is the lowest level of ethnocentrism. People and groups at this level treat others as equals (do to others as you would have them do to you). While they may notice diversity between themselves and others, they see the other peoples' customs and ways of thinking and behaving to be equal to their own. Cooperation is likely under these circumstances, as is effective communication, and problem solving. In political terms, these people treat each other as "allies." It is a "we" relationship.

Sensitivity is the second lowest level of ethnocentrism. People at this level see others as culturally diverse and recognize that this may be problematic. However, they want to better understand where the others are "coming from" and decrease the differences between themselves and the others if possible. They are willing to compromise with the others if they are willing to compromise as well. If the people from the other culture are also sensitive, the likelihood of successful communication between the two groups is good. They may be able to cooperate, compromise, and successfully work together. They may be able to convert "they" orientations to "we" orientations, at least on a temporary basis.

Indifference is the so-called moderate level of ethnocentrism. People at the indifferent level don't much care about people from other cultures, they prefer to communicate only with people like themselves. They reject diversity and embrace homophily. These people will not go out of their way to cause trouble for people that are different from themselves. But if contact with diverse people is forced upon them (by the other people or by circumstances) they may react very negatively. Organizations undergoing change which requires cultural adaptation may have serious problems with people at this level. These are not people who should be sent on temporary (or permanent) assignments to other cultures, particularly highly divergent cultures. Nor should they be assigned to work under a person from a distinctly different subculture. If they are, any problems that occur are likely to be attributed by these people to the failings of the culture or subculture of the people they are forced to interact with. Extremely negative emotional outcomes are to be expected on the part of these people when forced to interact as an equal with people from cultures other than their own. They can be civil with people from other cultures, however, if they are only expected to do that and have no additional contact.

Avoidance is the second highest level of ethnocentrism. People at this level actively avoid and limit communication with people from other cultures to the maximum extent possible. They are especially averse to intimate contact with such people. In organizations they will avoid accepting any appointment which would require them to communicate with such individuals. They will actively resist hiring, retaining, or promoting diverse people if put in a position where they must participate in such decisions. They will not normally go out of their way to attack people from other cultures, but will do so if they feel their cultural orientations are being challenged.

Disparagement is the highest level of ethnocentrism. People at this level have no value for, nor do they respect, the cultures of other people. They are actively hostile to such people. They belittle them, and see them as inferior beings. Most cultures have terms for people who are considered inferior to others (mud people, untouchables, pagans, infidels, etc.). That is what people from other cultures are to these people. They reject communication with these people except to disparage them in every imaginable way. People at this level may be referred to as "bigots," however, they see themselves as defenders of their culture. They are often willing to take extreme measures to do so.

Highly ethnocentric groups see themselves as virtuous and superior, their values as universally correct, and their customs as original and centrally human. In contrast, they see members of other groups to be contemptible, immoral, inferior, and weak. They feel it is their responsibility to try to change those people and make them like themselves if at all possible. Most major religions have subgroups which are highly ethnocentric. Not all members of the religious group have these highly ethnocentric orientations, but their most extreme, fundamentalist factions frequently do. Fortunately, very few organizational cultures reach such extremes. While it is entirely possible you will find individual people working in organizations who are at the disparagement level of ethnocentrism, it is unlikely you will find it necessary to work as a subordinate in such an environment. If you do, do your best to find other employment!

Becoming Highly or Lowly Ethnocentric.   Ethnocentrism exists on a continuum of high to low. Therefore, everyone is ethnocentric to some degree.

Being at either end of the continuum can be disadvantageous (Gudykunst & Kim, 1997). There has been considerable dispute about how people come to be ethnocentric. Is it one of the genetically based orientations, or is it something that we learn? Since there is such high variability in ethnocentrism across people in any given culture, some have assumed that this must be a genetically-based trait. Recent research, however, has failed to confirm that belief. This research determined that ethnocentrism and homophobia (another trait generally considered to be anti-social) were highly correlated with each other ($r = .57$). However, neither were found to be associated with any dimension of temperament (Wrench & McCroskey, 2003). While this does not rule out the possibility that these two traits could be associated with some brain system(s) other than the ones controlling temperament, it does indicate that they are, at least, not associated with the genetic factors which have been seen to be highly instrumental in forming the foundations for many personality traits and communication traits. Hence, at this point, it appears that a view commonly expressed by people who regularly have to deal with problems associated with ethnocentrism is correct: "People have to be taught to hate, they aren't born that way." This learning may begin early in life when parents, and others in a child's culture, work to overcome a child's egocentrism by teaching them they are part of a group and not the be-all, end-all person in the world. Such efforts to open the child to others in their environment may provide the foundation of learning, or over-learning, to value members of their in-group and favor them over members of all other groups—the essence of ethnocentrism.

Positive Aspects of Ethnocentrism.   Ethnocentrism provides the foundation for the existence of a culture or a subculture. It helps people making up cultures and subcultures develop a sense of collective identity and group pride. It helps maintain the integrity of the culture or subculture in the face of external threats from people from other cultures (who also believe their culture to be the best one). Some people suggest that if there were no ethnocentrism, there would be no culture.

Ethnocentrism gives the people in an organization an identity and helps make them more homogeneous and cohesive. It promotes positive and effective communication among people within the organization. It results in people being more willing to follow the formal and informal practices of the organization, since the people in the organizational culture consider these practices to be the correct ones and the best ones for all normal people to follow. When conflict occurs with people from other organizational cultures (or subcultures), blame can be placed on the other group and that reduces potential conflict within the home group. Ethnocentrism provides the foundation for pride in one's organization.

Clearly, ethnocentrism is the first line of defense for any organizational culture, or any organizational subculture. Without it, an organization or a unit within it is open to rapid and extreme changes and is subject to losing its very existence. For this reason, people who lead subcultural groups within a larger organizational culture sometimes resort to very militant communication in the ethnocentric defense of their subculture. They recognize that in the absence of high ethnocentrism among the members of the subculture, it may be seen as weak and unimportant to others in the larger culture. If too few people think a subculture is worth preserving, it will not be preserved.

Negative Aspects of Ethnocentrism.   Like many other things, ethnocentrism in moderation can be positive, as we indicated in the previous section. However, if taken too far, ethnocentrism can become a very negative orientation for both individuals and organizations. It is particularly dangerous for either to have strongly ethnocentric beliefs and not recognize that they do. It is usually very easy to see ethnocentrism in others, but it is usually difficult to recognize it in oneself or one's organization. After all, our view of the world is the correct one, isn't it? Some of the people who complain the loudest about being mistreated by some other cultural or subcultural group are also among the most ethnocentric people you will find. However, they will deny their own ethnocentrism loudly while decrying this very evil in other people and organizations around them.

There are four potentially serious problems for communication in organizations which emanate from ethnocentrism which is too high: culture shock, stereotyping, prejudice, and excessive cohesiveness. We will consider each of these in turn.

Culture Shock.   While culture shock has been experienced by people for centuries, it was not fully identified and described until 1960 (Oberg, 1960). Culture shock is something almost everyone experiences when they move into a new cultural environment. Whether the move is from one continent to another, or just from home to a nearby college, some degree of trauma is likely to be experienced. Given the mobility of society today, this means that almost everyone will experience it at some time in their lives, and many will experience it several times. That trauma is now commonly referred to as "culture shock." If you have never experienced it, when you do, "shock" will not seem too strong a word to describe it. At the extreme, culture shock has been found to result in complete mental breakdown, and even suicide. The greater the actual difference between the old and new culture (or subculture) the greater the shock. Similarly, the higher one's ethnocentrism, the greater the shock.

While we don't always realize it, we become acculturated to work in our first job. We develop a concept of work based on that experience. Each time we take a new job, we have to revise that concept to fit the new organization's culture. When we take a new job in another organization, initially we take the old culture with us. If the new culture is not very different from the old one, or we have very low ethnocentrism, we may adapt to the new position quickly. If the new culture is very different, or if because we are highly ethnocentric we perceive the new culture to be very different, we are likely to experience severe culture shock and all that goes with it.

Highly ethnocentric organizations are not likely to recognize that new employees are experiencing culture shock. They see their culture as very open and accepting—and normal. Any problems in adaptation by new employees are seen as weaknesses or personality defects in the new people. More sensitive organizations develop programs to help new employees make the transition to the new culture. These programs socialize the new people to fit within the organization's culture. Over time, then, both the organization and the new employees adapt to each other and the new people are assimilated within the organizational culture.

Stereotyping is the process of forming generalizations about people based on their membership in a culture or subculture. Many stereotypes are fully accurate, others are partly but not fully correct, and still others are completely inaccurate (Lee, Jussim, & McCauley, 1995). Such generalizations serve as a means of organizing our experiences with others. We need them so we may better predict how people will respond to our communication efforts. It is important that we be able to recognize that individuals often differ substantially in important ways from other members of their own culture. Ethnocentrism interferes with this recognition. As a result, highly ethnocentric people are willing to generalize their stereotypes to people for whom the stereotype clearly (to less ethnocentric observers) does not apply. The more ethnocentric an organization's culture, the more absolute will be the stereotypes in the collective consciousness of its members. Even if an individual employee recognizes the falsity of the stereotype (her sister works for the stereotyped company), they may feel strong pressure to remain silent.

Prejudice refers to "a priori judgements" based on inadequate stereotypes. The term "a priori judgements" references judgements made in advance of the time when they are employed. By "inadequate stereotypes" we mean the basis for the stereotype is insufficient or inaccurate information.

While "prejudice" suggests a negative judgement, that is not always the case. There are instances where the pre-judgement is positive, even though it was based on insufficient or inaccurate information. However, this is the exception rather than the rule—and much more likely to occur within one's home culture than in intercultural encounters. Like stereotyping, the root cause of prejudice is ethnocentrism. And since virtually all of us are ethnocentric, at least to some degree, it is likely that we have some negative stereotypes of people from other cultures or subcultures, and it is likely that we have some prejudices about some groups of people and their culturally based behaviors—including communication behaviors. And, of course, it is highly likely that people from other cultures and subcultures have negative views of us for the same reasons.

Excessive cohesiveness may at first appear to be an oxymoron. We want our work groups to be cohesive. Cohesiveness is good. It enables people to work together. All true, but as is usually the case, it is possible to have too much of a good thing. Groups which share a highly ethnocentric organizational culture greatly exaggerate the "in-group"/"out-group" distinction we discussed earlier. Their own cohesion is extremely highly valued, while members of other groups—even within the same organization—can be seen as enemies. Extremely high cohesiveness increases stereotyping and prejudice against out-group members and leads to a decline in decision-making quality. In the "worst case scenario," it can lead to what is called "groupthink." We will consider this phenomenon in more detail in Chapter 14.

Organizations exist within cultures and cultures exist within organizations. To fully understand how an organization works (much less why) we must make ourselves aware of both of these powerful influences. As peons in an organization, nothing may be as we see it initially. Consequently, we need to exercise great caution in drawing any conclusions, good or bad, about what is going on in our new cultural world. We must take time to get more information, be aware of our own ethnocentrism as well as that present in the organizational culture, and remain open to changing any conclusions we may draw.

REFERENCES AND RECOMMENDED READINGS

DeVito, J. A. (1997). *Human communication,* 7th ed. New York: Addison Wesley Longman.

Gudykunst, W. B., & Kim, Y. Y. (1997). *Communicating with strangers: An approach to intercultural communication.* (3rd ed.). New York: McGraw-Hill.

Hanna, M. S., & Wilson, G. L. (1998). *Communication in business and professional settings.* (4th ed.). New York: McGraw-Hill.

Hofstede, G. (1991). *Cultures and organizations: Software of the mind.* London: McGraw-Hill.

Klopf, D. W. (1998). *Intercultural encounters: The elements of intercultural communication.* (4th ed.). Englewood, CO: Morton.

Lee, Y. T., Jussim, L. J., & McCauley, C. R. (1995). *Stereotype accuracy: Toward appreciating group differences.* Washington, D. C.: American Psychological Association.

Neuliep, J. W. (2000). *Intercultural communication: A contextual approach.* Boston, MA: Houghton Mifflin.

Oberg, K. (1960). Cultural shock: Adjustment to new cultural environments. *Practical Anthropology, 7,* 176–182.

Pacanowsky, M. E., & O'Donnell-Trujillo, N. (1983). Organizational communication as cultural performance, *Communication Monographs, 50,* 128–146.

Rogers, E. M., & Steinfatt, T. M. (1999). *Intercultural communication.* Prospect Heights, IL: Waveland.

Samovar, L. A., Porter, R. E., & Stefani, L. A. (1998). *Communication between cultures.* (3rd ed.). Belmont, CA: Wadsworth.

Wrench, J. S., & McCroskey, J. C. (2003). A communibiological examination of ethnocentrism and homophobia. *Communication Research Reports, 20,* 24–33.

STUDY GUIDE

1. Define "culture" and "organizational culture."
2. Relate culture to communication.
3. Explain: subculture, intracultural, intercultural, cross cultural, international, interethnic, interracial, pancultural, diversity.
4. Distinguish between biological sex and gender.
5. Explain the concept of "ethnocentrism."
6. Distinguish between in-groups and out-groups.
7. List and explain the five levels of ethnocentrism.
8. List and explain the positive aspects of ethnocentrism.
9. List and explain the negative aspects of ethnocentrism.

CHAPTER 13

COMMUNICATION AND CHANGE

Why is it that when someone in an organization says the "c" word, people immediately start hyperventilating? The word *change* always seems to invoke feelings of anxiety, hostility, and frustration. Probably the primary reason people have such feelings when the word *change* is mentioned is that they have been through many changes that were total disasters. This chapter reviews why people generally resist change and then discusses factors that assist in promoting change or preventing change.

WHY PEOPLE RESIST CHANGE IN ORGANIZATIONS

People resist change for numerous reasons. Probably the most significant reason people resist change is that they are fearful that their position or status in the organization might change—for the worse. This is not to suggest that people are always opposed to change, for some changes would enhance their position in the organization. However, many persons are satisfied with their position, or at least secure in it, and do not want to play with fire. The possibility of making things significantly better is not worth the risk of making them significantly worse. For example, take a manager who has been supervising a unit for eight years. She has the routine down in terms of who does what, when reports are due, how to do things, and she is competent at what she does. Any change within the system might impact her role and ultimately change her position so that she would have to start all over and learn a new role. With all that effort, she would only get back to where she was before the change. Is it any wonder she would be resistant?

In conjunction with this, many employees fear change because it might require their workload to be increased or altered so they would have to do something they disliked. Many, many employees are satisfied having a routine job with routine functions and do not want to change the routine. Whether you are a teacher or a factory worker, you may have scheduled routines that you have established and you feel comfortable with things the way they are. Granted, some routines can be boring, but most people would rather have a boring routine than have to learn a new job or have their workload increased. And many times change means altering one's workload or increasing it, for a time at least.

People also resist change because they have had past experiences with change processes that have been failures. Changes can fail for a multitude of reasons. For example, if most people are not in favor of the change, it will be undermined. If the organization does not have the resources for funding the change, it probably will fail. Many schools have tried to implement the use of computers to teach computer literacy for their students. However, only those schools with sufficient funding to buy and maintain a sufficient number of machines have successfully created a high-quality computer program for all. In many schools only a select few get to use the computers, because there are not enough for all students and teachers.

Employees also fear that a change might alter their economic status in a negative fashion. One of the first questions people will ask in organizations when approached about a change is, "How will this change impact my salary?" If the change will impact a person's salary or company benefits in a negative way, then he or she will be highly resistant to the new idea. Even if the change is going to improve his or her economic status, he or she wants to know "how much improvement, when, and what do I have to do for the improvement?"

People also resist change because they are fearful that it will create chaos. In other words, the system will be disorganized and dysfunctional for an indeterminant amount of time. We know of a system that discontinued the graduate school in favor of centralizing graduate processing functions in various departments and units. It took several years before personnel knew how to transfer students from one unit to the next, new forms had to be created, new rules and policies had to be created, and of course new personnel had to be hired and some older personnel were moved or their jobs changed. This type of a major change can cause incredible amounts of chaos, which makes the process so unpleasant that the next time someone mentions a change of such magnitude, many in the system will say, "Hell no, the last time we did something like this, it was a mess for years."

In conclusion, people resist change because they have had past experiences that have not been positive, fear an economic decrease or workload increase, and most of all are afraid of all the chaos that can accompany a change. The primary argument given by most persons against change goes something like this: "It will cause confusion, more work, and a lot of chaos, so why should we change?" The majority of the workforce is generally reluctant to accept a change unless it is a clearly desirable change for the majority of the personnel. How then do we get a change or new idea successfully diffused throughout a system?

Everett Rogers, along with a number of co-authors, has published several in-depth, comprehensive reviews of research and theory related to the diffusion of innovations in societies and organizations. This chapter draws heavily on the Rogers influence; it reviews the types of persons involved in the change process and their impact on diffusion and change.

Before we review the types of persons involved in the diffusion process, we need to define what we mean by an innovation or change. We use the definition posited by Rogers (1995): "An innovation is an idea, practice, or object that is perceived as new by an individual or other unit of adoption. It matters little, so far as human behavior is concerned, whether or not an idea is 'objectively' new as measured by the lapse of time since its first use or discovery. . . . If the idea seems new to the individual, it is an innovation" (p. 11). We use the words *innovation* and *change* interchangeably. Rogers suggests that he does "not find it fruitful to make much of the distinction. The communication patterns for change and innovation in organizations are rather similar" (Rogers & Agarwala-Rogers, 1976, p. 153).

Regardless of the innovation being anticipated, persons within both the formal and the informal communication networks must support the change. It is clear to most that if they are going to introduce a change and want a chance for success, their immediate manager (a person who is clearly part of the organization's formal structure) must support the change. The persons in the informal network (those not clearly found on the organization's hierarchical chart but may have the potential to be influential) are an integral and necessary component of any successful change process. The next section reviews roles of people in the informal network who might influence the success of an innovation's diffusion.

INFORMAL COMMUNICATION NETWORK ROLES

All of the roles discussed are representations of individual communication roles that various employees might hold in the informal communication network system in an organization. Each role affects the diffusion of a new idea in some manner. The influence of each role on change is discussed.

A *bridge* is "an individual who links two or more cliques in a system from his or her position as a member of one of the cliques" (Rogers, 1995, p. 297). In other words, this is an individual who belongs to one primary group but communicates with other groups or individuals from his or her position as a member of a primary group (see Figure 13.1). This person has strong ties with the primary group and can at the same time communicate with a number of other groups or persons. This person is highly interconnected within the system because of his or her connections with one primary group and willingness to communicate with other groups and persons. For example, a teacher might belong to the Washington Elementary

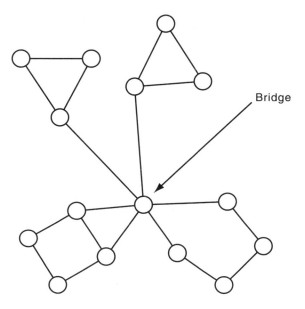

Bridge

FIGURE 13.1   Bridge

School group as his or her primary group but have strong ties with other people in other schools in the district.

Bridges are important persons in the change process because of their communication connections and influence in the primary group and with other groups and persons. The bridge has a close-knit relationship with his or her primary group and yet can establish strong communication links with other groups. Hence, in the process of change, the bridge has the potential to be highly influential. He or she is influential not only within the primary group, but also with others. This is an individual who should be sought out to assist with introducing a change or diffusion of an innovation. If a bridge can be influenced to accept a change, then he or she might persuade the primary group and possibly influence other groups in a positive manner about the change.

A *liaison* "is defined as an individual who links two or more cliques in a system, but who is not a member of any clique" (Rogers, 1995, p. 111). In other words, this is an individual who does not have a primary-group connection but links other groups or individuals (see Figure 13.2). This person is sometimes called a "linker" or "linking pin" within organizations. "Thus liaisons are positioned at the crossroads of information flows in an organization. Liaisons have been called the 'cement' that holds the structural 'brick' of an organization together; when the liaisons are removed, the system tends to fall into isolated cliques" (Rogers & Agarwala-Rogers, 1976, p. 135).

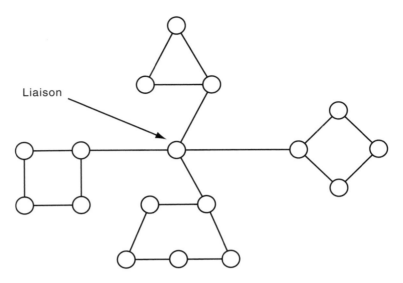

Liaison

FIGURE 13.2   Liaison

Liaisons are crucial persons in the change process because of their communication connections with many groups or persons. For example, substitute teachers might be liaisons in a school system. They really have no primary-group connection but have communication links with many groups and persons because they may work in one school one day and a completely different one the next day. They are in the "crossroads of information" or mainstream of information and could influence people to accept or reject a change. They know what is going on in a number of different systems and can be influential in a change process because of their communication links.

A *gatekeeper* is "an individual who is located in a communication structure so as to control the messages flowing through a communication channel" (Rogers & Agarwala-Rogers, 1976, p. 133). More recently, Rogers (1995) described the gatekeeping role as the "communication behavior of an individual or individuals who withhold or reshape information that they control as it flows into their system" (p. 354). In other words, the gatekeeper is a person who is in a position to screen or filter information as it flows through a network (see Figure 13.3).

As with the bridge and liaison, gatekeepers can be critical in the change process because of their role which allows them to have control over information and screening of information. For example, a secretary might be in a gatekeeping role. He or she has the opportunity by function of his or her role to monitor and have access to much information that flows through the organization. In fact, some organizations have recognized the important role a secretary plays, beyond his or her formal assignments, and spend

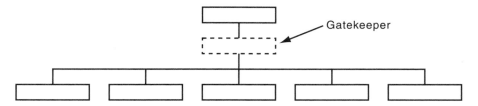

FIGURE 13.3   Gatekeeper

much money and effort training secretaries on how to screen information. A good gatekeeper is irreplaceable.

The gatekeeping function has the potential to be influential in the change process because gatekeepers can decide what information to pass on and what information to "sit on." For example, employees who cross a secretary may not get their messages when needed, their phone calls may be placed a little late, and their supervisor might receive negative information about them. Hence, people should value a person in a gatekeeping role and understand the impact this person can have on communication and change in the organization.

Another critical role in the diffusion of change process is the *opinion leader*. This person provides information or advice about innovations to others in the system. "Opinion leadership is the degree to which an individual is able to influence other individuals' attitudes or overt behavior informally in a desired way with relative frequency. It is a type of informal leadership, rather than a function of the individual's formal position or status in the system" (Rogers, 1995, p. 27). Opinion leadership is earned and maintained by competence, accessibility, compatibility with others (followers), similarity with others, and a willingness to communicate about new ideas and change (see Figure 13.4).

Opinion leaders are usually quite innovative and may be perceived to be of slightly higher social status than some of the other employees. Of course, the other employees (those who follow the opinion leader's advice) give them the higher social status.

Opinion leaders can be quite influential in the change process. Because of their influence over others in the system, they can support a proposed change or reject it. Their support or rejection can often influence others to accept or reject. Because they generally conform to the system's norms, opinion leaders are also privy to more information and have more exposure to communication channels about any changes. Any intelligent manager or employee will try to locate the "person others go to for information or advice on issues at hand" and get their opinions and support before they propose a change to others. If opinion leaders are willing to support a change, the likelihood of success is quite high.

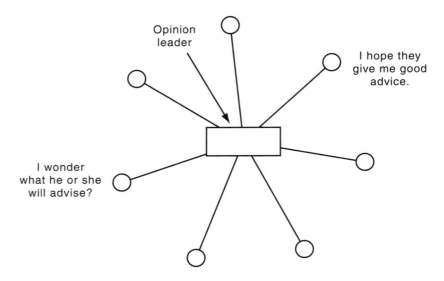

FIGURE 13.4 **Opinion leader**

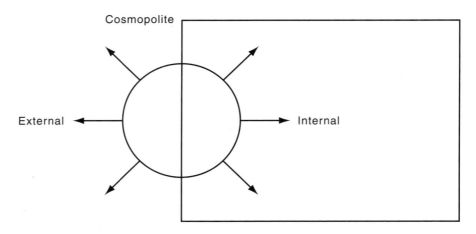

FIGURE 13.5 **Cosmopolite**

A *cosmopolite* is "an individual who has a relatively high degree of communication with the system's environment" (Rogers & Agarwala-Rogers, 1976, p. 133). These people are similar to gatekeepers in that "they control the communication flows by which new ideas enter the system" (p. 140) (see Figure 13.5). The cosmopolites are usually well-versed, well-traveled persons who have affiliations with national and international groups or organizations, and are in a professional occupation that has a

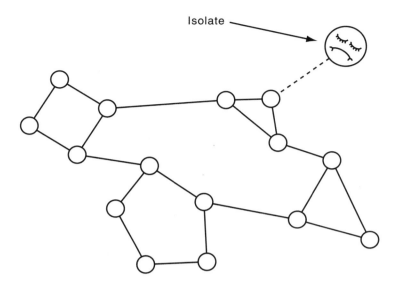

FIGURE 13.6   Isolate

high migration rate, such as a college professor, salesperson, public relations person, or minister.

These people are a great resource to most systems and have the potential to be influential in terms of change. They usually are well versed in areas that relate to new ideas coming into their field and have the ability to predict needed future changes in their units. Because of their expansive contacts outside their own unit or organization, these people provide openness to the system and can assist the system with needed changes.

An *isolate* is "an individual who has few communication contacts with the rest of the system" (Rogers & Agarwala-Rogers, 1976, p. 130). This person theoretically has no communication connections, but we all know that isolates talk to at least one other person occasionally (see Figure 13.6). In addition to one isolated individual, there can be isolated dyads or groups. People can become isolates for a number of reasons: They do not like their colleagues or are disliked by the colleagues; their position in the organization isolates them; they may be shy and prefer to be left alone by others; they may have body odor; they will not conform to the system's norms; they are getting ready to leave the system and isolate themselves (are "short-timing it"); or all their colleagues have left.

It is obvious that isolates would have little influence in the change process. Since they have few, if any, communication connections with others in the system, they would not be good persons to select to assist with a change. Some isolates stay so "isolated" that others rarely see them, much less speak with them. For example, the researcher who is assigned to work in the "annex" separated from the main building might be so isolated it is difficult to establish communication with colleagues. In scientific organizations, the lab technicians or scientists sometimes are so isolated in their labs that hardly anyone in the organization knows them. In business organizations, people not in the central headquarters are considered "out in the boonies" by those in the headquarters. Hence, out of all the persons we have discussed, these are the least influential. In fact, they may not even know a change is taking place until it has taken place.

Last, we have established another group of persons we think might have the potential to be influential in the organizational change process. We call these people the *"old boys and old girls."* These persons are individuals who have been in the system longer than the rest, have communication connections throughout the system, and know who is really talking to whom and about what. These persons know where all the skeletons are buried, and they probably buried a few themselves!

These people can be highly influential because they know the system's informal communication network better than others, because they have been in the system longer than others. This is not to suggest they are "old" in the sense of chronological age (although they could be). They are simply those who have been in a system longer than others, and they usually know the communication networks better. These people can be highly influential in assisting with a change or highly influential in stopping a change. It depends on how they are treated by others. Sometimes the old boys and girls can be good or they can be bad. If you "step on their toes" they will not assist with your change; they will quietly but surely try to destroy it. They do not even have to do anything in a direct fashion. For example, you want to make a change, but ignore the old girl's suggestions; the supervisor asks the old girl one day while they are at lunch what she thinks of your change. Her reply is something like this; "Well, I'd wait awhile and see how things work out. After all, this employee is awfully young and new. Has some good ideas, but they need some seasoning." Then you wonder why your supervisor gives a resounding *No* to your idea.

In conclusion, the individual communication roles we have discussed all exist in organizations. They all have some impact on the change process. It is important that these persons be respected and utilized when making any changes or the idea might not be accepted by the system. Most of the roles we've mentioned have the potential to be influential (except the isolate) in the change process. The question is, Do you want them on your side or against you?

The next section reviews how a person's willingness to change impacts the innovation and change process. All people do not adopt innovations at the same time—they will adopt in a "time sequence," and often they are classified into adopter categories by their willingness to adopt a new idea. Next we review the adopter categories and discuss why each is relevant to the change process.

INNOVATIVENESS: THE WILLINGNESS TO ADOPT

It is obvious to all of us that when a new idea is introduced into a system, some members of the system are more willing to adopt than others. Some persons simply have a higher level of *innovativeness* than others. Innovativeness is "the degree to which an individual or other unit of adoption is relatively earlier in adopting new ideas than other members of a system" (Rogers, 1995, p. 242). It is of practical importance that a person thinking of introducing a change (a potential change agent) know how to identify potential adopters versus those who are not likely to adopt willingly (see Figure 13.7).

Innovators can be described by one word—"venturesome." It is almost an obsession with innovators. "They are very eager to try new ideas. This interest leads them out of a local circle of peer networks and into more cosmopolite social relationships" (Rogers, 1995, p. 248). This person is usually willing to gamble, and even occasionally take a setback in finances, in the hopes that he or she will make it up elsewhere. He or she is usually rash, daring, and a risk taker. Such a person is also able to deal with a high degree of uncertainty and ambiguity.

Most of us are not innovators. In a normal population only about 5 people in 200 (2.5 percent of the population) are innovators. Although they may be small in number and not fit into the local peer networks, they are definitely desirable in the diffusion process. They are willing to take risks and "launch" new ideas into the system. They understand that others may not want to take the risk, so they will take the risk of being the first to adopt a new idea. The biggest drawback to being an innovator is that

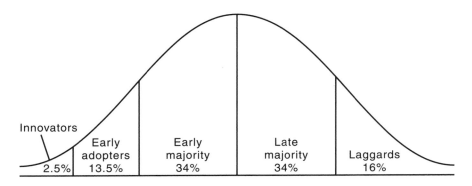

FIGURE 13.7   Adopter Categories

innovators cannot communicate informally with their peers as easily as people in some other adopter categories.

Early adopters also can be described by one word—"respectable." These people are more integrated into the system and usually can communicate on a similar level with others. Whereas innovators are in the cosmopolite communication network, early adopters are in the localite communication network. "This adopter category, more than any other, has the greatest degree of opinion leadership in most social systems. Potential adopters look to early adopters for advice and information" (Rogers, 1995, p. 249). These are the people known in the system as the "individual to check with" before using a new idea.

Some of us may be early adopters. Approximately 13.5 percent of the population fall into this category. Early adopters are respected and held in high esteem by others in the system. They often are able to take the innovators' ideas and help diffuse them successfully into a system because others respect them and are willing to listen to their advice. They help decrease uncertainty about the respectability of the innovation.

The *early majority* are usually referred to as "deliberate." These people "adopt new ideas just before the average member of a social system. The early majority interact frequently with their peers, but seldom hold leadership positions" (Rogers, 1995, p. 249). They are unique in that they are between the very early to accept a new idea and those late to adopt a new idea. They provide "interconnectedness" in the system.

Approximately 34 percent of the population are in the early majority. They are "deliberate" and think about the innovation for quite awhile before adopting. They usually adopt with "deliberate willingness" but rarely lead the way. Their motto, as Alexander Pope put it, is "Be not the first by which the new is tried, nor the last to lay the old aside."

The *late majority* can be described best as "skeptical." These people "adopt new ideas just after the average member of a social system." They usually adopt because of increasing peer pressure or because of economic necessity. For example, some people would not give up their typewriters in favor of word processors until most of their colleagues were using them, or until they found they could not get their typewriter fixed any more. These people approach all innovations with an air of caution and skepticism.

Approximately 34 percent of the population are in the late majority, just as there were in the early majority. They will wait until most of the system has adopted before they adopt. They want to see that the innovation works and have most of the uncertainty about the innovation removed before they adopt.

Finally, we have the *laggards*. They are the "traditional" people in the society. They are the last in the system to adopt and "the most localite in their outlook of all adopter categories; many are near-isolates . . . and the point of reference for the laggard is the past. They possess almost no opinion leadership" (Rogers, 1995, p. 250). Whereas the late majority may be skeptical, the laggards are truly *suspicious* of any new idea. They rarely will interact with cosmopolites; they prefer to interact with localites with traditional views such as their own. When they do adopt something, it is no longer an innovation to most people in the society. It may even have already been superseded by another, newer idea. For example, laggards might adopt typewriters (rather than cursive) when almost everyone else has moved to word processors.

Approximately 16 percent of the population are in the laggard category. These people will slow down the change process when they can, and often do not understand why others adopted. This is not to suggest that laggards are bad people. They are not—they are simply not change-oriented. Most people in the society recognize that change is not always good, but these people go a step farther. They think change is never, or almost never, good. Sometimes it turns out that they are right, but it can be a problem if laggards dominate a system. Some systems are so laggardly that they eventually "put themselves out of business" by not being willing to change when change is needed.

In conclusion, the rate at which persons adopt innovations can influence how quickly a change is diffused throughout an organization. The categories mentioned demonstrate the various categories of potential adopters. Anyone attempting any change in any organization must be aware of the above. He or she needs to know that all are present in organizations and that some stimulate change and others impede change. In addition, employees also need to know what type of a system they work in—is it change-oriented or not? For example, if a highly innovative person is working in a laggardly system, he or she might be completely dissatisfied and need to move. If a laggardly person is working in a highly innovative system, then he or she might be completely dissatisfied and need to move. Change will be successful only if the persons who can promote the change are persuaded that it is a needed change.

INTRODUCING CHANGE

What elements influence others to "buy into" an idea or a product? Researchers and practitioners ask that question each time they want to "sell" an idea or a product (an innovation). There are three factors that usually come into consideration.

First, the product should have some intuitive appeal to the consumer. For instance, new and improved hand calculators had instant appeal to almost all users. It just seemed like a good idea to have something you could put into your pocket that would perform all the mathematical operations a normal person would have any need for. Second, the product or idea must be attainable and affordable. For example, most of us can afford $10 (or less) for a pocket calculator. However, most of us could not afford a Ferrari, no matter how good an idea it might be. Third, the idea or product must give the results it promises. For example, if a company buys a campaign to sell a product, sales are expected. If we buy the calculator, we expect it will compute accurately.

Even if the proposed innovation meets these three initial tests, that does not necessarily mean it will be accepted. The process of decision making with regard to accepting something new involves five stages. At any point in this process, even the best innovation can wind up being rejected.

Stages of the Adoption Process

The adoption process involves stages one goes through from the point at which you first gain basic knowledge of an innovation to the point where you know you are going to maintain the innovation into the future. This process can be followed by individuals or by entire organizations when deciding whether to accept or reject a new idea. Various persons within the system may go through the process at different rates, and some persons may even skip a stage in the process. Regardless of the rate at which an organization or individual goes through the adoption process, the fact remains that all persons eventually go through some type of decision-making process when evaluating a new idea, reducing uncertainty about the new idea, and making a decision about the acceptance or rejection of the new idea.

The first phase of the process, the *knowledge stage,* involves obtaining basic exposure to the innovation's existence and some understanding of how it functions. (For a depiction of the stages, see Figure 13.8.) This initial stage is when someone in the organization (a manager or an employee) becomes aware of or gains interest in a new idea that might help the organization. Or there might be a need in the organization to create or find an innovation to satisfy the need. Regardless of how the innovation is developed, whether it be by people outside the organization or by people within the organization, persons must first have some knowledge or interest or awareness of the innovation in order to consider adoption. In the knowledge stage, the organization or individual usually learns about the innovation ei-

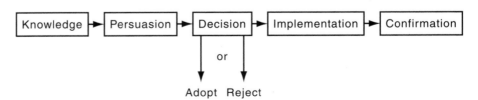

FIGURE 13.8   **Five Stages in Innovation-Decision Process**

ther through mass media channels or from other individuals. For example, in this country much of our information is generated through some form of the media (television, radio, newspapers, computer bulletin boards, and so on). Hence, the initial awareness can come from seeing something on television or reading about a new idea in some printed material. For example, many people see or learn about a new car that they might like to purchase from some media ad. Let's say we heard about the 500LX we might want; now what do we do?

Now that we have an interest in or awareness of a new idea, we must start investigating whether the new product is compatible with our needs. We must also remember that simply being aware of an innovation is quite different from actually adopting and using the idea. This leads us to the next stage.

The *persuasion stage* involves forming a favorable or unfavorable attitude toward the innovation. In the knowledge stage, the thinking was more on a cognitive level. The main type of thinking at the persuasion stage is on the affective or feeling level. We begin to develop a positive or negative feeling toward the new idea. We investigate the innovation more thoroughly by actively seeking information about the new idea, by talking with persons whom we respect who have tried the new idea, and by asking ourselves a series of questions about the new idea. We will often ask, "What are the advantages and disadvantages of this new idea? How will this help me in my work? Will this be harmful to my work? Will I be pleased with this idea? How will my boss react to this idea?" What we really are doing is mentally applying the new idea to our situation and determining whether it is something we should try. We are evaluating the potential effects of the idea without really being able to use the idea on a permanent basis and see the real effects. For example, with the 500LX we think we might want, we might talk to friends who have a 500LX and get their opinions about the car at this point. We would think about potential problems or benefits, and we probably would form some feeling for the car.

The *decision stage* involves choosing to adopt or reject the innovation. In this stage we have two choices: adopt or reject. If we adopt, we are accepting the innovation. If we reject, we are refusing the innovation. Much of our decision to adopt or reject is influenced by peers who either volunteer advice on the new idea or respond to our request for information about the new idea. At this stage peer influence is quite high and usually plays a significant role. If people we respect and like have accepted the idea, then we are more likely to accept the idea. For example, the 500LX we want is being driven by two close, respected friends and they spoke favorably about the car in the persuasion stage. When we get to the decision stage we might be influenced to buy the car. Some friends of the authors of this text bought their teenage son a red car as a surprise. Someone asked them why a "red car"? They replied, "All his friends drive red cars and we doubt he'd like any other color." They were right. All of his friends drove red cars and he wanted a red car. Any other color would not have made the car as appealing. Hence, the parents were influenced by their son's friends, knowing that he liked what his friends had and would want a similar car that was red.

The *implementation stage* involves putting an innovation into use. Until this stage, the decision-making process has been "strictly a mental process." But this stage involves actual behavior. This stage will usually present more problems for an organization than for an individual. After all, an organization is a collection of individuals, all of whom may or may not want to implement the new idea. This is why change sometimes can be very slow. Trying to get an entire organization to implement a change can take years. Much time has to be spent in the persuasion stage giving personnel favorable attitudes about the new ideas, and then much time has to be spent polling personnel to determine how many will actually adopt the new idea. Both of these stages must be completed before successful implementation can take place.

If a change is forced on personnel, they probably will find a way to sabotage it. Hence, in order for implementation to go smoothly, the other stages must be completed. In addition, in this stage there may have to be some redesigning, modifying, or reinventing of the new idea to make it more compatible with the personnel and the overall organizational structure. For example, not every innovation can be adapted to every organization without some minor modification. When you buy clothes, even though you wear a certain size, some clothing may require slight modification so it fits more comfortably. The same is true with innovations. The implementation stage can take a long time depending on the innovation being introduced and the number of people who have to implement the change.

Now back to our car. Here we actually buy the car and drive it off the lot. It is ours and we must begin making payments. But the process still is not over.

The final stage, the *confirmation stage,* involves seeking reinforcement for our decision. We may still reverse the decision if exposed to conflicting information, such as if the car does not run. In some cases dropping an innovation can be easy and inexpensive. In the case of our car, it could cost us a lot of money to return it to the dealer and say we no longer want it. But it still could be done. In an organization, if we spent years implementing a change and then decided we no longer want the change, it still could be reversed, but it could cost us our job and our reputation.

However, rather than discontinuing the innovation after having previously adopted it, we usually seek out information that helps reduce our uncertainty or "dissonance" about whether or not we made a good decision. It is not uncommon for new car owners to notice ads about the efficiency and durability of their new car and disregard ads or communication with others to the contrary. When an individual feels uncomfortable about a change, he or she usually will seek information that supports or confirms that the decision to adopt and implement an innovation was good. It usually is less difficult to resolve this feeling of dissonance or discomfort than it is to change one's previous decision and have to admit to making a bad decision.

In conclusion, the stages an individual or an organization go through when deciding whether to accept or reject an innovation are critical to the successful implementation of a change. Although some stages may receive less time than others (because some people need little persuasion on some ideas), it is clear that people go through stages and these stages can affect an organization for years to come if a change is accepted that should have been rejected. Hence, it is always wise to thoroughly investigate any potential change for problems and review the possible consequences of the change. Although we know that people go through the various stages at various times and paces, we need to know what attributes or characteristics of an innovation might prompt one to consider adopting an innovation.

Characteristics or Attributes of Innovations

Some innovations (such as the pocket calculator) diffuse rapidly throughout systems, whereas others linger or even die. What factors impact the eventual success of an innovation in an organization? Rogers (1995) has suggested five characteristics of innovations that are mutually exclusive and universally relevant. The five attributes are relative advantage, compatibility, complexity, trialability, and observability. These characteristics either must be present in the innovation or must be explained so that the potential adopter will be likely to adopt.

Relative advantage "is the degree to which an innovation is perceived as being better than the idea it supersedes" (Rogers, 1995, p. 213). The innovation must be better than what already exists in the system. The first question any potential adopter should ask about a new idea is, "Why is this idea or product better than what already exists?" In other words, one must be prepared to demonstrate the advantages of adopting the new idea over the current existing idea or thing. Relative advantage is often shown in either economic profitability or some increase in status for the individual. In 1974 one of the authors of this book purchased a moderate-size calculator with a square root function for $175. Now a smaller, better version of the calculator sells for approximately $15. Nevertheless, it was difficult for the author to accept that something so cheap was really better than something she had spent so much money to purchase.

When attempting to get someone to "buy into an idea or thing," the innovation's advantages must be better than what already exists in the system. For example, if an organization wanted to restructure itself and become more streamlined, there must be many advantages to restructuring that outweigh the current structure. The relative advantages of an innovation are positively related to the number of people wanting to adopt and the rate of adoption. The relative advantages must outweigh what exists, or the idea might fail.

Compatibility "is the degree to which an innovation is perceived as consistent with the existing values, past experiences, and needs of potential adopters" (Rogers, p. 223). Ideas that are perceived by organizational members to be compatible with the values, beliefs, attitudes, and norms are much more likely to be accepted than ideas that are in extreme opposition to the values, beliefs, attitudes, and norms of the members. It is easier to accept a proposed change when it can be "fitted into" the system. Innovations need to be named and positioned so that they seem compatible with the system's norms. Years ago an American car manufacturer tried to sell the Nova in a Latin American country with little success. The primary reason for the failure was that Nova could be roughly translated as "no go" in the language of that country. Most people were not really interested in buying a car that was named the "no go" car.

Potential users of the new idea want to know that the new idea is compatible with their way of life or work. Most of us are not willing to try change anyway, so in order for a change to have a chance to be successful, it must be compatible with existing norms. The perceived compatibility of an innovation is positively related to the number of people wanting to adopt and the rate of adoption.

Complexity "is the degree to which an innovation is perceived as relatively difficult to understand and use" (Rogers, p. 230). Potential users usually place innovations on a continuum from complexity to simplicity. The more complex an innovation is perceived to be, the smaller the number of people wanting to adopt and the slower the rate of adoption. In other words, complexity is negatively related to rate of adoption. People in organizations are hesitant to adopt because it might cause chaos, loss of status, and so on. Hence, if an innovation is introduced that seems complex, then people will simply reject it out of hand.

Employees will often ask, "Why is this so complex?" Employees want to adopt ideas that are presented in a simple, easy-to-understand manner. We want to adopt things or ideas that seem to be "user friendly." A rule of thumb is the KISS motto (Keep It Simple, Stupid!) when introducing a new idea. Even though you may be well versed in terms of the innovation, keep it simple for the rest of the people in the organization or they will simply turn a deaf ear when you try selling your idea.

Trialability "is the degree to which an innovation may be experimented with on a limited basis" (Rogers, 1995, p. 231). Although not all innovations can be tried on a full-scale basis, if there is a way of trying the innovation on a small-scale basis, this will increase the likelihood for adoption. People like to try out new ideas or things. For example, Apple has been successful in getting public schools in many areas to buy its whole computer line by initially giving the school a free Apple for trial. People tried it, determined they liked it, and bought more. As we said earlier, clearly not all innovations can be tried, but you can show others where the innovation has been tried and show the results, or perhaps you can try the innovation in your unit and show others the results. Trialability is positively related to the number of people wanting to use the innovation and the rate of adoption.

Observability "is the degree to which the results of an innovation are visible to others" (Rogers, p. 232). Some results are easy to observe; others are more difficult to observe. Some results take a longer time to observe; others take a shorter time to observe. In any case, you need to design a way in which others can see the positive results of your idea or innovation or they can see your suggestion working in another organization. If people can see things working, they are more likely to buy into them. Observability is positively related to the number of people wanting to use the innovation and the rate of adoption.

In conclusion, the number of people adopting and the rate of adoption or "relative speed with which an innovation is adopted" (Rogers, p. 132) are affected significantly by the introduction and explanation of the characteristics of any innovation. If employees see advantages, feel the innovation is compatible with norms, think it is easy to handle, and can try it or at least see it being tried and observe positive results, then an innovation has a high likelihood of adoption and continued use. The reason change fails in most organizations is that people fail to consider the stages in the adoption process and the attributes of the innovation. Failure is practically guaranteed. Another reason is that they usually present the change in such a complicated, highly complex manner that most people immediately are turned off to the idea. Remember, most people in organizations do not have a high willingness to change; hence, we must use all the communication strategies available to us when attempting to institute a change. Communicating the five basic attributes is a step that will increase the likelihood that change will be accepted, not rejected.

On the other hand, if you want to stop a change that is being diffused in your organization, simply make it seem complex, show there are few relative advantages, show it is not compatible, and demonstrate that it does not work well—and the change probably will be a failure. In conclusion, you can center your communication on the attributes of an innovation to increase change or to inhibit change.

SIX CONDITIONS NECESSARY FOR SUCCESSFUL CHANGE

There are six conditions that must be met for a change to be successfully diffused throughout an organization. If any one of the conditions is not met, the change probably will be a failure. Let us examine each of these.

1. *The system must have, or create, slack resources.* Resources are things such as finances, personnel, time, or space. "Slack" resources are those resources that are available but not allocated, or ones that can be reallocated easily. If you want to start a business, you must provide all of these resources. If any one of them is unavailable, you might not be able to start your business. For any change, some type of slack resources are usually needed. Hence, when introducing a change in your organization, you must have planned for any necessary slack resources. If your change requires more personnel, where will these people come from? What can be given up to make people available? If your change requires more financial assistance, where will the money come from? What can we stop doing so as to free up the needed money? Your supervisor will not be responsive to ideas that have not anticipated where the slack resources are that might be needed. The world is full of good ideas, but it is short on resources to make those good ideas realities. If you cannot figure out how to pay for it, your idea has little chance for adoption.

2. *The new idea must be supported by both the formal and the informal leaders in the organization.* Again, we can see why this might inhibit the change process. If either your supervisor (formal leader) or an informal leader (opinion leader, old boy or girl, and so on) opposes the new idea, it might not be accepted into the system. The formal leaders can simply say, "No, it's not beneficial to the system at this time or viable at this time." The informal leaders will use the informal communication network to sabotage the new idea. Thus, for a new idea to have a chance at success, it must have the support of both groups of leaders, and this can be accomplished only through communication. If you try to implement without the support of these people, failure is virtually assured.

3. *Persons implementing the change should be involved in the change process.* This does not mean that every person who will be using the change must be involved, but it does mean that key personnel—such as opinion leaders, bridges, liaisons, old boys and girls, and so on—should be involved or at least made aware of the change in order for it to have a chance to succeed. Organizations can always use the forced-compliance model of change, which says "You will adopt whether you like it or not," but we know that model is only successful as long as scrutiny is present. Hence, the model that involves people who might diffuse the change is much more successful. If you want people to implement the change without hovering over them to ensure compliance, it is necessary that they be involved in the decision to make the change. Remember, people tend not to like change in the first place. They like it even less if it is "sprung" on them.

4. *The change must be adapted to each specific organization.* Do not assume that if a change worked at IBM it will work at GM. What works in one system may or may not be compatible with another system. Personnel differ, norms differ, and values, attitudes, and beliefs differ. Hence, a change that is successful in one organization may be a total failure in another. Each change must be made compatible with each specific organization. Perhaps portions of a change can be transported from one organization to another with some things being redesigned to fit the second organization. Sometimes major problems occur unexpectedly. Hence, if implementation hits a snag, time must be taken to work out adaptations or the innovation is almost certain to fail.

5. *The change must show obvious, positive results soon.* This seems to be a fact of human nature for Americans. If we cannot see our positive results immediately, we want to discard the new idea or thing. In a world that is constantly changing, we want results fast. Hence, when introducing a change we should let personnel know when to look for results and what to look for. In fact, we should even plan small successes for them to experience in the change process. For example, if we are trying new word processors, we should take people step-by-step through a learner's manual and make sure each phase works. This will ensure that employees have a success experience while using the system. Many, many changes fail because positive results are not demonstrated soon enough for the majority. We should tell people what the results will be and when to look for them, and assist them in seeing the positive results.

6. *The change must be implemented in a carefully organized and gradual manner.* Changes that are unpredictable, disorganized, disorderly, and quick tend to be rejected because people feel they had no input into the change and because it creates chaos. Quick, massive change should be avoided unless it is an absolute necessity. Through the use of interpersonal communication channels, sources (managers) can get information from receivers (employees) about what changes are needed in a system and how to go about making the needed changes. This is the appropriate way to pursue change, and it also involves the people who will be implementing the change. When people who will implement the change are involved in the process, they will be more committed to the change. Once the information concerning the change is gathered, the process can be implemented gradually and carefully so that all will have an opportunity to adapt to the change and make it work.

In conclusion, change can be enjoyable, profitable, and manageable. By understanding the stages a person goes through when deciding whether to accept or reject a change, one can see the time a change might take. Managers and employees alike can effect positive change if they communicate the five basic attributes of an innovation to others, and meet the six conditions listed above. There is no reason for change to be a feared concept in organizations. The primary reason changes fail is that someone failed to plan and communicate the plan in an appropriate manner.

REFERENCES AND RECOMMENDED READINGS

Richmond, V. P., (1999). Communication, people, and change. In G. Stone, Singletary, M., & Richmond, V. P. (1999). (pp. 132–139). *Clarifying communication theories: A hands-on approach*. Ames, IA: Iowa State University Press.

Rogers, E. M. (1995). *Diffusion of innovations*. (4th ed.). New York: The Free Press.

Rogers, E. M., & Agarwala-Rogers, R. (1976). *Communication in organizations*. New York: The Free Press.

STUDY GUIDE

1. What are some of the reasons people oppose change?
2. Define *innovation*. Give three examples of innovations you have experienced.
3. Explain how we might recognize each of the following types of people in informal communication networks, and indicate their function in the diffusion process:
   a. Bridge
   b. Liaison
   c. Gatekeeper
   d. Opinion leader
   e. Cosmopolite
   f. Isolate
   g. Old boys/girls
4. Identify the five adopter categories and indicate how people in each category are likely to communicate about change.
5. Identify the stages of the adoption process and indicate the type of communication that occurs during each stage.
6. Identify and explain the characteristics or attributes an innovation must have to be adopted by most people. Why is this information important to understanding communication in organizations?
7. What are the conditions necessary for a change to be successful in an organization? Why is this information important to understanding communication in organizations?

■ ■ ■ ■ ■

CHAPTER 14

DISAGREEMENT, CONFLICT, AND GROUPTHINK

To agree or not to agree, that is the question. Many managers spend more time helping employees deal with problems between themselves and other employees, or supervisors, than on any other task. An effective supervisor knows that problems left unsolved or disagreements that get out of control can lead to severe interpersonal conflict. Let us look at the following meeting about a new proposal for the reorganization of a unit. We have Mike, Vickie, John, Larry, and the manager, Lee.

Mike: (To the group) Well, I have seniority and I think since we have to reorganize, the persons with seniority should call the shots. After all, we're the ones with experience and know-how. We don't want some kid who's still wet behind the ears running the place.

John: (To Mike) Well, I don't have seniority and frankly I don't want you calling the shots for me. You've been around too long. (To the group) I may still be a kid who's wet behind the ears, but at least I'm a breathing, functioning person.

Mike: (To the group) That's the kind of infantile crap we don't need in this organization. (To John) Is that what they taught you in that fancy MBA school?

Vickie: (To the group) Let's keep personal feelings out of this and behave like adults. We have a job to do.

Larry: (To Vickie) Now, now, Vickie. (To the group) Isn't that just like something you would expect a woman to say? (To Vickie) Always trying to be the little peacemaker, aren't we?

Vickie: (To Larry) Well, at least I work. What would you do if you had a real job?

At this point, Lee intervenes and suggests that perhaps a meeting is not the best way of determining the reorganization. She says she will ask each person for his or her advice and then submit a proposal based on that advice to another, more objective committee. The group agrees this is the best solution, since they obviously will not be able to come to any agreement because of their feelings.

Clearly, situations like this should be avoided. They usually lead to feelings of discomfort and dislike on the part of the participants. However, as long as we are in contact with other human beings, there always will be potential conflict situations. Even though the occurrence of conflict in interpersonal relationships is inevitable, the frequency with which it occurs and the severity of the conflict can be reduced by effective communicators. Although we cannot reasonably expect to eliminate conflict from our interpersonal communication with our colleagues, we can learn to manage it and keep it under control. To understand the nature of conflict, one needs to distinguish between "conflict" and "disagreement."

DISAGREEMENT AND CONFLICT

Disagreement is a difference of opinion between persons. It usually is seen as functional or positive within the organizational framework. We can disagree with another and still maintain a good working relationship. We may disagree on facts, on what the facts imply, or on what we might wish to do about those facts. Disagreement is usually classified into two types: substantive and procedural. Substantive disagreements are about the topic or issue at hand. Procedural disagreements are concerned with procedure, how a decision should be reached or how a policy should be implemented. In other words, disagreements usually arise in organizations when certain topics are discussed or certain procedures are discussed. People may disagree—even disagree extremely strongly and loudly—without entering into conflict.

Many researchers and practitioners have suggested that disagreement probably is good for the growth of an organization. When people disagree without moving into conflict, some positive outgrowths can be seen. For example, people can affirm or disconfirm their viewpoints, they can see others' viewpoints, they may see other possible solutions to the problem they had not been aware of before, brainstorming often will occur and many solutions can be generated, we see informal leaders emerging within the group, we find out who the opinion leaders are in certain topic areas, people feel they have had the opportunity to communicate their opinion to others, and an overall higher quality of decision making might emerge as a result of disagreement.

Although disagreement does not necessarily lead to conflict, in any situation where people are disagreeing the potential exists for conflict to raise its ugly head. Disagreement can lead to conflict, but this will occur mainly when the level of affinity between the communicators is not high, such as in the case study given at the beginning of this chapter. Clearly,

Mike, John, Vickie, and Larry did not enter the meeting with high affinity for one another. They immediately started discussing each other's failings, real or imagined.

Conflict has been described by McCroskey and Wheeless (1976): "Conflict between people can be viewed as the opposite or antithesis of affinity. In this sense, interpersonal conflict is the breaking down of attraction and the development of repulsion, the dissolution of perceived homophily (similarity) and the increased perception of incompatible differences, the loss of perceptions of credibility and the development of disrespect" (p. 247). McCroskey & Richmond (1996) suggest that conflict is characterized by hostility, distrust, suspicion, and antagonism. If we really like another person in our work environment and that feeling is reciprocal, the incidence of conflict is greatly reduced, and when it looks as if it might occur, one or both of the participants are likely to realize that the relationship is more important than conflict and move to resolve their disagreement. *Conflict* can be defined as "disagreement plus negative affect" or a "difference of opinion between persons accompanied by feelings of dislike for the other person."

Conflict is the product of communication. What and how we communicate with another in the organizational environment will determine how others react to us. We need to think more before we open our mouths. Once something is said, you cannot take it back and expect people to forget. One might ask, "Why then in marriages can people say some extremely ugly things and still have a relationship?" The answer is simple—the affinity or liking for the other person is higher. In organizations we have liking for others, but it usually is not as high as in marriage. Hence, in marriage we might endure a lot more disagreements and unkind remarks than we would in the organizational environment before we feel we are in true conflict with our spouse. Conflict in the organization may be much like "irreconcilable differences" in a marriage.

It takes only one person, not two, in a relationship to perceive conflict, and if one perceives it, it exists. If one person dislikes another or thinks another dislikes him or her; or that this person does not agree with him or her on issues; or that they have a value difference, he or she eventually will verbally or nonverbally communicate these feelings and the conflict will exist.

It is clear that disagreement can have positive outcomes and should be encouraged in organizations. However, *conflict has no positive outcomes*, and it should be avoided in organizations. Conflict can be likened to an ugly, putrid, decaying, pus-filled sore. If picked at it grows, festers, and finally spreads throughout the organization. Conflict has many negative outcomes: Good working relationships are destroyed, it can escalate to involve many persons (this has happened in companies throughout the United States where management and labor cannot agree and an arbitrator has to be brought in to handle the conflict), and it can permanently damage an organization's reputation and the people in the organization can have their reputations damaged. In addition, it will inhibit open, honest communication between persons.

Whereas disagreements can be resolved and the relationships still be intact, *conflicts cannot be resolved, only managed*. Although disagreement is one of the critical components in conflict, the way a person habitually deals with disagreement has more to do with whether disagreement will lead to conflict than with the simple presence or absence of disagreement itself. People differ in the extent to which they can tolerate disagreement and, thus, avoid entering into conflict.

TOLERANCE FOR DISAGREEMENT

Perhaps you have noticed that some people with whom you interact in your organization tend to become hostile whenever you or anyone else disagrees with anything they say, yet others tend to remain relatively unemotional even when someone takes a view directly counter to theirs. If these persons respond to others in ways similar to the way they respond to you, they are evidencing differing levels of tolerance for disagreement. Tolerance for disagreement is defined as *the amount of disagreement an individual can tolerate before he or she perceives the existence of conflict in a relationship*. A person can have a high tolerance for disagreement (TFD) or a moderate TFD or even a low TFD. A person's general level of TFD represents a general trait, a personality orientation of that individual. However, this trait can be pushed higher or lower in a given situation by other people with whom one interacts. No matter what our level of TFD in general, since we have more affinity for some people than we do for others, we will enter conflict with different levels of provocation from different people.

Figure 14.1 demonstrates an example of a high tolerance for disagreement. A major degree of difference of opinion must be expressed or a substantial increase in negative affect must be present in order for conflict to result. In organizations everyone needs to have a high tolerance for disagreement, but especially managers. A manager is often caught between a rock and a hard place. No matter what he or she does, someone is going to react emotionally. Sometimes employees are put into similar situations. Hence, all of us need to try to develop a higher tolerance for disagreement. Let's face it. Some situations, problems, and issues are worth arguing about, and some are not. Even fewer are worth getting into conflict over.

An example from our experience with some students might illustrate this distinction. When students in our classes want to argue over one or two points on a test or a paper, we usually say, "Wait until the end of the term. If two points is truly keeping you from a higher grade, then come see us." We may have graded the paper right or wrong, but it makes little difference

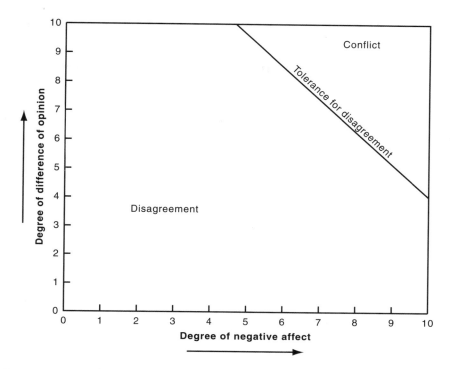

FIGURE 14.1   **High Tolerance for Disagreement**

in most cases. Thus, it makes no sense for either us or our students to argue over one or two points, unless it is absolutely certain that such a small difference will make a real difference. In short, there is no reason to risk conflict when it is of no real consequence who is right and who is wrong. An argument over two points could cost the student and us a relationship that could have enhanced the communication in that class. A compromise that says "You may be right, we may be right, but let's wait until the end of the term" is better than a needless argument that could lead to conflict and a negative outcome for all concerned.

In Figure 14.2 we see a moderate tolerance for disagreement being demonstrated. This figure shows that there is a moderate level of liking for the other person, and a moderate level of disagreement, before people feel as if they are in conflict with one another. Here, the personality of the individual and the situation may greatly affect the tolerance for disagreement level.

In Figure 14.3 we see a low tolerance for disagreement being demonstrated. This figure shows that there is a low level of liking for the other person, and even a modest level of difference of opinion will lead to the

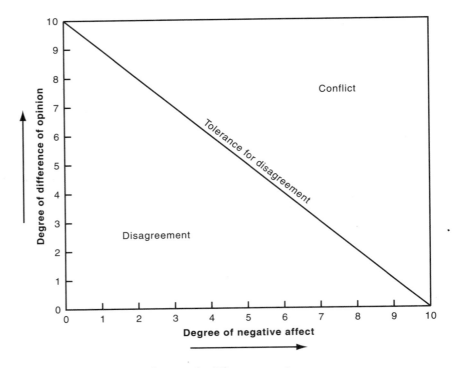

FIGURE 14.2   Moderate Tolerance for Disagreement

perception of conflict. People with this type of personality orientation are likely to be in conflict much of the time. Other people have to be extremely careful in their communication with such people to avoid conflict with them. This becomes doubly difficult because such people tend not to be liked by their peers.

Would you, for example, try to make friends with a person in the work environment you do not like just to avoid conflict? In many communication contexts, people do not feel this is worth the effort; hence, conflict most likely will occur. Because much of our lives is devoted to our organization, we often try to avoid conflict by attempting to be friends with persons we do not care for so that we will not be uncomfortable with them for years to come. But because we really do not like them, they do not have to push us too far before we will give in to the pressure to strike back, and conflict is there.

No matter how well we communicate with another, sometimes the other person will still perceive conflict when we do not. Remember, conflict is experienced by an individual, not by a dyad. It is quite possible for one person in an interaction to perceive a high degree of conflict while at the

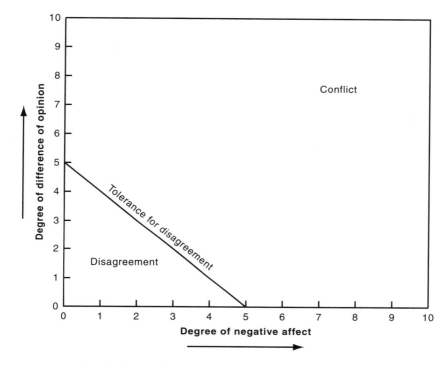

FIGURE 14.3   Low Tolerance for Disagreement

same time the other person experiences no conflict at all. When this occurs, the probability that the other person will also experience conflict later is substantially increased. The person experiencing conflict (person A) is likely to react harshly to the other person, thus reducing affect of person B toward person A. Now person B begins to feel threatened and responds in kind. The more A and B talk, the worse it gets. Conflict feeds on communication. When conflict is present, communication is more likely to increase it than to reduce it. We expand on this point later.

CONFLICT PREVENTION

As noted earlier, conflict is destructive to the organization and should be avoided. Although this is true, it may not always be easy to prevent conflict completely. However, there are some methods for preventing conflict that can be attempted when one feels it arising.

First, if we can communicate similar attitudes about the topic of issue at hand while at the same time expressing some difference of opinion, we may reduce the potential for conflict. If we express our agreements before we express our disagreements, our communication is far less likely to be seen as an attack by the other person. For example, you might say, "I agree with Bob's general suggestions. Clearly he has some good ideas. Based on his ideas, however, we might be able to . . ."

Second, if we have mutual liking or high affect for each other, the differences of opinion that will occur in communication about the topic or procedures will most likely remain at a disagreement level rather than move into conflict. For example, two employees who have mutual respect and liking for each other can express differences of opinion at a vehement level and walk out of the meeting friends. On the other hand, if mutual liking and respect are not present and one has a low tolerance for disagreement, one or the other might leave the meeting feeling that conflict has arisen. But if we like each other it is hard to stay angry with our colleague for long. If we don't like each other to begin with, it may not be hard to dislike him or her. Expression of positive affect, particularly when sincere and previously acknowledged, blunts the potential for disagreements growing into conflict. For example, you might say, "Nancy, you know how much I respect you and your work in this company. I certainly do not mean anything personal by this, but in this instance I think . . ."

Third, if we know there are topics that some of our colleagues find unpleasant or dislike discussing, we might try to avoid bringing these topics into discussions. This does not mean that discussions on these topics will never occur. It means that we should not dwell on things that have the potential to make people angry or make them feel as if they are being "singled out." Follow the old saying, "Never discuss religion and politics" and whatever else might push one into conflict. If someone has a topic that sets him or her off, try to avoid bringing it up in the conversation; if it comes up, try to steer conversation in another direction. After all, ask yourself the question, "Is it worth it to lose a colleague?" Remember, you may have to work with this person for years to come. Who knows, he or she might be your supervisor one day, or you his or hers.

Fourth, do not constantly remind others of their past failures. Particularly do not remind them of their past failures in front of their other colleagues. If you constantly remind people of their failures and embarrass them in front of their colleagues, you cannot expect their feelings to remain positive about you. No one likes to be reminded of past failures. Instead talk about their successes or the progress they have made in the organization. Focus on the positive, not the negative. In other words, in some situations if you "have nothing good to say, don't say anything." Most people do not need reminding of their failures; they remember them well enough without your being there to remind them.

Fifth, when you feel an argument arising, try to stay objective and keep an open mind. Communicate about the common goals and express areas of similarity, such as common attitudes, beliefs, and values. Do not get so involved in the issues that you cannot think objectively about them and never, never start using name calling as a technique to get your point across. Do not make ugly inferences about the person because of his or her gender, race, parentage, and so on. Communication should always be as positive and as reinforcing as possible, not negative. Tactics such as name calling only alienate persons. Of course, if a fight is what you want, that certainly is a good way to get one!

Sixth, some issues are just not worth arguing about to the point that conflict might be created. Pick the issues you want to argue about and pursue them. Do not argue just for the sake of argument. Highly argumentative personality types must be cautious about this behavior. On occasion they will argue for the pure enjoyment of it. Other highly argumentative people will enjoy rising to the occasion. Unfortunately, people with a low argumentativeness orientation do not get the same enjoyment out of an argument. Sometimes it is best just to let your colleague have his or her own way. At worst, you can remind him or her of it later, if you feel you have need to irritate him or her.

Finally, a method of preventing conflict from occurring is to raise your level of tolerance for disagreement. This may be more difficult than some of the other methods of preventing conflict; however, it will allow you to be more accepting of other people's views and reduce the potential for conflict. The "Just say NO" to conflict approach is a good idea, but one that often is hard to follow. On the positive side, it gets much easier with practice.

Clearly, there is no one best method for the avoidance of conflict. However, if you raise your level of tolerance for disagreement, reduce the importance of issues in your communication, and increase the level of affinity between yourself and others in the work environment, then the likelihood that conflict could occur will be decreased. We might have little effect on the basic personalities of our peers, but we can understand the impact of conflict and learn how to prevent it so that we might have a more peaceful work existence.

CONFLICT MANAGEMENT

If we cannot prevent conflict, we have tried and failed, then what do we do? This next section reviews methods for managing conflict. Remember, most conflict cannot be resolved, short of an extended leave from the other person or intervention by a skilled psychologist. It can only be managed. We must remember that even a "leave" from the other person or "intervention" may not resolve conflict. After all, once you truly dislike (perhaps even despise) another person it is very, very difficult—often impossible—to restore positive affect. Hence, you might not work with him or her for

15 years, but see him or her at a meeting and all the feelings will come rushing back. Even before you say a word you realize you still dislike this person and will always be in conflict with him or her. With the assumption that most conflict cannot be resolved, only managed, let us review methods for the management of conflict.

Although we have discussed methods for preventing conflict, in the real world we cannot create a conflict-free existence. We are going to find ourselves in conflict from time to time in spite of our best efforts to avoid it. It is important, then, to understand the options we have when such situations arise.

First, we might try to change the topic of discussion. In some cases we can simply note that the present disagreement cannot be resolved; thus there is no useful purpose served by discussing the topic further. A person skillfully employing this technique will shift the topic of discussion to one that the parties agree on. Because disagreement is no longer being expressed, the level of conflict can drop sharply in a relatively brief period.

Second, we might try halting the communication that is stimulating the conflict. One method of doing this is to leave physically, to break off communication and leave the presence of the other person. Although this approach may not actually reduce the conflict, it will at least make it less immediately relevant and may prevent it from escalating.

Third, we might try to stop communicating (at least verbally) about the topic with the other person. When employing this method, one lets the other person have his or her say but does not respond with a contrary opinion. If you do this, you may continue to disagree privately but not say so. Hence, the communication that would permit the conflict to escalate is not present.

Fourth, we might try to separate persons who are clearly in conflict or not have them work together. This might be a bit difficult to manage and the supervisor may have to initiate this step. If two employees are clearly not in agreement on anything and cannot get along, they should be separated so that conflict does not escalate. Here you are mainly trying to keep a bad situation from getting worse. You do not need each one trying to pull his or her friends into the conflict and expecting them to take sides. If at all possible give them different assignments, different offices, and different duties. Make sure their paths cross as little as possible. Try never to have the one employee evaluating the other one they dislike. Above all, do not try to get them together to resolve their differences. They know their differences and forcing them to discuss them probably will only escalate the situation, and you may become the common enemy.

Fifth, negotiation and compromise with third-party intervention has also been a method used to manage conflict. For example, when management and labor are in conflict, sometimes a third party intervenes and assists them to negotiate and compromise to find acceptable solutions. Obviously, if you must take this step, the conflict is out of control. Communication in this setting functions in three ways: (1) Communication is used to discover what settlements both parties are likely to accept; (2) communication is used to influence or persuade both parties to modify their range of acceptable solutions; and (3) communication is used to provide both parties with rationalizations for acceptance of previously unacceptable positions or solutions. Although this is not the best or the easiest method for managing conflict, it may be one that has to be used when conflict is out of control.

Obviously none of these methods are ideal for managing a conflict situation. However, once you are in conflict, the communication has become of a destructive nature and it is difficult to control communication. Subordinates as well as supervisors want to avoid conflict. But if in conflict, employees must realize they are risking their job and reputation. For example, if an employee decides he or she is dissatisfied with his or her supervisor and wants to have the supervisor removed, then he or she had better prepare for a long, hard battle, one the subordinate most likely will lose. In many cases, the supervisor will manage to get the subordinate removed, not the other way around. Hence, before pushing yourself into conflict with your immediate manager, you might want to consider your chances of winning, the impact on the organization, and the amount of time the conflict will take.

GROUPTHINK: TOO MUCH AGREEMENT
FOR THE GOOD OF THE ORGANIZATION

Conflict is bad. Agreement is good. By agreeing, we can avoid conflict. But can we have too much of a good thing? This section reviews the situation when agreement gets out of control. Although most of us would rather be in a state of agreement than disagreement or conflict, excessive agreement can be detrimental to the functioning and decision making of any organization. The situation where excessive agreement exists has been labeled "groupthink" in the writing of the leading scholar in this area, Irving Janis (1971, 1972, 1982).

Janis has suggested that decisions made at critical periods in our history have been disastrous to the United States (for example, Bay of Pigs, Vietnam, Korea, Pearl Harbor, and the Watergate coverup) because of the desperate striving for consistency and agreement by key decision-making groups. Although the *Challenger* and *Columbia* Shuttle disasters happened after Janis's last book in this area, they too are prime examples of groupthink.

Just what is groupthink? Janis says he uses the term *"groupthink* "as a quick and easy way to refer to the mode of thinking that persons engage in when concurrence-seeking becomes so dominant in a cohesive ingroup that it tends to override realistic appraisal of alternative courses of action" (1971, p. 43). It is when cohesiveness goes beyond rationality, when the tendency to agree interferes with critical thinking. It usually takes place in groups that are highly cohesive and are afraid that any disagreement might lead to rejection by the group. "Groupthink refers to a deterioration of mental efficiency, reality testing, and moral judgment that results from in-group pressures" (Janis, 1982, p. 9). Following are some symptoms of groupthink that might be exhibited by decision-making groups. For groupthink to be present, a group must exhibit a number of the symptoms, not just one.

Illusion of Invulnerability.   Most, if not all, members of the group share an illusion that they are invincible or invulnerable; they cannot lose. They feel that they can take risks with no real chance of loss. They base this on their past experiences where they have taken risks and have not failed. Because of this illusion, they might make rash decisions that could cause great damage to the organization. The longer this illusion persists through increasing numbers of risks, the more risky the ventures of the group become.

Rationalization.   Here the group ignores warnings or refuses to recognize warnings that might impact their decision making. They collectively construct rationalizations to ignore warnings or negative feedback. They can explain away any intimations that they have done or are doing anything wrong.

Illusion of Morality.   Here the group members believe unquestioningly in their inherent morality. They think they are right and usually ignore signs that indicate otherwise. Because they feel they are good, they believe any decisions they make must be also. Many of the catastrophes generated by religious groups throughout history are traceable to this illusion.

Stereotyping.   The group holds or creates stereotypes about other groups or persons. For example, they might see another organization or group as "evil," "incompetent," or "stupid." "If 'those people' believe it, we know it is wrong." Even if some members of the group do not believe in the stereotypes, they will rarely speak up for fear that they might be ostracized from the group.

Peer Pressure.   Victims of groupthink will apply direct pressure to any person who even remotely acts as if he or she might not agree with the group. If someone tries to present arguments against the decision, the group will directly apply peer pressure to get the person to stop any further disagreement. For example, they might say things such as, "You always think that way," "You don't know what you're talking about—go along with the group," "Be a team player," or "Don't rock the boat."

Self-censorship.   This is when people in the group avoid presenting disagreements or arguments contrary to the group consensus. They keep silent about their concerns and even minimize their concerns to them-selves. They do this because they are afraid that if they express disagree-ments, they might be excluded from the group, be subjected to peer pres-sure, or be embarrassed.

Illusion of Unanimity.   This is the illusion that "all agree," when they really do not. Many simply will not voice disagreement. Whereas most will voice arguments in favor of a certain decision, many will remain silent. Often it is assumed that since those who stayed silent did not voice any disagreements, then they must be in agreement. This can lead to the illusion that "all" support the decision. Again, many who have misgivings will not speak up for fear that they might be expelled from the group.

Mindguarding.   Sometimes victims of groupthink will appoint themselves as "mindguards." Mindguards are similar to "bodyguards." They will keep contrary information or advice from reaching the group or their leaders. They will go to fellow members and obtain the information and interpret the information from their own vantage point for the group.

In conclusion, several symptoms have to be present for groupthink to exist. But remember, it thrives in cohesive groups, groups where positive in-terpersonal affect is high and people are afraid to communicate disagree-ments for fear of rejection by the group. Groupthink can be as destructive to an organization as conflict. Groupthink stifles communication, whereas con-flict creates hostile communication. In a groupthink situation, not all mem-bers of the group are satisfied; they are simply reluctant to communicate their misgivings. Hence, although on the surface groupthink might be ap-pealing, because there is no conflict, it is no more desirable than conflict. Fol-lowing are some communication strategies for preventing or avoiding groupthink.

Although cohesiveness is desirable, it can be accomplished through high affinity and people can still be encouraged to voice their opinions without fear of reprisal. Some steps that should be taken are:

1. Disagreement should be encouraged throughout any decision-making process.
2. Occasionally, each member of the group should be assigned the role of critical evaluator. Since these people are playing a role, they usually will feel free to question information and ideas.
3. Sometimes key members (such as managers or people with vested in-terests) should stay out of the decision making. Often people will try to please their "boss" and will not make an honest decision. Keeping the boss out of the process will tend to keep his or her influence from dominating the decision reached.

4. Outside experts should be used when necessary to provide needed information that might impact the final decision. This will overcome the tendency to keep conflicting information from the group.

5. Occasionally someone should play the "devil's advocate," without creating conflict. This person's charge is to attack everything and force the remainder of the group to defend it. Even "sacred cows" get challenged by a devil's advocate. Hence, rationalization and stereotyping are challenged.

6. Keep the communication channels open to information from many sources. This means that all information must be allowed in, even that which comes from a "hated" group.

7. Never assume silence means consensus. Force everyone to vote privately if groupthink is feared. That way, people who are in silent disagreement can express that disagreement without being identified.

8. Be open to change and new ideas. Express your willingness to hear others' ideas and express a willingness to change for the good of the organization.

9. If the project is too large for one group, have some smaller subgroups work on it. Then you have input from a variety of sources. Listen to what key individuals (competent people) in the groups tell you.

10. Do not ignore warning signals or suggestions from concerned sources that the decision being made is a bad one for the organization. Concerned people outside the group are likely to evaluate the degree of risk in a decision much more accurately than the group members themselves if groupthink is a problem.

11. If at all possible, give sufficient time for discussing the issue, and after a preliminary decision is made, put it aside for awhile and then perhaps rethink it. The illusions that arise during decision making under conditions of groupthink are likely to be more visible over time than they are immediately.

Although none of these suggestions is workable in every group under all conditions, it is essential that groupthink not become the norm in your group or organization. It may seem desirable because everyone "seems to agree," but it is not. Thus, it is essential that as many of the preceding suggestions are employed as are feasible in a given group.

In conclusion, Table 14.1 demonstrates the impact of conflict, disagreement, and groupthink on communication. In disagreement situations, communication is encouraged and opinions are exchanged. In conflict situations, defensive, hostile communication is the norm. In groupthink, communication is stifled to the point that people will rarely express an opinion contrary to the group. Both conflict and groupthink can lead to the destruc-

TABLE 14.1   Continuum of Conflict, Disagreement, and Groupthink, and Their Impact on Communication

CONFLICT	DISAGREEMENT	GROUPTHINK
Hostile, defensive communication	Communication encouraged; opinions exchanged	Communication stifled; disagreement stifled

tion of an organization. Conflict will tear it apart; groupthink will allow it to die because no new ideas will be generated. Disagreement is the only viable option available to us without creating conflict or groupthink. Disagreement encourages communication without resentment. Disagreement must be encouraged and conflict and groupthink avoided.

REFERENCES AND RECOMMENDED READINGS

Janis, I. L. (Nov. 1971). Groupthink. *Psychology Today, 43–46,* 74–77.

Janis, I. L. (1972). *Victims of groupthink: A psychological study of foreign-policy decisions and fiascoes.* Boston: Houghton Mifflin.

Janis, I. L. (1982). *Groupthink: Psychological studies of policy decisions and fiascoes.* (2nd ed.). Boston: Houghton Mifflin.

McCroskey, J. C., & Richmond, V. P. (1996). *Fundamentals of human communication: An interpersonal perspective.* Prospect Heights, IL: Waveland Press.

McCroskey, J. C., & Wheeless, L. R. (1976). *An introduction to human communication.* Needham Heights, MA: Allyn and Bacon.

Teven, J. J., McCroskey, J. C., & Richmond, V. P. (1998). Measurement of tolerance for disagreement. *Communication Research Reports, 15,* 209–217.

STUDY GUIDE

1. Define and distinguish between "disagreement" and "conflict." When is conflict desirable? Why? When is disagreement desirable? Why?
2. Explain the concept of "Tolerance for Disagreement." Discuss the types of TFD.
3. How are tolerance for disagreement and interpersonal liking related? Explain.
4. Identify and explain six communicative techniques for conflict prevention.
5. Identify and explain five communicative techniques for conflict management.
6. Identify and briefly explain the eight symptoms of "groupthink."
7. Choose and identify the five methods you believe are the best ones for avoiding groupthink.

■ ■ ■ ■ ■

CHAPTER 15

EFFECTIVE SUPERVISORY AND SUBORDINATE RELATIONSHIPS

One of the major concerns of managers in most organizations, whether the organization is profit or nonprofit in orientation, is how to obtain more productivity. Often this can be achieved through introducing new equipment or work procedures. However, much of the time the only way to increase productivity is to have employees who work harder. This can be achieved by hiring harder-working employees, which usually is not possible, or by getting current employees to work harder.

In Chapter 9 we introduced you to the two major approaches to management which were developed early in the twentieth century—the scientific approach and the human relations approach. Although these two approaches were different from each other, they had one thing in common. They were concerned with how to get workers to be more productive. One focused primarily on the working conditions and sought to make the work more efficient; the other focused on the workers and sought to make them more motivated. Each approach met with some success in terms of increasing productivity: One found that there was only so much that could be done to increase efficiency and the other found that there was only so much that could be done to make workers happier. Each approach was limited by the underlying assumption that it was exclusively management's task to make the worker more efficient.

Fredrick Herzberg (1966, 1968) challenged this assumption when he advanced his motivator–hygiene theory of management. He suggested that employees will be motivated to produce at high levels if they believe certain needs will be satisfied by this behavior. Herzberg suggests that there are two types of factors that impact work behavior: satisfiers (motivating factors) and dissatisfiers (hygiene factors). For ease of reading in this chapter, we refer to these simply as *satisfiers* and *dissatisfiers.* Herzberg saw no overlap in these two categories. That is, his view was that the things that make us satisfied are not related to the things that make us dissatisfied. Hence, it is possible to be both satisfied and dissatisfied at the same time. The traditional view holds that our reaction to our job falls on a single continuum ranging from "dissatisfied" at one end to "satisfied" at the other.

Satisfied_____Not satisfied

Dissatisfied_____Not dissatisfied

or

Satisfied_____Not satisfied

Not dissatisfied_____Dissatisfied

FIGURE 15.1   Satisfaction and Dissatisfaction Continuum

Herzberg's view is that we have two reactions to our job. One falls on a continuum of "dissatisfied" to "not dissatisfied" and the other falls on a continuum of "not satisfied" to "satisfied" (see Figure 15.1). Although the hard research has not always been fully supportive of this fully dichotomous view, the distinction is strong enough to be helpful for us to gain insight as to what is happening to us in our organization and why we may be responding the way we do.

Our reactions on the satisfaction continuum are based on such factors as the possibility of personal growth in the job, recognition, the work itself, responsibility, opportunity for advancement, and achievement. These are sometimes thought of as representing "higher-order" needs. Some people have strong needs of this type—the people we referred to as "high achievers" in Chapter 6. In contrast, the people we described as "indifferents" have little concern for these matters. In Herzberg's view as well as the view we expressed in Chapter 6, these people are unlikely *ever* to be motivated by anything having to do with the job, since the job is not a valued concern in their lives.

Our reactions on the dissatisfaction continuum are based on such factors as salary, interpersonal relations with other subordinates and peers, status, interpersonal relations with your supervisor, working conditions, policy and administration (too many rules or nonsensical policies), job security (lack of it), and technical supervision. These are sometimes thought of as more "basic" needs. Some people have particularly strong needs of this type, the "indifferents" in particular. These are people who tolerate the job only to have enough money to support the rest of their existence—the important part. Others may be willing to sacrifice some of these needs to build for the future, such as those we identified in Chapter 6 as "upward mobiles," without actually becoming dissatisfied.

According to this view, factors relating to the "job" itself (the satisfiers) influence employee satisfaction, whereas factors relating to the "work environment" (the dissatisfiers) influence employee dissatisfaction. Hence, as we've noted, there are two continua influencing employee satisfaction and dissatisfaction in the organizational environment. Consequently, it is quite possible for employees to be neither satisfied nor dissatisfied. They are simply not satisfied and not dissatisfied. They are neutral or impartial on both continua. There are numbers of employees that, when you ask them if they are satisfied, say "Not really, but I'm not dissatisfied either." This can occur when the person's basic needs are being addressed, but his or her higher needs are not. The person may be quite willing to continue working in that job for years, or be constantly looking for a better position. It all depends on the strength of that person's higher needs. The "indifferent" has as good a job as he or she would ever want; the "high achiever" has to have more.

Dissatisfaction occurs when elements in the work environment, or dissatisfiers, are not acceptable. For example, most of us expect to have fairly decent working conditions, a decent salary, decent relationships with peers and supervisors, and some job security. These things are expected in most jobs and, when they are not present or provided for us, we become highly dissatisfied. For example, if for three years in a row management gives us a $1,000 pay increase but the next year gives us a $500 pay increase, we feel almost as if we have taken a $500 cut. This type of thing can cause great dissatisfaction. If we had a decent office and then a new person is hired and is given our office and we are assigned a less prestigious office, then we become highly dissatisfied. If we had had that office to begin with, it might have been just fine. We may think our salary is at an acceptable level, but if a new person is hired to do the same work we do at a higher salary, we may be incensed.

The unfortunate part of all of this is that management in most organizations tries to use the dissatisfiers to make us satisfied. Things simply do not work that way. The potential dissatisfiers, if not present, can make us highly dissatisfied; but if they are present, they will only make us less dissatisfied. Why? Because we expect decent salaries, working conditions, peer relationships, supervision, and so on. If we have them, it is because we have earned them and deserve them. If we do not, it is because management is stupid, uncaring, and discriminatory. Many organizations communicate with their employees almost exclusively on the dissatisfaction continuum and then wonder why employees only react in varying levels of dissatisfaction. This is particularly common in environments where unions represent the employees. Unions are started because employees are dissatisfied. They are only expected to work on reducing dissatisfaction. Management comes to center all of its attention on keeping the union "off its back" and ignores factors related to satisfaction altogether. Employees often are less dissatisfied after becoming unionized, but rarely are they more satisfied. In some cases they even redirect their dissatisfaction toward the union and away from management!

Satisfaction occurs when the satisfiers are being met—for example, when we feel that we can be recognized for our achievements, that we might be able to advance in our position or earn some credits, when we are given responsibility without others' scrutinizing our every move, or when we actually enjoy doing the work that the job requires. Many effective supervisors have come to realize that if they can provide decent "environmental factors" and can communicate to an employee how well he or she has done on the job, this is more likely to increase satisfaction than anything else.

An effective manager has to monitor the environmental factors to be able to identify potential dissatisfiers and do his or her best to make sure employees' needs are met in these areas to keep people from being highly dissatisfied. However, to increase satisfaction, the manager must also communicate about the potential satisfiers to keep employees moving in the direction of satisfaction. Employees in many companies (because of the size of the company) have figured out that their managers simply focus on the potential dissatisfiers because this is all they know. Hence, for many of us, the person who has to look out for our satisfiers is ourselves. Most of our managers do not have the time to come around and pat each of us on the shoulder and say "good job." If they did, this type of communication could mean a great deal to us.

If we want to be satisfied in our work, we have to focus our attention on the things that we enjoy in our work—to look for recognition, achievement, and potential for personal growth. We have to look for it *and* realize it when we have achieved it. For example, ask yourself, "Am I better at my job than I was a few years ago?" If so, then *give yourself* a pat on the back. If another notes how well you have done in your work, thank him or her, and give yourself another pat. In summary, who has to be your main motivator? You do. But you also can help new employees by pointing out their achievements and personal growth so they do not feel so neglected by the system. We need more people being satisfied in our environment. Is it not better to be around happy people than to be around whiners? Helping our co-workers become more satisfied and happy in their work is altruistic, selfish behavior!

It is clear that job and environmental factors can impact satisfaction and dissatisfaction. However, we also see that the attitude a person takes to a job goes a long way toward determining whether he or she will be satisfied in that job. The next section goes a step further to suggest that the attitude you communicate in your job may determine how satisfied others are going to be with you.

WHY SOME DO NOT SURVIVE: TEN COMMON COMMUNICATION MISTAKES

Have you ever met a person who has a series of tales to tell about terrible jobs and terrible supervisors he or she has had in the past? Maybe he or she even had terrible people to work with as well? Most of us have met at least one of these people, some have met many. At first the tendency is to feel sorry for them because of their bad luck to fall into so many bad situations.

However, as time goes by and we have more opportunities to get to know them better, we are likely to realize luck had nothing to do with the messes they got into. It was their own fault.

Some employees, from the time they walk through the organization's doors, are marked for failure. They become the target of the boss and the older, more established employees. Why does this happen? What mistakes do they make? Most of their mistakes are communication errors. It is almost as if they were to run down a hallway yelling, "Fire me! Fire me!"

Some employees are bound to fail because of their ineffective and/or inappropriate communication behaviors. They may know the appropriate communication, but fail to practice it. Or they may just not know what is appropriate communication. In either case, they are bound to fail. For example, we know of one employee who, within the first six weeks she was employed, managed to offend her immediate supervisor, a higher-level administrator, her male co-workers, and her female co-workers.

She began during the second week of her employment by informing her co-workers, many of whom had worked with her supervisor for years, that he was the worst supervisor she had ever worked for and needed to be replaced. It took about 10 minutes for them to pass that information along to him. Then she informed a high-level administrator that another high-level administrator was unqualified and incompetent to do the job she was in. This employee indicated that she would apply for that job if it became available, since she was much more qualified to do it right. This information passed through the ranks of administrators, and down to her supervisor, in less than a week. The third week she had a disagreement with one of her male co-workers and informed everyone in her division that he was "just like the rest of the pigs" in the organization, unwilling to accept the "views of a competent woman." She topped this off by confronting three of her female co-workers directly (and sending an unsigned note to another) criticizing them for "dressing like cheerleaders."

She was outraged when she was informed by her supervisor that, based on the advice given him by her co-workers, he had recommended she be fired. She claimed she was being discriminated against, that he made the decision because he did not personally like her. She was right; he didn't. But that was beside the point. When her background was checked more carefully than when she was first hired, it was learned that she had been asked to leave every position she had held previously because of similar kinds of behavior. If hers was a rare case, it could be thought of as somewhat amusing and forgotten. Unfortunately, it is not rare. The behaviors she exhibited are not even among the most extreme we have seen, but they are representative of inappropriate communication behaviors many employees exhibit that doom them to failure. There are several types of communication behaviors that can virtually ensure you will not survive in your organization. We refer to the people who consistently engage in these behaviors as "DOA" employees. *DOA* refers to "dead on arrival" in the organization. It does not matter what the organization is, believes, or does; they are DOA. Let us examine some of the behaviors DOAs are likely to exhibit.

1. Many DOAs hold their supervisors solely responsible for their growth and motivation. They often will be heard saying things like "My supervisor doesn't do enough to improve my life or help me grow" or "My supervisor just will not give me a chance to show what I can do." They have not realized that they have to be their own main motivators. They want to blame their supervisor and the system for their lack of success. They do not realize that they must earn opportunities in most organizations.

2. DOAs often think they know it all and will refuse assistance from other employees, or even their supervisor, when offered. They say things like "Of course I know how to do that" or "Anyone can do something that simple." When most of us learn that we are working with someone like this, we keep our advice to ourselves and let them fail. This know-it-all behavior often reflects the DOA's insecurity and fear of looking inadequate to others. However, it is seen by others as arrogance, and the others are more than delighted to watch arrogant DOAs fall flat on their faces.

3. DOAs love to say things like "Do you still do it that way?" or "It is silly to do that. We stopped that years ago where I worked before" or "This place is so out-of-date." These statements are usually highly offensive to established employees, who are put on the defensive with the new employee. They are likely to think, if not say, things like "Why don't you go back to that place then? We can live without you!"

4. DOAs want all the rewards available in the system without paying any dues or putting in the time to earn them. They will complain that co-workers with more seniority get things they do not, and often they will be complaining to some of those same co-workers. "Why does everybody else get the day off they want but I don't?" They are not willing to do the "grunt work" others have done in order to earn the respect of their co-workers and supervisors. They simply want it all without doing the work.

5. DOAs often are deviants in terms of the norms. They do not conform to the common norms such as being on time for meetings, wearing certain apparel, and so on. Worse, they may even openly criticize the norms. They are oblivious to the fact that the very person to whom they are talking may have helped establish the norms.

6. DOAs enjoy arguing over insignificant issues simply to get attention. Unfortunately, they do get attention—the wrong kind. Many other people will ignore the DOA, even if he or she does have a good idea, because they figure they are going to have to argue over some insignificant issue.

7. DOAs are constantly "poking their nose" into everyone else's work or business. They like to be "in the know." They try to gain access to the rumor mill by telling others what they learn from their snooping. After a

while, people stop communicating significant issues with this person for fear anything they say will be misinterpreted or used against them.

8. DOAs usually step on the toes of the good old boys and girls. They will often point out to others around them that these people do not seem to be as "productive" as the rest, that they seem to get all the benefits, or that they are out-of-date. DOAs forget that the old boys and girls established much of the system and have friends "where you would least expect them" to be.

9. DOAs usually will talk negatively about their boss and their co-workers behind their backs, such as at social gatherings or functions outside the immediate work unit. They usually think this will help them obtain higher status, when in fact all it does is keep them from being considered for higher positions. Nobody wants to hire individuals who talk negatively about their boss and co-workers.

10. DOAs try to get things done without following the proper communication channels in the organization. They tend to want to jump proper channels, such as "bypassing" their immediate supervisor when they want something they think the supervisor will not agree to. Rather than trying to make their idea compatible with the supervisor's ideas, they simply go above him or her with their ideas. This is a stupid move. Almost any supervisor (even an amiable) will become upset with an employee that ignores the chain of command and goes above him or her. And almost anyone at a higher level will inform the supervisor that this has happened, often within minutes.

These are 10 common communication errors that cause discomfort in the system. Many of these mistakes can even lead to your being forced out of the system. Use these approaches and you too can be DOA. Instead, however, you might like to try the communication strategies outlined in the next section. These include several strategies that you might be able to use to get supervisors and co-workers to like, respect, and trust you. They might even try to keep you around for a while!

HOW TO SURVIVE: COMMON COMMUNICATION STRATEGIES FOR SURVIVAL

Whether we are in a work organization or in a social group, most of us feel the social needs for affection and inclusion. We want our colleagues to like, respect, and appreciate us—to have *affinity* for us. McCroskey and Wheeless (1976) referred to affinity as "a positive attitude toward another person" (p. 231). They went on to suggest that "at the heart of being able to develop affinity with another person is understanding the principle of affinity. This principle is as follows: Generally, the more people believe that we like them, the more they are inclined to like us" (p. 232). They suggest that there may be exceptions to the principle, but in general, affinity is "the direct result of how another person perceives us. People will like us or dislike us based on the way they see us" (p. 232).

Bell and Daly (1984a, b) have taken a broad view of interpersonal relationships and have posited a typology of 25 affinity-seeking strategies that can be utilized in a variety of contexts to increase liking and affect between two people. They define affinity seeking as "the active social-communicative process by which individuals attempt to get others to like and to feel positive toward them" (1984b, p. 91). They continue by suggesting that "the ability to evoke positive feelings is a favorably regarded and often envied skill" (p. 91). This is further substantiated by the reasoning that affinity seeking is an "important communication function" (p. 91) and that those who lack these strategies often "suffer from a variety of social and personal turmoils" (p. 91). In their research they found that in six relationships (work supervisor, romantic partner, close friend, acquaintance, roommate, and neighbor) there was a strong link between affinity seeking and interpersonal attraction, life satisfaction, and social success. They also found that people "who were thought to use many affinity-seeking strategies were judged as likeable, socially successful, and satisfied with their lives" (p. 111).

More recently, McCroskey & Richmond (1996) suggested that we engage in the process (of affinity seeking) when coming together in new relationships and when trying to salvage relationships that are coming apart. Often we use affinity seeking to gain the positive regard of our teachers, coworkers, and superiors. Richmond, McCroskey, and Davis (1986) suggest that affinity seeking not only is useful in "developing and maintaining relationships in our everyday lives but could be invaluable in the work environment" (p. 182). For example, the subordinate who gets along with his or her supervisor is much more likely to be satisfied than the subordinate who doesn't. The same would hold true for the supervisor. Effective use of affinity-seeking strategies can enhance supervisor–subordinate relationships and prevent potential conflicts.

There are 25 affinity-seeking strategies, in the context of supervisor–subordinate relationships. They are presented below in alphabetical order, not in order of effectiveness for any given situation. All of these techniques have been found to be effective in the development of affinity in some interpersonal relationships. However, not all are equally effective for use in working with your supervisor. We note these specifically later, but you probably will recognize them right away. Each strategy is discussed in the unique context of the work environment. The focus is primarily on what will work and what will not work for the subordinate when attempting to get his or her supervisor's respect and liking. You may be interested in learning how these can also be used in other contexts. This is the concern of the recommended readings listed at the end of the chapter.

Altruism. The subordinate attempting to get another individual (for example; primarily supervisor but could be co-worker) to like him or her tries to be of help and assistance to the supervisor in whatever he or she is currently doing. For example, the person holds the door open for the other, offers to get him or her something to drink, takes his or her coat, and is generally available to assist with duties or errands. He or she also gives advice when it is requested.

Assume Control. The subordinate attempting to get the supervisor to like him or her presents him/herself as a leader, a person who has control over what goes on. For example, he or she directs conversations held with the other person, takes charge and mentions examples of where he or she has taken charge or served as a leader in the past.

Assume Equality. The subordinate attempting to get the supervisor to like him or her presents him/herself as an equal of the other person. For example, he or she avoids showing off, does not act superior or snobbish, and does not play one-upmanship games. He or she generally treats the other individual as an equal, rather than a superior.

Comfortable Self. The subordinate attempting to get the supervisor to like him or her acts comfortable in the setting in which the two find themselves, comfortable with him/herself, and comfortable with the supervisor. He or she is relaxed, at ease, casual, and content. Distractions and disturbances in the environment are ignored (such as, loud noises, obnoxious people). The subordinate tries to look as if he or she is having fun, even if he or she is not. The impression the subordinate tries to convey is "Nothing bothers me."

Concede Control. The subordinate attempting to get the supervisor to like him or her allows this person to control the relationship and situations the two individuals find themselves in. For example, he or she lets the other take charge of their conversations and decide what they do and where they go. The subordinate attempting to be liked also lets the supervisor influence his or her actions by not acting dominant.

Conversational Rule Keeping. The subordinate attempting to get the supervisor to like him or her follows closely the culture's rules for how people are to socialize with one another by demonstrating cooperation, friendliness, and politeness. The subordinate works hard at giving relevant answers to questions, saying the right thing, acting interested and involved in the conversation, and adapting messages to the particular characteristics of the supervisor. The subordinate avoids changing the topic of conversation too soon, interrupting the other person, being pushy, dominating the conversation, or excessive using self-references. He or she also avoids topics that are not of common interest to both parties.

Dynamism. The subordinate attempting to get the supervisor to like him or her presents him/herself as a dynamic (but not overly so), active, and enthusiastic employee. For example, he or she acts physically animated and lively while interacting with the other person. (He or she does not sit like a lump of clay.) He or she varies intonation and other vocal characteristics and is outgoing and extroverted in the presence of the supervisor.

Elicit Other's Disclosures. The subordinate attempting to get the supervisor to like him or her encourages the supervisor to talk by asking questions and reinforcing them for talking. For example, the subordinate inquires about the other's feelings, interests, opinions, views, and so on and responds as if these are important and interesting and continues to ask more questions of the other person.

Facilitate Enjoyment. The subordinate attempting to get the supervisor to like him or her seeks to make situations in which the two are together enjoyable experiences when the situation calls for it. For example, he or she will do things the other would enjoy, be entertaining, tell jokes and interesting stories, and say funny things. The subordinate tries to make the environment conducive to enjoyment within limits.

Inclusion of Other. The subordinate attempting to get the supervisor to like him or her includes the person in his or her social activities and group of friends. For example, he or she introduces the other to friends, makes the supervisor feel like "one of the guys" or "one of the girls."

Influence Perceptions of Closeness. The subordinate attempting to get the supervisor to like him or her engages in behaviors that lead the supervisor to perceive the relationship as being closer and more established than it has actually been. For example, he or she uses nicknames when addressing the other, and talks about "we" rather than "you" and "I." He or she also mentions any prior activities that included both of them.

Listening. The subordinate attempting to get the supervisor to like him or her pays close attention to what the supervisor says, listening actively. He or she focuses attention solely on the supervisor and pays strict attention to what is said. Moreover, the subordinate demonstrates that he or she listens by being responsive to the other's ideas, asking for clarification of ambiguities, being open-minded, and remembering things the supervisor says.

Nonverbal Immediacy.   The subordinate attempting to get the supervisor to like him or her signals interest and liking for the supervisor through various nonverbal cues. For example, the subordinate frequently tries to make eye contact with the supervisor, sits or stands closer to him or her (without invading his or her personal space), and smiles and looks positive when interacting. The subordinate also uses nonverbal signs of interest, such as leaning forward, frequent head nodding, and directing much gaze toward the supervisor. All of these nonverbal cues indicate that the subordinate is interested in what the supervisor has to say.

Openness.   The subordinate attempting to get the supervisor to like him or her is open to the supervisor. For example, the subordinate discloses information about his or her background, interests, views, and perhaps even insecurities, weaknesses, and fears to make the supervisor feel special and trusted ("just between you and me").

Optimism.   The subordinate attempting to get the supervisor to like him or her presents him/herself as a positive individual—an optimist—so that he or she will appear to be a person who is pleasant to be around. He or she acts cheerful, tends to look on the positive side of things, avoids complaining about things, avoids talking about depressing topics, and avoids being critical of him/herself and others. In short, the subordinate makes a concerted effort to avoid being a "drag" or a "downer."

Personal Autonomy.   The subordinate attempting to get the supervisor to like him or her presents him/herself as an independent, free-thinking person—the kind of person who stands on his or her own, speaks his or her mind regardless of consequences, refuses to change his or her behavior to meet the organizational expectations, and knows where he or she is going.

Physical Attractiveness.   The subordinate attempting to get the supervisor to like him or her tries to look as attractive as possible in appearance and attire. He or she wears nice clothing, practices good grooming, shows concern for proper hygiene, stands up straight, and monitors his or her appearance. He or she dresses appropriately for the job and any occasions correlated with the job. For example, at the annual Christmas party, he or she would dress a bit more formally than most of the other employees.

Present Interesting Self.   The subordinate attempting to get the supervisor to like him or her presents him/herself as a person who would be interesting to know and with whom to work. For example, he or she highlights past accomplishments and positive qualities, emphasizes things that make him or her especially interesting, expresses unique ideas, and demonstrates intelligence and knowledge. The subordinate also tries to discreetly drop the names of impressive people he or she knows or has worked with. He or she might even do outlandish things to appear unpredictable and amusing.

Reward Association. The subordinate attempting to get the supervisor to like him or her presents him/herself as an important figure who can reward the supervisor for associating with him or her. For instance, he or she offers to do favors for the other, and gives this person gifts and information that would be valuable. The subordinate's basic message is, "If you like me, you'll gain something."

Self-concept Confirmation. The subordinate attempting to get the supervisor to like him or her demonstrates respect for the supervisor and helps him or her feel good about him/herself and the job he or she does. For example, the subordinate treats the supervisor like an important person, occasionally complimenting him or her, saying positive things about how he or she does the job, and tells others what a good supervisor he or she has.

Self-inclusion. The subordinate attempting to get the supervisor to like him or her sets up frequent encounters with the supervisor. For example, he or she initiates casual encounters with the supervisor, attempts to schedule future encounters, and places him/herself physically close to the supervisor. The subordinate puts him/herself in a position to be invited to participate in the supervisor's social activities.

Sensitivity. The subordinate attempting to get the supervisor to like him or her acts in a warm, empathic manner toward the supervisor and tries to communicate concern and caring about organizational matters. He or she shows concern for the supervisor's problems and anxieties, and will spend time understanding the supervisor's problems. The subordinate sends a message that says, "I care about you as a person and I understand being a supervisor is not always an easy job."

Similarity. The subordinate attempting to get the supervisor to like him or her tries to make the supervisor see how the two of them are similar in terms of attitudes, values, interests, preferences, personality, and so on. The subordinate expresses views that are similar to the views of the supervisor and agrees with the supervisor on issues. Moreover, the subordinate will deliberately avoid engaging in behaviors that would suggest extreme differences between the two.

Supportiveness. The subordinate attempting to get the supervisor to like him or her is supportive of the supervisor and is encouraging and reinforcing. The subordinate avoids criticizing the supervisor or saying things that might hurt his or her feelings, and sides with the supervisor in disagreements he or she has with others.

TABLE 15.1   Affinity-Seeking Strategies Subordinate Use and Impact on Supervisor

1. Altruism	Positive
2. Assume control	Negative
3. Assume equality	Negative
4. Comfortable self	Positive
5. Concede control	Positive
6. Conversational rule keeping	Positive
7. Dynamism	Positive
8. Elicit other's disclosures	Negative
9. Facilitate enjoyment	Depends on situation
10. Inclusion of other	Depends on situation
11. Influence perceptions of closeness	Negative
12. Listening	Positive
13. Nonverbal immediacy	Positive
14. Openness	Negative
15. Optimism	Positive
16. Personal autonomy	Negative
17. Physical attractiveness	Positive
18. Present interesting self	Depends on situation
19. Reward association	Negative
20. Self-concept confirmation	Positive
21. Self-inclusion	Depends on situation
22. Sensitivity	Positive
23. Similarity	Positive
24. Supportiveness	Positive
25. Trustworthiness	Positive

Trustworthiness.   The subordinate attempting to get the supervisor to like him or her presents him/herself as trustworthy and reliable. For example, the subordinate emphasizes his or her responsibilities, reliability, fairness, dedication, honesty, and sincerity. The subordinate maintains consistency among his or her stated beliefs and behaviors, fulfills any commitments made to the supervisor, and avoids "false fronts" by acting natural at all times.

Although not all the strategies presented will increase affinity between supervisor and subordinate, most will. Subordinates who employ a majority of the more positive affinity-seeking strategies (see Table 15.1) will have supervisors who have formed a more positive impression of them and will trust them more than other subordinates.

Subordinates have many potentially effective strategies among which to choose when attempting to get their supervisors to like them. However, seven of the strategies—assume control, assume equality, elicit other's disclosures, influence perceptions of closeness, openness, personal autonomy, and reward association—appear to be potentially negative if used extensively or without great care. Four others—facilitate enjoyment, inclusion of other, present interesting self, and self-inclusion—appear to be helpful in some circumstances but might be harmful in others.

Subordinates may use the remainder of the affinity-seeking strategies with confidence that they will be helpful. The most positive ones to use are altruism, comfortable self, concede control, conversational rule keeping, dynamism, listening, nonverbal immediacy, optimism, physical attractiveness, self-concept confirmation, sensitivity, similarity, supportiveness, and trustworthiness. Of course, not all 14 options may be fully compatible with a given subordinate's personality or with a particular supervisor–subordinate relationship. Fortunately, sufficient options exist so that no subordinate can argue that there is nothing he or she can do to improve relationships with the supervisor. Face it—if your manager doesn't like you (or your co-workers don't like you), what *haven't* you done to modify your attitude or behavior?

Some people believe that it is inappropriate to employ these affinity-seeking techniques strategically to attain more positive relationships in the workplace. They often use very derogative descriptions of this behavior, such as "kissing up," "brown nosing," "sucking up," "selling out," and "apple polishing." We prefer to describe this behavior as "interpersonal public relations." Our advice: Reject those who are not smart enough to work to build good interpersonal relationships in the workplace and their ignorant attitude. Smile at them as you get your raise and promotion. Be a competent communicator and make work, work for you. Some people are going to get the "goodies" that your organization has to offer. Why shouldn't one of them be you?

REFERENCES AND RECOMMENDED READINGS

Bell, R. A., & Daly, J. A. (1984a). Affinity-seeking: Its nature and correlates. Paper presented at the annual convention of the International Communication Association, San Francisco.
Bell, R. A., & Daly, J. A. (1984b). The affinity-seeking function of communication. *Communication Monographs, 51,* 91–115.
Herzberg, F. (1966). *Work and the nature of man.* Cleveland: World.
Herzberg, F. (1968). One more time: How do you motivate employees? *Harvard Business Review, 46,* 53–62.
McCroskey, J. C., & Richmond, V. P. (1996). *Fundamentals of human communication: An interpersonal perspective.* Prospect Heights, IL: Waveland Press.
McCroskey, J. C., & Wheeless, L. R. (1976). *An introduction to human communication.* Boston: Allyn & Bacon.
Richmond, V. P., McCroskey, J. C., & Davis, L. M. (1986). The relationship of supervisor use of power and affinity seeking strategies with subordinate satisfaction. *Communication Quarterly, 34,* 178–193.

STUDY GUIDE

1. Distinguish between "satisfiers" and "dissatisfiers" and provide three examples of each.
2. Why is the above important to an understanding of communication in organizations?
3. Who has to be an individual worker's primary motivator? Why?
4. Explain the concept of organizational "DOAs" and give five examples of the type of things these individuals might do in the organization.
5. Explain the concept of "affinity seeking" and explain why it is important to communication in the organizational context.
6. What is the "principle of affinity"?
7. Select and identify the five affinity-seeking techniques you believe would be most effective in working with a manager you have now or had recently. Explain why these techniques would be particularly effective.